SPORTS
MARKETING
THE VIEW OF INDUSTRY EXPERTS

DANIEL J. BRUTON, MBA
President of SportRx

JONES & BARTLETT
LEARNING

World Headquarters
Jones & Bartlett Learning
5 Wall Street
Burlington, MA 01803
978-443-5000
info@jblearning.com
www.jblearning.com

Jones & Bartlett Learning books and products are available through most bookstores and online booksellers. To contact Jones & Bartlett Learning directly, call 800-832-0034, fax 978-443-8000, or visit our website, www.jblearning.com.

4847–3

Production Credits
Chief Executive Officer: Ty Field
President: James Homer
Chief Product Officer: Eduardo Moura
VP, Executive Publisher: David D. Cella
Publisher: Cathy L. Esperti
Associate Editor: Kayla Dos Santos
Editorial Assistant: Sara J. Peterson
Production Assistant: Alex Schab
Senior Marketing Manager: Andrea DeFronzo
Art Development Editor: Joanna Lundeen
Art Development Assistant: Shannon Sheehan
VP, Manufacturing and Inventory Control: Therese Connell
Composition: Cenveo Publisher Services
Cover Design: Michael O'Donnell
Rights and Photo Research Coordinator: Ashley Dos Santos
Cover Image: © David Lee/ShutterStock, Inc.
Printing and Binding: Courier Companies
Cover Printing: Courier Companies

Library of Congress Cataloging-in-Publication Data
Bruton, Daniel J.
  Sports marketing : the view of industry experts / Daniel J. Bruton.
    pages cm
  Includes bibliographical references and index.
  ISBN 978-1-284-03409-7 (alk. paper)
  1. Sports--Marketing. I. Title.
  GV716.B78 2016
  796.0688--dc23
                        2014044442
6048

Printed in the United States of America
19 18 17 16 15   10 9 8 7 6 5 4 3 2 1

Contents

About the Author

Daniel J. Bruton teaches sports marketing at the University of San Diego and sports licensing at the San Diego State University Sports Management MBA program. A former college basketball player, Ironman and multiple marathon finisher, and now 20-year veteran of the sports marketing industry, Dan ran marketing for the Upper Deck Company when they were a top licensee in sports. His team managed the image and likeness for trading cards and memorabilia for such sports icons as Tiger Woods, Michael Jordan, Kobe Bryant, and Peyton Manning. Dan is currently the president of the e-commerce company SportRx, the leading provider of sports prescription eyewear to athletes. SportRx was recently ranked as the tenth best place to work in America by *Outside Magazine*. He has been a frequent speaker on the subject of sports business for many media outlets, including ESPN, FOX, NBC, CBS, *Forbes, U.S. News & World Report,* PBS, and the *Washington Post.*

Acknowledgements

To Steve Schaller: What can I say but thank you? This book wouldn't have been completed without your constant editing and suggestions. Your perspective on each chapter added a great deal to the content.

To Danielle Werner: Thanks for sticking with me from the start. You are a great writer and your contributions to this book made it a better experience for the reader. Congratulations on completing your sports MBA. You are going to do great things in this industry.

To all of the featured industry experts: I can't thank you enough. You are the leaders in sports business and are incredibly busy. For you each to take the time to contribute to this book so students can learn how the industry works means a great deal to me. Your real-world knowledge gives each student a behind-the-scenes look at the world of sports business.

To my beautiful wife, Kathy, and my two wonderful babies, Orlagh and Fiona: Thank you for the unending support through this process. This may be the only book ever completed while carrying a baby in one arm and typing with one finger.

Thank you to everyone at Jones & Bartlett Learning for guiding me through this process. Each one of you was fantastic to work with the entire time. Thanks for believing that a book based on real-world experience has a place in the world of textbooks.

Preface

Sports Marketing: The View of Industry Experts was written to provide the reader a behind-the-scenes look at how the sports marketing industry operates. This is the first sports marketing textbook based entirely on real-world experience. The goal of the book is to provide the reader exposure to the many niches in the sports marketing industry while also providing the insights of top experts in the field of sports marketing.

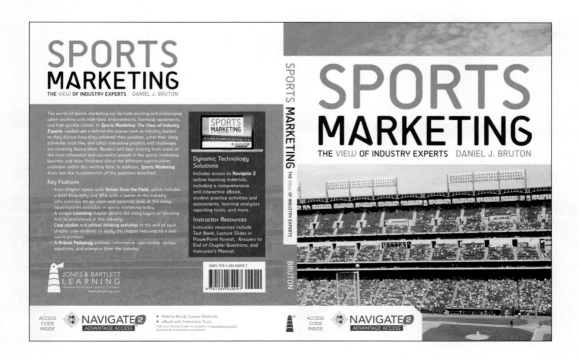

Key Features

Biographies and Interviews of Industry Experts The book features bios and inter-views with 13 of the top experts in the field of sports marketing, including:

- NBA super-agent **Bill Duffy** discusses how he builds the business portfolios of athletes such as Yao Ming, Joakim Noah, and Andrew Wiggins.
- NFL Players Union President **Keith Gordon** shows readers what it's like to run one of the most powerful unions in sports.
- Leading sports marketer **Bill Sanders** takes readers behind the scenes of the advertising and endorsement world while he works with some of the biggest names in sports.
- USA Olympian **Holley Mangold** gives us a look at the field of sports market-ing from the eyes of the athlete. Her perspective gives a view rarely seen in a marketing textbook.

How the Five Ps Affect Athlete Marketing Throughout, this book clearly breaks down how the Product, Price, Place, Promotion, and Progress of that chapter topic impacts athlete marketing.

Case Study A real-world scenario is presented to the readers at the end of each chapter with questions to provoke discussion and application of knowledge.

Critical Thinking Activity Ideas for projects that can be used for in-class discussion or homework assignments are included to enhance the learner's experience of the text.

Chapter Questions Each chapter also offers questions to help readers assess the information gained from the chapter.

Key Topics

Chapter 2, Licensing, is a chapter based on material rarely covered or understood in academics. In sports marketing, everything is controlled by licensing. Companies are either officially licensed or are working around the various rules and regulations of the governing body. This chapter reviews how a team, company, or athlete must navigate through the strict rules of the licensing game. The chapter includes an example of a sports licensing contract along with the author's notes explaining each section.

Chapter 3, Properties Groups and Players Unions, discusses how professional sports leagues are run. Knowledge of the inner workings of a professional sports league is rarely covered in the classroom setting. Understanding the differences between the properties groups and players unions will help the reader navigate the hurdles of building a sports marketing strategic plan.

Chapter 16, Review of Sports Marketing Through the 2012 Olympic Games, reviews how each of the concepts covered in the book applies to the Olympics. USA Olympian Holley Mangold gives her perspective on what it's like to be an athlete competing not only for gold medals but also for available sports marketing dollars. The readers can see how all of the sports marketing concepts play out in a single sporting event.

Sports Marketing: The View of Industry Experts will give the reader exposure to the many positions in the industry and a strong base to secure their dream job in sports.

Instructor & Student Resources

- Test Bank
- Lecture Slides in PowerPoint Format
- Sample Syllabus
- Instructor's Manual

Reviewers

Darrin C. Duber-Smith, MS, MBA
Marketing Professor
Athletic Training Department
Metropolitan State University of Denver
Pueblo, CO

Todd Hall, PhD, MBA, BS
Assistant Professor
Davis College of Business
Jacksonville University
Jacksonville, FL

Thomas Kernodle, BS, MBA, PhD
Business, Management, and Economics
    Department
Empire State College
Staten Island, NY

Jordan Kobritz, JD, CPA
Professor and Chair
Sport Management Department
SUNY Cortland
Cortland, NY

James Padilla, JD
Associate Professor of Law and Sports
    Management
Business Law and Sport Management
    Department
Tiffin University
Tiffin, OH

Mauro Palmero, PhD, MS, BS
Assistant Professor
Kinesiology, Sport, and Recreation
    Management Department
East Tennessee State University
Jonesborough, TN

Kevin T. Wayne, BS, MBA, DBA
Associate Professor
Business Administration Department
Rivier University
Nashua, NH

SPORTS
MARKETING
THE VIEW OF INDUSTRY EXPERTS

Chapter 1

Introduction

CHAPTER OBJECTIVES

- Learn how to become a complete marketer.
- Learn the five Ps.
- Review the fundamentals of marketing.
- Discuss sports as a business.
- Learn how to build a sports résumé.
- Review potential first jobs in sports.

CHAPTER OVERVIEW

This chapter reviews the fundamentals of marketing and takes a broad look at the field of sports marketing. It also focuses on how you can start a career in sports marketing.

Introduction

Welcome to sports marketing. This book introduces one of the fastest-growing segments in the discipline of marketing. Throughout, it features leaders in various niches of the industry. These experts give you a behind-the-scenes look at what it is like to work in the industry and how the fundamentals of marketing apply to their jobs. Sports marketing has developed because brands want to attach their products to the passion and loyalty that fans feel toward their favorite teams or players. (I use *brand* to mean a product, a company, or a symbol of that company.) Tapping into the excitement created by sports can help a brand quickly develop a loyal following. Companies realize that a fan's excitement can translate into sales, even for products that have nothing to do with the sports industry. This text explores the experiences of the leading experts in the industry and how the fundamentals of marketing apply to their jobs.

Book Objectives

When you finish reading this book, I want you to be a complete marketer, someone who can look at a project not only from a creative perspective, but also from the financial, sales, and production sides of its development. We marketers often get a bad rap for wanting to work only on the creative side of a project. In order to become a complete marketer, you need a solid blueprint and the tools to make your plan a reality. This text shows that successful leaders in the industry are all complete marketers. Although they are creative, they also look at projects from many different angles of development. Each complete marketer brings a vision and an action plan to his or her respective industry. The plans must constantly evolve because marketing is not a static endeavor.

Another objective is to expose you to many of the possible jobs in the industry. Most people think of sports marketing as working for a team or a sports-related corporation such as Nike. There are many other opportunities. Consider the many aspects that make up the industry. There are interesting niches in licensing, public relations, advertising, and media training and with agents and colleges, among others that are rarely discussed. This text explores these themes. Learning what it takes to work in this industry from experts in the field gives you a good overview of each job. The experts also provide sound insights and strategies so that you can springboard into a niche that interests you.

For the recent graduate, the most available position in sports marketing often is with the sales department of a team. Those positions can be grueling. You may be asked to make cold calls all day to try to sell season tickets. It's not the glamorous job that you may have envisioned when you imagined being a part of a professional team. Typically, if 12 new people are hired, 2 or 3 will realize that cold calling just isn't for them and will quit. Two or 3 will not make their quota and will be asked to leave. Two or 3 will find work with another team, and the rest will stay with their organization and move up the ranks in sales or marketing. Each year, it's a game of survival of the fittest. One of the keys to making it through this process is the willingness to move from position to position with different teams. If you are working for the Chicago Bulls and there is a chance for advancement with the New Orleans Saints, then you have to be willing to pack the car and get to New Orleans as soon as possible. In the first few years at the start of your career, you may work with multiple teams.

Beyond the teams, there are many other opportunities to work in sports. As this text explains, most sports have players unions and properties groups, and just about every company that sells a product featuring a team or player has a sports marketing department. There are products such as plates, coins, lunch boxes, mugs, and pens that provide interesting opportunities in licensing and product development, and that most people would never associate with sports marketing. There are advertising, events, and public relations companies that focus on sports. In addition to marketing, these companies need employees in accounting, finance, legal, and sales. My goal is to open your mind to all of the options that the sports industry offers.

One of the best things that you can do as a student to help find your first job in sports is to secure an internship. A small number of companies and organizations have formal internship programs to which you can apply. Most others have no formal program—but that does not mean there are no internship possibilities. My most successful students have done a good job of targeting companies that interest them and networking with employees of those companies. Networking can be done through social media sites such as LinkedIn or by attending industry events and meeting people face to face. By building a network, students can offer their services to companies and secure internships. Although the majority of internships are unpaid, the experience is invaluable. Most students who want to pursue a career in sports have no sports industry experience to list on their résumé. As a new grad, featuring an internship on your résumé could be just the thing that distinguishes you from the masses and secures that first job in the industry. In addition, understanding the major themes discussed in this text provides a solid foundation for your career in sports marketing.

Before You Jump, SWOT

SWOT analysis is one of the most used resources in business decision making. SWOT (strengths, weaknesses, opportunities, and threats) analysis enables you to compile an inventory of a company's strengths and weaknesses while you look for external opportunities and threats. In marketing, SWOT analysis helps provide an objective overview before a project is given the green light and money is spent to conduct research. It also helps to develop and confirm the goals and marketing strategy before pushing forward. It can help you find opportunities worth pursuing as well as identify the critical issues that need the company's attention.

Strengths: When thinking about strengths, list both tangible and intangible attributes. What does the company do well? Remember to also list the resources that are readily available. Strengths are the competitive advantages your company has over other companies.

Weaknesses: No one likes to think about their weaknesses, but to market a new product or to expand a company, this is a must. List factors that are within your control and that can undermine the competitive advantage you listed as strengths. Knowing your weaknesses is a great advantage. The more honest you are about pinpointing possible internal weaknesses, the better off the company will be in the long run for this potential new launch.

Opportunities: Opportunities is the category in SWOT analysis most people enjoy filling out. This step represents the purpose of this new product or service and why it will do well in the marketplace. How will this product or service fulfill a need consumers have?

Threats: Last is to identify threats in the marketplace. Under weaknesses, you listed factors within your control that could hinder this product or service from doing well. Threats are factors beyond your control that could put the launch or the company at risk. The hope is that there are not many threats; however, it is best to list all threats in order of severity, ranging from serious to possible.

Market Research

Before you roll out a product or service to take the world by storm, you conduct research. Although the opinions of friends and family might be encouraging, true market research is the gathering of information about consumers' needs and preferences. This digs deep into the size, location, and makeup of a product market. Potential questions that can arise during this process help uncover the key factors of consumer buying behavior in the areas to be investigated. There are two types of market research: primary and secondary.

Primary market research is conducted by you or your company. You have direct contact with the customers and general public through surveys, focus groups, or polling. Surveys can be handed out, verbally completed, or conducted on a tablet device. They can be lengthy or short and sweet. Typically, existing customers are questioned about their current buying habits. Focus groups can be successful but tricky to conduct. A group facilitator walks the small gathering of participants through a series of questions, concepts, images, and so forth. The issue that can arise with focus groups is that some group members are overshadowed by a boisterous, opinionated member. It is the role of the group leader to notice this and to rein in the rowdy member. Polling is a fast, easy way to gain information quickly. Soft drink companies often conduct polls at grocery stores and sporting events by asking consumers to try a new brand of beverage and provide feedback. Polling can be as simple as conducting a taste test and then asking whether the individual preferred product A or B.

Secondary market research is more formal. Information has already been collected and published. There are four prime channels for this type of research. The first is trade associations. The major trade association for sports marketing is the National Sports Marketing Network (NSMN). Another channel to find this information is government, state or local resources, or the U.S. Census Bureau. Chambers of commerce are another avenue. Last, educational resources can be a big help. Examples of sports marketing–related resources are the *International Journal of Sport Management and Marketing, International Journal of Sports Marketing & Sponsorship*, and *Sports Marketing Quarterly*. Keep in mind that journals such as the *Sports Business Journal* are trade publications and are not considered scholarly.

Introducing the Fifth P

The four Ps of marketing are product, place, promotion, and pricing. After you finish your college marketing classes, you may never hear of the four Ps again. Why, then, are they featured in just about every marketing book ever written? The answer is that they affect nearly every decision that you will make as a sports marketer. Your boss will probably never ask you about the four Ps. You may never hear them formally discussed in a marketing or creative meeting. However, every marketing decision is affected by your choice of product attributes, advertising and promotion, pricing, and distribution. The four Ps are often referred to in textbooks as the marketing mix, the set of variables used to achieve a company's marketing goals.

Let's take a look at the four Ps and how they relate to sports marketing.

PRODUCT When discussing products, most people think of tangible items such as Nike shoes or Spalding basketballs. In sports, products take many forms. Teams, websites, personal training, events, and even the athletes themselves are all products of the industry.

PLACE Most businesspeople don't automatically think of distribution as part of marketing. It's easy to overlook because most of the focus is placed on creating and promoting the product or service. Yet, where you sell the product (place, placement) is a key component of successful sports marketing plans. Will it be sold online, through distributors, or directly to consumers through infomercials? These decisions say a lot about what type of product you have. A product sold at a big box discount retailer is viewed differently than a product featured at an expensive boutique. Between the products there may not be a huge difference in quality, but the way the products are marketed through their placement creates a perception for the consumer.

PROMOTION Promotion includes advertising, public relations, personal selling, discounts, and sampling. Each can play a role in a marketing mix.

PRICING Price is the amount charged for a product or service. Although there are many ways companies determine price, in the end price often is determined by how much the buyer is willing to spend. A carefully marketed product can create demand and command higher price levels. Often, the price of tickets to see your favorite team rises if the team is successful or wins a championship. Although the product is the same, fans pay the increase when their team is successful.

And now, introducing the fifth P.

PROGRESS There has never been so much change happening at one time in the world of marketing. The days of simple TV, radio, and print advertising are over.

Although those methods will always be options for a marketing mix, they are no longer the automatic go-to options. Social media has changed the game. Almost daily, new options to help market products develop. Some companies have completely abandoned the old-school marketing methods and have created a marketing mix solely on the Web. Companies must stay alert and on top of the latest methods that progress affords them to keep ahead of their competition.

Some progressive methods are obvious. Facebook, Instagram, and Twitter have changed the way companies market. Other new methods are still developing. Many companies are taking a long look at options such as QR codes, Pinterest, Foursquare, social analytics, and other new trends to determine whether they fit into their marketing mix. I'm certain that by the time this book is published, there will be many more options available. That is why I have created the fifth P, and why progress is critically important to any marketing plan. This text examines how the five Ps affect specific niches in the industry.

Sports and the Fundamentals of Marketing

Many companies have chosen to use the field of sports as a way to reach their target market. The target market is a segment of the population to which a company has chosen to promote and sell its product. Targets are chosen from market segments. Market segments divide a specific population into categories based on demographics, geography, psychographics, and product choices:

Demographics: Demographics define a population by gender, age, family status, income, education, and ethnicity.

Geography: Geography divides a population on the basis of where people reside. It can include broad categories such as countries, cities, rural, or urban. It can also be further defined by naming a particular neighborhood within a city, for example.

Psychographics: Psychographics define a population by lifestyles and interests.

Product choices: Product choices define a population by the products that people use and the frequency with which they use them.

In your marketing career you will use all of the fundamentals mentioned, but the world of sports changes faster than just about any other industry. Companies in the sports industry are not selling product based solely on need. When hype, fandom, loyalties, and excitement are the main driving forces of the buyer, the marketer must be nimble. Whereas it is important to have long-term plans, as in traditional marketing, sports marketing is a different animal. Popularity, loyalty, and following can change overnight. One great play, game, or season can turn an average consumer into a superfan. Likewise, one misstep by a team or player can destroy years of consumer loyalty built up by marketing programs. Successful sports marketers who are fundamentally sound follow a strategic long-term plan but are positioned to change that plan whenever necessary. The fluidity of the marketing plan is what separates good sports marketers from great ones.

The Power of Sports Marketing

Each semester I start my first sports marketing class with a discussion of the marketing of trading cards. The product is the most amazing example of pure sports marketing. Trading card companies have created a product that is approximately a nickel's worth of ink on paper. But, through marketing, they have made the product exciting, collectible, and sought after.

The challenge to sports marketing product development teams is how to keep a simple printed product fresh and exciting. I typically show examples of how cards have developed through the years. The first cards showed posed photos of players holding a bat or mitt. They were printed on cardboard and had a white border and a matte finish. Then, companies developed cards using full bleed (no more white borders), action photography. Next, they created limited editions and autograph cards and randomly inserted these into packs so consumers would start to chase these cards and buy more product. Later, companies started to imbed small pieces of game-used equipment into their cards as a way to bring fans closer to favorite players. This game-used concept includes jerseys, balls, helmets, bases, bats, floors, and just about anything else that could be laser cut into small pieces. This was also a way to create card sets around legendary former players who still had uniforms and equipment available for the companies to use.

In class, after discussing the minimal costs of creating a simple trading card, I pass around some examples. I mention that the autograph and game-used cards often start trading at around $175. The final card that I show is a Tiger Woods game-used shirt card from one of his championships, which recently sold for $21,000 on eBay. These values show the power of sports marketing and the value to companies of the passion of the loyal fan.

From now on I want you to be more than just a fan. When you watch a game on TV, think about the commercials in the broadcast. Do they reach the demographic of the viewers? When you attend games, look at the signage of sponsors and ask yourself whether the sponsors are a good fit. When you see a name on a stadium, ask whether the venue-naming rights were worth the price paid. The average consumer never thinks about many aspects of the business of sports. It's time to look beyond your team loyalties and see the business of sports unfolding in front of you.

Building Your Résumé

Each semester, I have a leader in the sports human resources industry work with my class. She brings many years of sports experience to my students. I think that we can all learn a thing or two about how to market ourselves as job candidates from her main discussion points.

First, she says that when she is hiring she looks at a prospect's résumé for 3 to 6 seconds on average. Let's stop and think about that for a second. You may work for weeks building your résumé. You probably get help from your career services office and friends. You might spend hours polishing it before you deem it good enough to submit for your dream job. In turn, the person in human resources (HR) at that company may scan it for as few as 3 seconds. In those precious seconds, you must make an impression that lands your résumé on the save pile. (When I worked at Upper Deck, it was not uncommon for us to receive 500 or more résumés for an open position. From that group, 10 to 20 candidates would receive phone interviews and 5 would make it to an actual in-person interview from which the new hire was chosen.) So, do not waste any space on your résumé. Make each line count. This is your chance to market your skills. If you include an objective statement, make it specific. Too many times I see résumés that state that the candidate is energetic and a hard worker. That tells me nothing. Use those few lines to reiterate your goal and further highlight your experience. If you have specific sports experience, explain in your objective statement that you want to build on your experience with XYZ Sports Company to achieve your goals. This is a great chance to name-drop and get noticed. Also, references or even the statement "references available upon request" should not appear on your résumé. If a company wants references, it will ask you to provide them. Stating that you are proficient in Word and Excel is a waste of space unless such skills apply to a specific position—companies will assume that you can work the most simple business programs. Instead, use that space to further differentiate your résumé from your competition's. Finally, if job seekers have any experience, I prefer they place the education section at the end of their résumé. Almost every graduating senior places their education at the top of the résumé. Instead, feature your experience and help HR representatives find what they are looking for in those precious 3 to 6 seconds.

Second, the HR expert relates how her office looked out on the parking lot, so she would watch candidates enter the building for an interview. She said that with almost 100% accuracy she could predict whether a candidate would be a fit for the company before the person even entered the building. What does that mean? To me, it shows that candidates must think of every detail throughout the entire hiring process: how your résumé looks, what your cover letter says, how you conduct yourself on the phone, how you dress for an interview, what your body language conveys, whether you make eye contact during the interview, and even how you hold yourself when entering the building.

After teaching our very first class together, the HR expert called me to say that she saw three students in class who she thought were sharp and could do well in the industry. One of those 3 had asked a question, and the other 2 had just listened to her presentation. So, she had picked those 3 from a group of 40 with almost no direct interaction. If I had to rate the class from top to bottom, those 3 would have been my top picks, too. By evaluating eye contact and body language, the HR expert was able to determine the best of the best. This should demonstrate that there is a lot more to getting a job than simply submitting a résumé online. Don't miss any details when trying to secure your dream job. The bad news is that these sports jobs are difficult to obtain. The good news is that most candidates will *not* use all the tools available that can give them an advantage in getting their résumé transferred to the save pile and securing an interview—but you can.

These days, traditional paper résumés often are replaced by digital résumés. LinkedIn profiles were an early entry, and now dozens of sites can help you construct and share your résumé online. Monster.com is a well-known site where you can create and upload your résumé. Tech-oriented sports marketing firms may prefer electronic submissions. The digital format offers some advantages, including the ability to link to social media references and projects created by the applicant. There is also the disadvantage of making links to embarrassing social media pages available to potential employers. Video interviews and presentations are easily linked to a résumé. Employers may screen digital résumés by trolling for keywords appropriate for a job. Savvy applicants research the right terms to place on the résumé.

The most common problem I see on résumés is that most students lack experience in sports marketing. There are three ways to combat this shortcoming on your résumé. First, determine which skills that you have developed in other jobs translate to the job you are trying to secure. Even if you have worked in construction or waiting tables, skills and duties of those jobs can translate into business experience. For example, you can spin the phrases *working on a team*, *organizing a schedule*, *achieving goals*, and *completing tasks in a timely manner* to catch the eye of the HR representative.

Second, include any class projects on your résumé. For example, if in your sports marketing class you had to complete a project for a company in the industry, make sure to include a section on your résumé entitled Sports Industry Experience. Word it something like "completed group project for the VP of Marketing at XYZ Sports Company." Explain the project's objectives and your solutions. Students rarely think that a class project is worthy of including on their résumé. Remember, all you are trying to do is get your résumé into the save pile. Also, remember that someone in the HR department may look at your résumé for only 3 seconds. Their eyes are trained in that short time to pick up keywords that tell them you have the experience they are looking for. A mention of a well-known company in the industry will often warrant a closer look at your résumé. Because most students applying for their first job in sports have no sports industry experience, even the mention of a small sports-related project could be enough to get you ahead of the competition.

Third, secure a sports-related internship. An internship is a great way to gain experience while in school. Most students assume that an internship in sports, like a first job in sports, is impossible to get. Whereas many big companies offer formal internships that might be difficult to secure, smaller companies are typically happy to have an intern help them build their business. There are small to midsized sports companies everywhere. Around San Diego, where I teach, there are more than 40 sports companies, many you may have never heard of. Almost all of these companies are open to interns. The common theme that I hear from these companies is that they would love to have an intern, but they don't know how to secure one. If you are willing to work for free (in most cases), you can secure an internship because very few companies will turn down an offer for free labor. Do your homework and find all of the companies in your area. LinkedIn is a great way to find local companies in sports. You will probably be surprised that there are sports companies nearby. Don't be afraid to contact the companies directly or through LinkedIn to tell them that you are taking a sports-related class and that you are interested in being an intern to gain experience. You will be surprised by the response. Once again, most students will not do this, so you will be one step ahead of your competition.

Your First Job in Sports

I got my first job in sports 10 years after I graduated from college. However, I made my first attempt to enter the industry just after I obtained my MBA. The Minnesota Timberwolves franchise was entering the NBA, and it had entry-level ticket sales positions available. I applied and did everything that I could think of to get noticed. This was pre-Internet and e-mail days, so I sent letters, made phone calls, and I remember sending an overnight package congratulating the new head of marketing. Despite all of that, I didn't get the job. I did send a follow-up note that said I had a lifetime of sports knowledge, I played college basketball, I had an MBA, and that all I wanted was an entry-level sales position—I was asking, "What's the deal?" They were nice enough to respond and say that they received thousands of responses, many from applicants with industry experience who were willing to take a pay cut to get in the door. It was hard to argue with that. I then proceeded to work in an industry about as far away from sports as possible, a small company in the environmental industry. When I had my shot to apply to Upper Deck a few years later, I used the strategies discussed earlier to try and make my résumé attractive to the HR department. Fortunately, many skills and duties of my then-current job translated well to working at Upper Deck. Also, the environmental company had grown significantly during my tenure, and Upper Deck was looking to grow its business at a rapid pace. So, if you want to work in this industry and have no experience, it's your job to figure out what skills you have that will translate to your desired sports position.

In the next few paragraphs, I describe some entry-level positions to give you an idea of what types of jobs are available in each niche of the industry that this book covers. First jobs in sports licensing, product development, and advertising typically are titled something like "Marketing Coordinator." An example of a typical marketing coordinator position follows:

POSITION

SPORTS MARKETING COORDINATOR

SUMMARY *Overview of the position.*

Support company's marketing team and efforts. Coordinate the creation and distribution of marketing materials to staff, distributors, and vendors. Provide support for events, promotions, and sponsorship programs.

ESSENTIAL DUTIES AND RESPONSIBILITIES

Create, review, and edit marketing materials.
Be responsible for on-time delivery of all marketing materials.
Work with operations and purchasing to secure best available pricing and timeliness of the production of marketing materials.
Work with brand managers to secure appropriate licensing approvals.
Coordinate the on-time delivery of all POP and advertising materials to retail locations.
Be responsible for the execution of all sweepstakes, including legal copy, bonding, and delivery of prizes.

INTERACTION

This position reports directly to the sports brand manager and will interact with the VPs of Marketing, Licensing, and Events.

EDUCATION/YEARS EXPERIENCE

Bachelor's degree in marketing, advertising, or business or 2+ years of experience

SKILLS AND ABILITIES

Team player
Ability to keep a timely schedule
Strong knowledge of sports
Strong communication skills
Ability to network and build relationships
Ability to travel
Strong organizational skills

As you can see, many of the requirements are skills that are transferrable from different jobs and experiences.

For agent and athlete marketing positions, most entry-level jobs are in an athlete support role. On the agent side, you may work directly with a group of athletes, attending to their needs. On the marketing side, your supporting role would include reaching out to companies to create potential endorsements and helping with the athlete's social media plan.

For a team marketing position, you will most likely start in a sales role. Many find this uncomfortable because it involves a lot of cold calling. Most of the people that you talk to do not want to hear from you. You have to get used to a lot of rejection. Most students entering this position have great excitement and expectations that they will be around the team and a professional sports organization. Although technically they are, the initial days require them to sit in a cubicle and make as many cold calls as they can. It's not as glamorous as expected, and many new employees are quickly disappointed in what they thought was a dream opportunity. Those who can stick it out usually succeed in the industry.

For college marketing positions, the path includes a start in the athletic office. Introductory positions include game day operations, event management, and sponsorship sales. Jobs vary by the size of the university.

First jobs in the properties and players union groups usually entail working with licensees. This could include being part of the current licensee's product approval process or reviewing new licensing applications.

For sports advertising, most initial jobs involve helping to develop the strategic brief for a campaign and monitoring all deadlines for each step. Advertising coordinators must be organized and have the ability to keep all involved, informed, and on target to meet a campaign timeline.

Initial positions in the sports events industry almost always involve on-site coordination and execution of events. One position recently posted by the sunglasses company Spy Optic included the coordination of all the company's outreach to its business-to-business partners. This may include promotions at various doctors' offices or at cycling, triathlon, and running events.

Cause marketing positions almost always involve working with the development of sponsorship proposals. The ability to create proposals is a sought-after skill. This may be one of the times when including your proficiency in Word, PowerPoint, Photoshop, Acrobat, and other software applications may be warranted.

Finally, positions in media training are probably unique in sports. Most media training companies are run by a single individual who does most of the direct work with the client. Staff positions usually include the scheduling of clients and the promotion of the business. Trainers come from many different backgrounds.

First jobs in sports marketing are similar to entry-level positions in traditional businesses. Necessary skills include organizational skills, ability to communicate, and work ethic. If you can focus on and build these skills, you will have a shot at securing your dream job. My final word of advice to secure a job in sports is *network*! Go to as many events, talks, and sports trade shows as you can. Speak with every sports-related person who comes to your campus. Be a prolific LinkedIn user. Don't wait—start now and follow your dream.

Chapter 2

Licensing

CHAPTER OBJECTIVES

- Understand licensing.
- Learn the history of licensing.
- Understand how the five Ps affect licensing.
- Identify key benefits of licensing to both licensee and licensor.
- Learn the key components of a licensing plan.
- Review team, league, and athlete licensing deals.
- Review a licensing contract.

CHAPTER OVERVIEW

This chapter covers the fundamentals of sports licensing. It discusses how the rules of licensing control almost everything that a sports marketer does. It includes a sample licensing contract and reviews the most important aspects of the document.

Voices from the Field: Linda Castillon
Biography

Linda M. Castillon describes herself as a "product person." She has more than 25 years of experience working in the licensed sports, entertainment, and brand industry creating exceptional and best-selling products. Her expertise in creating these licensed products has generated millions of dollars in revenue for the companies that she has worked for.

She has been in charge of the licensing departments for such sports brands as Upper Deck Company, The Original Ball Bag Company, Fathead, and Skinit. Along the way, she has handled licensing deals for icons of sports, including Michael Jordan, Tiger Woods, Kobe Bryant, and many others. Her experience with the NFL, NBA, MLB, and NHL is unparalleled in the industry.

Linda started her career in the gift industry in Los Angeles and Texas. She then entered the wholesale arena in New York in categories such as sleepwear/lingerie, jewelry, and accessories. Her next stop was Seventh Avenue to work on selling licensed apparel.

That's when her career in licensing really took shape. She worked with Jim Benton on selling his new evergreen property, "The Misters," for Sharkys, Apparel, Trevco, and Apparel America. She built a successful licensing program that placed millions of dollars worth of this property on T-shirts that sold into retail. One of her "real big" successes was helping to launch a new product category in sports and entertainment: The Real Big Fathead line of life-sized wall graphics was an instant hit.

Linda appreciates the power of licensing and understands how to build a business from the ground up. She knows how to market and sell the licensed product that she helps to create, and she knows how to build brands. "I love working with the licensors, licensees, celebrities, agents, athletes, artists, and the manufacturers who develop quality products." Her nickname is "The Licensing Guru."

Q&A

Q: *What is your current position?*

I am the Senior Vice President of Licensing at CARD.com. We produce high-quality skins for electronic devices.

Q: *How did you become an expert in your field?*

Well, nothing beats hands-on experience. I constantly strive to learn and get better. I've worked in many niches of the licensing world, learning a bit in each one.

Q: *Tell me about your department. Who works with you?*

I typically have a few sport and entertainment licensing managers, an occasional student intern.

Q: *How is it structured?*

I like to give the people who work with me direct contact with the licensors. It's the only way to truly learn the business. I will have each person handle the day-to-day with a few licensees. I usually divide it by sport or entertainment category. I always try to teach my team so that they learn as much as possible and get hands-on experience.

Q: *What is the most exciting thing about the field of licensing?*

Licensing changes every day. Teams or players get hot, break records, or win a championship. The companies that can respond first to those events win. Sometimes it feels like you are part of the sport. You have to stay on top of everything that is happening on the field or court and be positioned to take advantage of opportunities when they arise. It's very exciting.

Q: *What advice do you have for students interested in licensing?*

Study the industry. Learn how licenses are awarded. Understand the league structure of properties and players unions. And, if possible, get an internship while you are still in school. Always be learning.

Courtesy of Linda Castillon.

Introduction

Sports licensing is one of the most important things that you will learn from this book. A license is *the* legal link between a league, team, or player and a paying client or sponsor. Negotiating a license agreement is a central skill set in this business. You must learn to maneuver easily through all the brands, governing organizations, players associations, contracts, and rules and regulations. Knowing the guidelines that govern licensing is paramount to success in the consumer products, sports licensed industry.

Licensing occurs when the owner of intellectual property (IP)—copyrights, trademarks, indicia, or "licensed marks"—grants use of the IP to a third party (licensee) in exchange for a fee. The licensor is the owner of the property. The licensee uses the property for a fee.

History of Licensing

Licensing is not a new phenomenon. Examples actually reach back centuries. However, licensing really started to blossom with the advent of television. Weekly shows and cartoons spawned image and likeness use of many characters, from Mickey Mouse to Superman.

Table 2-1 Historical Retail Sales of Licensed Products by Property Type					
Property Type	**2002**	**2007**	**2010**	**2011**	**2012**
Entertainment/character	$49.9B	$52.4B	$46.0B	$48.0B	$49.3B
Corporate/brand	$24.2B	$24.7B	$19.7B	$21.2B	$21.6B
Fashion	$19.5B	$17.7B	$15.1B	$16.0B	$16.5B
Sports	$14.0B	$15.0B	$11.8B	$12.3B	$12.6B
Art	$4.7B	$5.1B	$3.8B	$3.9B	$3.9B
Collegiate	$3.4B	$3.7B	$3.6B	$3.8B	$3.8B
Music	$2.6B	$2.8B	$2.6B	$2.7B	$2.7B
Nonprofit	$844M	$931M	$736M	$758M	$779M
Publishing	$941M	$857M	$690M	$752M	$732M
Others	$211M	$190M	$63M	$63M	$63M
Total	**$120.4B**	**$123.4B**	**$104.0B**	**$109.3B**	**$112.1B**

Modified from: SportsBusiness Daily. Licensing Revenue Rising in U.S., Canada. June 18, 2013. Sportsbusinessdaily.com http://www.sportsbusinessdaily.com/Daily/Issues/2013/06/18/Research-and-Ratings/Licensing.aspx

Licensing is used to enhance and add value to consumer products and goods in many assorted industries. Art, nationally known consumer product brands, celebrities, sports, entertainment, music, and several types of proprietary software are the major intellectual properties in focus in consumer products licensing. Sports are one of the leaders in the field of content licensing and one of the most visible—after all, football is king in the United States, and baseball is as good as Mom's apple pie. According to Forbes, retail sales of professional sports and collegiate licensed products have been as high as $15.15 billion in a single year.[1] (See **Table 2-1**.) For decades, entertainment companies such as Disney have been licensing the rights for use of their characters' images on products. Elvis is one of the biggest revenue-generating celebrities year after year. The music industry accounts for a large number of licensing deals and, with the death of Michael Jackson, looks to capitalize on more and more licensing revenue. Music's big revenue generators also include the Beatles.

The National Football League (NFL) and Major League Baseball (MLB) propel sports to the forefront of revenue generators year after year, even during strikes. (See **Table 2-2**.) Sports licensing is fueled by the passion that consumers feel for their sport, team, and favorite athlete. Fans want something tangible to link them to their heroes, and even if a game is locked out, the consumer who loves sports can still share his or her passion for the game. Retailers happily supply licensed T-shirts, caps, mugs, and cell phones.

As the featured speaker at the 2009 NFL Licensing Summit, Jerry Jones, owner of the Dallas Cowboys football team, delivered this message, which struck a chord with me. I paraphrase: *Some folks will never get to go to a Dallas Cowboys game at Cowboys Stadium, but by buying some licensed Dallas Cowboys products, they'll be able to, even in a small way, feel the passion and wonderment that going to a live game delivers. By*

Table 2-2 2012 Estimated Licensing Revenues—U.S./Canada	
Property Type	**Licensing Revenue (in millions)**
Art	$134
Character (entertainment, TV, movie)	$2550
Collegiate	$206
Fashion	$755
Music	$122
Nonprofit (museum, charities)	$36
Sports (leagues, individuals)	$685
Trademarks/brands	$928
Publishing	$35
Other	$3

Reproduced from: SportsBusiness Daily. "Licensing Revenue Rising in U.S., Canada." June 18, 2013. Sportsbusinessdaily.com
http://www.sportsbusinessdaily.com/Daily/Issues/2013/06/18/Research-and-Ratings/Licensing.aspx

watching a game on television and seeing our brand new stadium, that fan will feel like he's actually there. That comment sums up why these products are so successful. Sports licensed products provide fans with a way to show support and fuel their passion for their team.

Before a third-party company or sponsor is willing to pay for a sports license, team, or player, the owner/licensor needs to have already developed brand equity to leverage. Very few consumer product companies or athletes have enough brand equity to sell a license on their own. The entire team/roster or organization is needed to offer the chance of success for the product line.

That's why powerful and popular brands such as the NFL and National Basketball Association (NBA), as well as athletes like Michael Jordan, have been able to create large revenue streams through licensing deals. These are carefully crafted brands, built over time, and that brand equity can be leveraged to make it profitable.

How the Five Ps Affect Licensing

PRODUCT   The product in licensing is an intellectual property. Although not the typical tangible product that one thinks of in business, an IP can be a valuable asset to it rights holder.

PRICE   Licensing fees take a number of different forms. Some have a fixed fee, whereas others may have a royalty-based price structure. Most have some combination of a minimum guarantee and a royalty.

PROMOTION   There are many different aspects to promoting in the licensing industry. First, the owner of the IP must promote and build its brand in order to attract other companies to it. Companies paying for the rights to associate with an IP must then promote that association with the goal of increasing sales of their product.

PLACE   Once the owner of an IP has decided to license that IP to other companies, it must choose which companies it wants to partner with. Many times, IP owners will license only one company in a category. It is critical for the owner of the IP to perform due diligence and determine the best company with which to place its brand.

PROGRESS   In the past, licensing deals were pretty clear-cut contracts. Often, they took the form of an IP holder allowing another company to use the IP holder's logo on a product. For example, the NFL may license a T-shirt manufacturer the right to include team logos on their shirts. The continued development of the Web has created many opportunities for the use of an IP to help promote a brand. These new opportunities can make the rights portion of a licensing contract extremely complicated. The lines become particularly blurred with the use of images on fantasy sports websites. Whereas progress creates opportunities, it also creates rights questions in licensing.

Why License?

Consumer product licensing allows the licensor (brand owner) and licensee (consumer products company) to capitalize on each other's strengths. For instance, the NFL doesn't have the knowledge or infrastructure to produce or distribute anything other than the management of its brand and the game. If the NFL wants to have trading cards produced for the teams and the brand, it must negotiate with all the major trading card companies to put together a licensed deal, whereby the brand and the teams are represented in great products and offered to consumers. Through the due diligence process, the NFL (property holder) can license with the best companies in an assortment of industries. The resulting mix of products will drive millions of dollars in sales and revenues. The NFL brand is enhanced while profitably satisfying the consumer sports fans.

Likewise, without a consumer products license from the league, the trading card company, as the licensee, doesn't have access to the star athletes or brand equity that the NFL controls. Both entities benefit from the partnership, and consumers have new products that further build their loyalty to the NFL brand.

Benefits to Licensor

New product offering: The rights holder or licensor can create a portfolio of products by leasing its intellectual property to manufacturers. This allows the licensor to spread its brand equity to multiple channels.

Creation of new and additional revenue streams: Licensing creates a revenue stream for the licensor through the flow of royalty payments from the licensee.

Expansion of brand equity and brand footprint: The licensor can use licensing as a form of advertising to reach many different demographics of consumers. The NBA has done a wonderful job of creating women's licensed clothing that reaches boutique clothing stores.

New channels of distribution: Through licensing, sports brands are now seen in hardware and grocery stores and in the bedding, toy, bath, and clothing departments of major retailers. These distribution channels could not be reached without a licensing program.

New demographics: Through licensing, the leagues have gone beyond the typical male-dominated demographic. Now, kids are using licensed toys, teens are playing licensed video games, and women are wearing licensed apparel. This exposure to new demographics has helped the leagues build their brand equity.

Benefits to Licensee

Minimal capital investment: Beside the royalty, an investment in a licensing program is minimal. Typically, companies simply add a league logo or player image to their existing product. The actual process is inexpensive.

Use of brand equity of licensor to make impact: Many sports properties are some of the most recognizable brands in the world. The ability to produce a product featuring one of those brands gives that product instant credibility.

Higher price points: Licensed products demand a higher price point. A plain cotton T-shirt may sell for $10 at retail. That same shirt with a Nike Swoosh and Michael Jordan's image may retail for $25.

Solid revenue stream: A well-planned licensing program should command higher price points and sell more product. This creates a revenue stream difficult to match without the use of a licensing program.

New distribution channels: Licensed products open doors at retail for companies. In the T-shirt example, the generic shirt has limited distribution possibilities. That same shirt with a sports license may be attractive to sporting goods stores, team shops, and stadiums. Through licensing, companies can create many different distribution opportunities.

Payment and Cost Structure

Although many types of licensed deal structures exist, the majority contain certain elements in common. Consumer products, sports licensing deals, and payment scenarios contain these elements:

- Advance
- Royalty
- Minimum guarantee

The licensor usually collects an agreed-upon advance payment on execution of the agreement, which means when the agreement is signed by both parties. The guarantees vary depending on the product category and the company. There is no set guarantee, and guarantees are completely negotiable. Royalties are also negotiable but tend to range from 8% to 15% depending on the product category, league, and length of license.

Typically, an **advance** is developed based on giving the licensor (brand owner) one-third to one-half the total minimum guarantee payment that the company (licensee) thinks it can deliver over the term of the agreement. This amount is calculated by forecasting sales of the product over the term of the agreement.

A **royalty** is a percentage of sales revenue to be paid by the licensee (product company) to the licensor. Royalties are based on whether the licensed products will be sold through wholesale channels or direct-to-consumer channels.

The **minimum guarantee** payment is what a licensor (brand owner) expects to make over the term of the licensing agreement from the licensee (product company). The minimum guarantee payment is typically built on a sales forecast (from wholesale or direct-to-consumer sales), and it is based on what the licensee expects to sell during the term of the agreement.

For example: Let's say that a company that manufactures action figures wants to make figures of NBA players. If the company estimates that it can sell $10 million in product in 1 year, then a reasonable minimum guarantee might be $1 million based on a 10% royalty. This is paid by the licensee to the licensor (brand owner). The final minimum guarantee payment is paid at the end of the agreed-upon term of the contract.

Securing a License

In its most basic form, securing a license takes three steps:

1. Product idea
2. Business plan
3. Financial proposal

PRODUCT IDEA

Product ideas can either be new or an innovation of a current product. As discussed later in Upper Deck's case, interesting product innovations can be enough to secure a sports license. In the other example, Fathead introduced a relatively new product concept. In each case, the licensor expects the concept to be interesting and well developed. Licensors are inundated each day with product pitches. Every company that applies for a sports license thinks that it has the next great idea. The job of licensing groups in each league is to evaluate the applications and choose the right products and companies. A well-developed product concept can help separate a company's application from its competition's.

BUSINESS PLAN

The business plan to support a product is a critical piece of a sports license. The plan should include features and benefits of the product, financial projections, competitive review of the territory requested, and distribution plan. Companies often overlook the value of a distribution plan. Helping a licensee reach a distribution category where it does not have a presence is a valuable asset. A company selling its product through direct-to-consumer, call-to-action TV commercials would give an athlete or league great exposure. These are the types of things that could help a licensee acquire a license.

FINANCIAL PROPOSAL

The bottom line in all licensing proposals is the revenue they drive. If the product concept and business plan are strong, the initial revenue numbers don't have to be spectacular. The long-term potential is just as important to the licensor. These projections can be the most difficult part of a business plan and licensing application. The initial thought is always to try to impress the licensor with how much revenue the company can create. The downside is that a high estimate directly drives up the minimum guarantee. Finding that fine line between creating excitement and overcommitting takes skilled negotiating.

Athlete and League Licensing

Most major sports have some version of a group license. This is often called a **group licensing authorization** or **agreement (GLA)**. The league players union attempts to get every player signed to a GLA as soon as a player is drafted. The GLA allows the league to market its players to potential licensees as an entire group. This makes it easy for a company to have access to all players in a sport without having to do many individual agreements.

The money generated is split between the league and the members of the GLA. The individual players split their piece evenly regardless of participation in a product. This sharing-of-the-wealth system allows even players without much marketability to receive an equal check from the league. As a marketer, understanding each sport's governing body's GLA is essential to building a successful sports licensing program.

Sports leagues have been able to expand their brands and increase their global footprint by licensing to leading consumer product companies in many different countries and industries. Apparel licensing is a key driver of revenue in the world of sports licensing. Other profitable avenues include licenses for video games, trading cards, signed and unsigned collectibles, home décor, and accessories. These consumer product licenses are negotiated with a small upfront investment (an advance), working against a fixed royalty (royalty) paid monthly or quarterly, against a back-end minimum guarantee (the guarantee).

Licensing is conducted in a similar manner across all of the major U.S. sports leagues, both domestically and internationally. As mentioned, some sports leagues have **players unions** that represent the players and control the use of their individual images and likenesses. Each sports entity also has a consumer products group, or **properties group**, that represents the owners and controls the use of team marks, copyrights, indicia, and uniforms.

The granting of most consumer licenses follows a common pattern. The licensor, the players union, or owners require the licensee to pay an advance against a royalty calculated across the term of the agreement. Royalties are paid on all product sales. Royalties are typically paid quarterly, during the term of the agreement. Some sports entities require monthly reporting but quarterly payments, and some sports entities require monthly payments.

As an example, a trading card company wants to show action shots of 50 NFL players in a set of trading cards. Because the players are being shown in their officially licensed uniforms, the company needs to have licenses in place with both the players union (NFL Players, Inc.) and the owners (NFL Properties). Both licensors require a royalty of between 8% and 15% on all sales, depending on the agreement. Each requires a minimum guarantee against that royalty. The guarantees vary greatly by product but often are in the low seven figures. Let's say that the minimum guarantee for NFL Players (the players union) is $2 million. That would mean, with a 10% royalty, that the trading card company would have to sell at least $20 million, at wholesale, in card sets to cover the minimum. If the trading card company does not reach $20 million in sales, it still must pay the $2 million guarantee.

The payment of these types of royalties is called a shortfall. Typically, the leagues and players unions are always "made whole" on shortfalls unless the product company has gone out of business. In some rare cases, it is actually acceptable for licensees to negotiate these shortfalls down or to try to negotiate them completely away. Much depends on the skill of the individual negotiating the licensing deal.

NASCAR and the Professional Golfers' Association (PGA) have a different licensing structure. They do not have properties groups or players unions that control image and likeness rights for their drivers or golfers. NASCAR recently started working for the assorted driver teams on a few licensed product categories, acting as the leagues do, as a governing body. It is having some success on die-cast cars and apparel. NASCAR would like to expand this management position into all product categories so that it will be much easier for product companies to work with NASCAR and the drivers without the need for separate deals with NASCAR and all the individual driver teams. One entity will review the business plan and financial proposal to strike a licensing deal.

Michael Jordan made a strategic licensing business decision early in his career. (See **FIGURE 2-1**.) He decided to opt out of (not participate in) the NBA's group licensing program. This meant that he would not take his share of the NBA's licensing revenue that is split evenly among players. Any company licensed by the NBA that wanted to feature Jordan in its products needed a separate agreement with Jordan to do so. This move meant that Jordan would not have to share licensing dollars with other NBA players. In addition, he could command lucrative contracts from any company wishing

FIGURE 2-1 Michael Jordan.
© John Swart/AP Images

to use his image and likeness. This small strategic move made millions of dollars for Jordan.

Throughout his long and illustrious career, Jordan has licensed his image to dozens of companies making a plethora of products. Jordan's name or image graces apparel, sports equipment, figurines, collectible coins, plates, limited edition gold cards, watches, limited edition signed and numbered photos, and signed fine art pieces. Each of these licenses created an additional revenue stream for Jordan. More importantly, these deals expanded and broadened his brand and reinforced his brand equity.

Nike and Jordan, even before his retirement, created Brand Jordan as a way to keep his name relevant. Despite his not playing since 2003, the Jordan name still sells. A select number of superstar athletes from different sports form the Brand Jordan team. This has allowed Nike to expand the Jordan reach beyond basketball and to create another brand with an exclusive feel that it can license. Of course, Jordan is involved with the athletes who get to be included in this exclusive club.

Tiger Woods built a mini-kingdom of licensed goods before his fall from glory in 2009. (See **FIGURE 2-2**.) Woods actually made it cool and relevant to play golf and to buy golf memorabilia and collectibles. He pulled the sport out of its exclusive, narrow space

FIGURE 2-2 Tiger Woods.
© David McNew/Getty Images News/Thinkstock

in the sports industry. The Tiger image injected the game and anything that had to do with golf with a certain amount of panache and glamour. Nike exploited the situation by branding an entire product line of equipment, clothes, and accessories with his name. Using his name and image, International Management Group (IMG), his agency of record, was able to create endorsement deals, sponsorships, and promotions to sell cars and insurance and to push financial institutions. All these deals needed a license in place to happen.

The golf industry has no licensing governing body, unlike the NFL, MLB, and National Hockey League. To license Tiger's name for a product line, companies had to have an endorsement deal (license) with Tiger directly through IMG. To make an even more authentic product, companies needed to arrange a deal with the PGA. The total fees likely were in the seven figure range.

History of a License: Upper Deck and Fathead

A product can be a completely new idea or an extension of an existing idea. In either case, in order to secure a license potential, licensees must convince the property rights holder that the idea is unique and needed in the industry.

FIGURE 2-3 Peyton Manning.
© Doug Pensinger/Getty Images Sport/Thinkstock

The start of the Upper Deck Company is a fascinating licensing tale.[2] For decades, the trading card industry was a stagnant marketplace. Little to no innovation had occurred, and no new licenses had been awarded in ages. With the advent of personal computers, counterfeiting started to become an issue. In particular, a late-eighties New York Yankee Don Mattingly card started showing up much more frequently than it should have. Collectors started to realize that their hobby had a developing counterfeit problem.

Upper Deck found a new way to fight counterfeits. The original owners of Upper Deck each had a unique skill set. One had knowledge of photography, one, holograms, and another, access to financing. Their combined abilities fit together to solve the counterfeit problem. Traditionally, sports trading cards depicted a player in a posed position and were printed on cardboard in a matte finish with a white border. One Upper Deck innovation was to substitute full-bleed action color photography. The second innovation was the hologram. A hologram on the back of the card made it difficult to counterfeit. Both seem like very simple solutions, but no one had done it before. They arranged to hold a photo shoot with a couple of Major League Baseball players and used those photos to create color, full bleed, action shot trading cards. Of course, they included a hologram on the back that made it all look very impressive and official. Cards in hand, they secured a meeting with Major League Baseball's licensing group. The group was blown away by the quality of the cards. Upper Deck obtained a license and began producing cards a short time after that.

In addition to the license and quality combination, Upper Deck also made one strategic marketing decision that helped it become the dominant company in the industry. It decided to designate the card of a minor league baseball player by the name of Ken Griffey Jr. as its number one card. (See **FIGURE 2-4**.) That year, no other company included Griffey in its offerings. Griffey debuted in April and had a sensational rookie season. Upper Deck struck gold by offering his rookie card, which became one of the most sought after cards in the history of collectibles.[3]

Fathead was also started with a simple idea: Passionate sports fans would love to display life-sized images of their favorite player on their walls. Linda Castillon was brought on board to secure all of the licenses. The company had two things that excited the leagues and helped Linda secure the deals.

First, the product concept was new and exciting. No one before had created a product where such large-scale, quality images could be mass produced. The "real big" concept brought something fresh to the passionate fan looking to decorate a kid's room or man cave. (See **FIGURE 2-5**.)

Second, the proposed method of distribution also piqued the leagues' interest. The direct-to-consumer model of distribution was new in this category. Fathead proposed to use NFL players in commercials to sell its product. Each one became a promotional piece for Fathead as well as for the leagues and players. Ben Roethlisberger appeared in the first commercial, and it was a great success. This is an example of Fathead not only using a new product idea but also leveraging a new distribution opportunity to help secure the license.

FIGURE 2-4 Ken Griffey Jr.
© Elaine Thompson/AP Images

FIGURE 2-5 Kevin Durant.
Courtesy of Fathead L.L.C. Used with permission.

Example Licensing Contract

This section introduces a typical league licensing agreement. Each contract is unique, but most share common language. It is critically important for you to understand what is covered in a licensing contract. In each part of the agreement, I share some common language, explain what that language means, and point out any tricks of the trade that you should be aware of.

LEAGUE LICENSE AGREEMENT

SAMPLE LANGUAGE THIS LICENSE AGREEMENT   is entered into by The League ("LEAGUE") and The Licensee ("LICENSEE") with regard to the commercial use of certain names, logos, symbols, emblems, designs, and uniforms and all identifications, labels, insignia, indicia, or trade dress thereof ("Marks") and names, nicknames, photographs, portraits, likenesses, signatures, or other identifiable features ("Attributes") of current players. License is only granted for the use of the Licensed Marks in the distribution, advertisement, promotion, and sale of the Licensed Products in accordance with this Agreement.

MEANING   "Grant of rights/scope of agreement": The brand owners and the sports leagues will attempt to grant very specific *product rights* to licensees. Licensees will attempt to get as broad a set of product rights as possible. For instance, a company that currently makes limited edition collectible coins may go to the NFL and request a broad collectibles license because it knows that in the future it plans to expand into other collectible products. The NFL will try to limit the license to only the coins that the company currently produces, which gives the league the opportunity to license other companies that manufacture other collectible products. These initial negotiations will determine the structure of the product license moving forward. An established company has more leverage versus a start-up company in negotiating for product rights because it has a track record to share with the brand owners.

INSIDER TIP   As you can see, the leagues are very specific about the use of their marks, logos, and player images. In contracts like this, very little is left to interpretation. It is important that your designers have a firm understanding of the rights granted under the contract.

A. LICENSED PRODUCTS

SAMPLE LANGUAGE   [Insert product description.] The above Licensed Products shall be manufactured, distributed, advertised, and sold under the "Company" label.
    LICENSEE must develop and offer for sale at least one product per team in the licensed product line.

MEANING   The league will request very specific descriptions of the company's products. Securing and negotiating product rights in a license contract can be one of the most difficult steps in securing a deal. There are many things to consider in the process of securing and carving out product rights. Is it a brand-new product? Is it a new variation of a product? Does the product offer the consumer something new and unique? How does the product differ from others in the same category of products in the marketplace? Licensees need to clarify to the leagues what value their products will offer.

INSIDER TIP   Companies need to be very specific about what they are manufacturing. All leagues will try to get a licensee to produce equal amounts of product for each team. This can be negotiated. Obviously, some teams or players sell better than others do. It is the job of the company to create some flexibility in this section of the contract so that it does not have to produce product for teams or players that aren't marketable.

B. TERM

SAMPLE LANGUAGE   The contract shall be for 1 year and shall be the period commencing on _____ through _____.

MEANING   Initially, the term of any license agreement is predicated on what is normal and customary in the product category being negotiated. Typically, a company with a great reputation and a history in the product category can negotiate a longer term than a new company or start-up can. When a licensee approaches a licensor with a brand-new product idea, it will be harder to negotiate a longer term than 1 year. Look at it from the point of view of the brand holder and you will understand the hesitancy to grant more than a 1-year term: No licensor wants to compromise brand image with shoddy merchandise. The new retailer is given a short-term contract. During the initial term, the licensee needs to produce terrific-looking product. Good sales and a strong royalty stream make longer terms easier to renegotiate.

INSIDER TIP   Many initial contracts are for a period of 1 year. Once established, contracts can be 3 years or longer. Licensee performance during the initial year will determine the possibility of contract renewal.

C. TERRITORY

SAMPLE LANGUAGE   Product may only be sold via LICENSEE's website and to consumers within the 50 United States, District of Columbia, Canada, and Puerto Rico (the "Territory").

MEANING   Territory means the approved geographic area where the company can market licensed products. Typically, domestic manufacturers want their territory to be the domestic United States, its territories, and its military bases. Licensees should add territories to the agreement only if they have sales coverage or a distributor in those territories working to sell and place products. Adding territories such as Canada and Mexico requires additional advance payments and more guaranteed dollars in the agreement.

INSIDER TIP   A contract should be only for territories where the company has distribution. Otherwise, licensees are paying for territories where they aren't going to make money. The contract should be as specific as possible.

If a product line is developed around a college, for instance, Ohio State University, it may not make sense to try and distribute those products internationally. Licensees may want to limit the scope of the agreement and focus on only the immediate area surrounding the particular team or brand. Ohio State currently handles its own product licensing but may in the future move its portfolio to Collegiate Licensing Company (CLC), Licensing Resource Group (LRG), or Strategic Marketing Associates (SMA), which all handle college sports licensing.

D. ROYALTY RATES

SAMPLE LANGUAGE   LICENSEE shall pay quarterly to LEAGUE a royalty equal to the percentage of "Net Sales" as defined in this agreement.

Licensed Products containing Player Attributes: 10%

MEANING   In consumer products licensing, royalty rates vary widely and are predicated on a number of factors: uniqueness of products, how many other companies are manufacturing the same or similar products, distribution capabilities, length of time in the category, and brand name. Apparel lines, which typically generate high royalties, tend to have lower royalty rates. Secondary product categories (in the hard goods categories, such as stationery, home products, and accessories) generally have higher royalties associated with them, but these products generate lower sales volumes than T-shirts, jerseys, caps, and apparel, so the licensor will try to compensate by requiring a higher royalty rate. With the development of the direct-to-consumer channel of distribution, and the proliferation of consumer-facing websites and stores, it has become necessary to develop two ranges of royalty rates. When a consumer products company collects payment directly from the consumer, the royalty rate is typically double that of products that are sold into the wholesale channel of distribution for placement at retail.

INSIDER TIP   Royalty rates can be negotiated but are typically between 8% and 15%. The leagues usually state that they have a standard rate. It is possible to negotiate these rates based on specific variables in a particular contract.

E. MINIMUM GUARANTEES

SAMPLE LANGUAGE   LICENSEE guarantees that its royalty payments for the contracted year under this Agreement shall be at least the amount set forth below:

1st Contract Year: $100,000

MEANING   The minimum guarantee is built on forecasts of sales of the licensed products, over time, and usually covers the first year in the term. Companies need to forecast how much of the licensed product they will sell in the assorted channels of distribution covered in the agreement during the term and at what price. Based on those predicted net sales, the minimum owed to the leagues, the brands, or the IP holder can be determined.

INSIDER TIP   These guarantees are payable to the league no matter how much product is sold. It is imperative to negotiate a minimum that the company can reach realistically. Understanding the sales forecasts helps in determining an acceptable minimum.

F. ADVANCES

SAMPLE LANGUAGE   At the commencement of each Contract Year, LICENSEE shall pay to LEAGUE against LICENSEE's annual Minimum Guarantee as set forth above:

1st Contract Year: $50,000

2nd Contract Year: $125,000

MEANING The advance is typically a small portion (a percentage) of what the licensee guarantees over the entire term of the agreement, paid when the agreement is finalized by both parties or executed. The advance lets the league partner know that the licensee company is serious and intends to move forward to develop licensed products, and that the company will deliver the new licensed products into the consumer products channel of distribution covered in the agreement. Most of the time, the advance is a third of what is required for the minimum guarantee. This payment gives the partner the confidence needed not to double-license the particular product category.

INSIDER TIP This is part of the minimum guarantee. These upfront payments show the league that the licensee is committed to the license. These are negotiable. The less money that a company has to pay upfront, the more that it has available to manufacture, market, and sell the product.

G. ADVERTISING AND PROMOTION

SAMPLE LANGUAGE League will devote 3% of royalties to advertising and promotional efforts of category.

When LICENSEE exhibits at trade shows or advertises product, at its sole cost, it agrees to show an equal selection of league products.

LICENSEE agrees to exhibit at a once-a-year LEAGUE-sanctioned trade show.

In addition to contractually required samples, LICENSEE agrees to provide the League with a $5000 merchandise credit.

MEANING Marketing, advertising, and promotion fund: Several brands, and some of the major leagues, write into their agreements a certain amount of money required from the licensee due during the term of the agreement that is earmarked and used for brand building, league advertising, and promotion. These charges can be for television spots, online and offline marketing efforts, e-mail blasts, features on the company website, press releases, ads in magazines, and banner ads with promotional or affiliate partners. This small percentage helps the licensor to offset the costs of unique brand building, marketing, and advertising efforts.

INSIDER TIP This money helps the league promote the licensees' category. It is imperative for the licensee to discuss upfront how this money will be used by the league. Without a specific plan in place, it is easy for this money to get wasted. The licensee wants to get value from every dollar spent. It is important for licensees to work with the leagues to make sure this money is spent in a way that helps sell the product.

H. TEAM REPRESENTATION; LIMITATIONS ON LICENSE

SAMPLE LANGUAGE   Unless otherwise approved in writing by LEAGUE, no license is granted for the use of the Marks of the LEAGUE Playoffs or Championships. The LEAGUE Logo may not be used by itself. When shown with a team logo, it must be shown with equal or greater prominence.

MEANING   Every licensing contract has limitations. In this case, the league sees a value in its championship logo and wants additional payment for logo usage. Each year unique Super Bowl, NBA Finals, and World Series logos are created.

INSIDER TIP   Notice that this license does not include the rights to the championship logo. If a company wants to feature championship product, it would need an additional license. It's a way for the league to make more money through licensing.

I. STATEMENTS AND PAYMENTS; REPORTING

SAMPLE LANGUAGE   Statement and Payments: By the thirtieth (30th) day of each month, LICENSEE shall furnish full and accurate statements of the agreed upon Net Sales. These calculations will be divided on a territory, unit, team, and player basis.

Failure to Comply: If LICENSEE fails to comply with agreed upon reporting terms, LEAGUE shall have the right to charge interest, fine, or terminate the agreement.

MEANING   Statements and reporting: Typically, companies are required to report quarterly, on or before 30 days past the quarter's end date. Some leagues and colleges make licensees report monthly but pay fees quarterly. Usually, it is a good idea for companies to have a specific employee dedicated to handling the accurate and timely reporting, accounting, and managing of the royalties. If companies report late or pay late, they can be held responsible for additional late changes.

INSIDER TIP   It's imperative that a company's accounting department understands the terms of the contract. Staying current and in compliance helps keep the relationship strong. Accurate and timely reporting increases the chances that a license will be renewed.

J. NONRESTRICTIVE GRANT

SAMPLE LANGUAGE   The LEAGUE has the right to grant other licenses in this category. Nothing in this agreement prevents the LEAGUE from granting additional licenses as it sees fit.

MEANING   This is a nonexclusive agreement that allows the league to license other competing companies. To achieve an exclusive license, companies typically need to pay a larger fee or have a unique product offering.

INSIDER TIP   In this case, the league has the right to issue other licenses in this category. This is not an exclusive deal. To obtain exclusivity in a category, the company needs to have a compelling reason to convince the league to protect it from competition in the category. Most of the time this is done by agreeing to increase the typical advance, minimum, and royalty.

K. PREMIUMS

SAMPLE LANGUAGE   LICENSEE shall not use product as a Premium without the prior written authorization of LEAGUE.

MEANING   There are separate agreements for products that will be sold as premiums. Premiums are typically sold for a lower price and may be subject to different royalty rates.

INSIDER TIP   The league is very specific about the method of distribution. It is important to inform sales groups of the company's rights in this section. Selling in a nonauthorized way will lead to issues with the licensor.

L. OWNERSHIP OF MARKS AND GOODWILL

SAMPLE LANGUAGE   LICENSEE acknowledges that the LEAGUE Marks are owned exclusively by the LEAGUE.

MEANING   Although the licensee manufactures, markets, and sells the product, it does not own the marks.

INSIDER TIP   The company is only leasing the marks from the league. The league is the sole owner.

M. QUALITY, APPROVALS, SAMPLES

SAMPLE LANGUAGE   LICENSEE shall submit both pre-production and post-production samples to the LEAGUE. All products will follow the LEAGUE-specific style guide for style, quality, and appearance.

MEANING   After securing a license, all new products must be approved by the licensor. This process typically takes 3 to 6 weeks depending on the league and complexity of the product. During contract negotiations, at what stage of the manufacturing process samples will be sent in for approval should be agreed upon. Obviously, it must be before products are manufactured, but samples must be as close to the finished product as possible. If the licensor requests changes, the licensee must make those changes and resubmit the product. Leagues never give companies the latitude to assume approval. Expiration of the "approval period" is not enough. Companies must have all approvals in writing.

Per the agreement, when product is approved and finalized, the licensee is required to send each licensor a specific number of approved samples of the products. The number of samples required should be worked out with each licensor prior to the final execution of the agreement.

INSIDER TIP Samples and approvals often become an issue between the leagues and licensees. Systems must be in place to make sure that the company complies with these standards. It can become difficult when a company is trying to get a product to market quickly. The approval process can be long. If the licensee has a good relationship with the league, it can occasionally get something approved quickly. When a quick approval is needed, it will depend on the relationship that has been built with the league contact. Companies must build the approval process into their product development timeline.

N. DISTRIBUTION

SAMPLE LANGUAGE LICENSEE shall use its best efforts to distribute licensed product in all areas agreed upon within this contract. If in any 90-day period LICENSEE fails to sell product, it will be deemed failure to use best efforts. LICENSEE will make best efforts to support LEAGUE promotional efforts with retailers.

MEANING The channels of distribution are the channels and markets that will sell these licensed products. Whether a licensee is selling strictly online through a proprietary website or in brick-and-mortar retailers determines what categories will be carved out in the agreement. If the company is selling into retail, the subcategories can become segregated as follows: mass retailers, national discount retailers, gift retailers, electronics stores, home specialty retailers, Internet retailers, office specialty stores, regional discount stores, mass retailers, television home shopping networks, wall décor stores, and others.

INSIDER TIP If licensees don't use their licenses, they will lose them. They should be very specific about how and where they will sell product and make sure that distribution is in place to support the agreement.

O. RECORDS, AUDITS

SAMPLE LANGUAGE LICENSEE shall keep accurate records covering sales, shipments, use of league holograms and hang tags, and shipment tracking. LEAGUE has the right at its sole discretion to examine and audit records.

MEANING Records and audits: Accurate books and records need to be available at all times at the licensee's place of business. The leagues and colleges typically audit companies every year or every 2 years. According to the agreement, should errors be found on any of the accounting forms, the company will be penalized and must pay those fees to stay compliant.

INSIDER TIP Involving the accounting department in any league license is important. Having organized and accurate records helps build trust with the league, which will help when it is time to renew the license.

Sublicensing

A lucrative niche in the licensing industry has developed in the sublicense arena. Although most league licensing agreements prohibit sublicensing, it does often occur. Usually, each opportunity is handled on an individual basis. A sublicense is when the licensee has the rights to license product rights to a third party. Companies such as Upper Deck have used this licensing strategy for many years. It includes both licensing and sublicensing rights in many of its contracts. Where it has a licensing agreement with the NBA and Michael Jordan to manufacture trading cards and other products, it also has sublicensing rights to market Jordan's image and likeness to other companies. Jordan allows Upper Deck to create and manage his collectibles category and create his licensing program. This has led to lucrative deals for collectible products such as plates, figurines, coins, and art pieces.

Case Study

Janet Varn is the head of licensing for a major university. She has been asked to devise a licensing program that will develop over the next 5 years and create a revenue base for the school. She has looked at the strategies used by similar universities. There seems to be two popular programs. Some schools have licensed the school's intellectual property in many categories. Others have taken a more exclusive approach and licensed only a small number of high-end products. Both seem to be lucrative strategies.

1. What strategy should Janet take?
2. Would you rather have a higher-end, more exclusive program or make sure that your fans could get products in all the areas that they desire?
3. Does the university have an obligation to its fan base to provide them with licensed products?

Critical Thinking Activity

OPPORTUNITY

Last night, LeBron James scored 103 points in the Cavaliers game against the Lakers, breaking Wilt Chamberlain's long-standing NBA record of 100 points in a single game. Greg Bertoni, the sports buyer at QVC, called to say that he can give you 1 hour of airtime to commemorate the event.

Challenge

Create seven products. The product mix should include retail price points from $20 to $1500. QVC will mark up the wholesale price 100%. The QVC sales goal is $4000 per minute, or approximately $250,000 for the 1 hour of airtime.

Develop a rough profit and loss statement (P&L) for one product. Your target is a 50% profit margin. Include raw materials, labor, league licensing fees of 20%, signature cost of $50 if applicable, and general and administrative expenses of 10%.

Goal

Convince the QVC buyer that he should give your team the airtime. You should be prepared to present your most unique product and convince the buyer (your professor) that your product is the one that will most excite his QVC audience. You can use a table like the one that follows to present your ideas.

Product	Retail Price	Projected Sales	Revenue

CHAPTER QUESTIONS

1. What is the difference between a royalty and a minimum guarantee?
2. How does geography come into play in a licensing agreement?
3. Go to your school bookstore and name three licensed products you find there.
4. What is the difference between NFL Properties LLC and NFL Players Inc.?
5. If your company's product features an action shot of LeBron James playing against the Lakers, what licenses would need to be in place to legally sell this product?
6. Find a sports advertisement where the company featured is fully licensed.
7. Find a sports advertisement where the company is not licensed.
8. Find an advertisement where a company that is not sports related is using sports as a way to reach a demographic.
9. Do you need a PGA license if your company's advertising campaign features Tiger Woods golfing? Explain.
10. Approximately how many dollars in royalties would an MLB licensed company pay MLB Properties if its product generated $25 million in revenue?

INDUSTRY CONTACTS

National Football League Properties: The Properties group is the collection of NFL owners. It is headquartered in New York City.

NFL Players Inc.: NFL Players Inc. is the football players' union. It is headquartered in Washington, D.C. The website is www.nfl.biz.

Major League Baseball Properties: The Properties group is the collection of MLB owners. It is headquartered in New York City.

MLB Players Union: The union represents the MLB players and is headquartered in New York City.

National Hockey League: The NHL represents the owners in hockey and is headquartered in New York City.

NHL Players Association: The NHLPA is headquartered in Toronto, Canada, and represents NHL players. The website is www.nhlpa.com.

National Basketball Association: The NBA represents team owners and is headquartered in New York City.

Major League Soccer: The MLS represents the professional soccer teams and is headquartered in New York City.

Major League Lacrosse: MLL is headquartered in Boston, Massachusetts, and represents the professional lacrosse teams. The Web address is www.majorleaguelacrosse.com.

Collegiate Licensing Company: The CLC is located in Atlanta, Georgia, and represents a large number of colleges for their licensing rights. The Web address is www.clc.com.

Licensing Resource Group: LRG represents a number of colleges for their licensing rights. They are located in Holland, Michigan. The Web address is www.lrgusa.com.

NASCAR: NASCAR governs and sanctions the sport of auto racing. It is located in Daytona Beach, Florida.

Licensing.org: LIMA is the international licensing association and is located in New York City.

Appendix

Following is an example of the NFL licensing application. All licensees start their application process by filling out this document. This sample form was copied from www.nfl.info.[4]

NFL PROPERTIES LLC
PROSPECTIVE LICENSEE INFORMATION PACKAGE

Thank you for your interest in becoming a licensee of NFL Properties LLC ("NFLP").

As you may know, NFLP serves as the exclusive representative of the National Football League and its professional football member clubs for the licensing of its and their trademarks and logos (the "Marks"). The Marks include, among others, the NFL Shield design, the Super Bowl and Pro Bowl logos, and the team names, nicknames, colors, symbols, emblems, helmet designs, and uniform designs.

NFLP licenses all commercial uses of the Marks (as herein defined) including the manufacture, distribution, and sale of products bearing any of the Marks. NFLP undertakes these licensing activities to promote and support NFL football, enhance fan interest and loyalty, and ensure that fans have access to a broad range of quality products representing the League and its member clubs.

NFLP grants licenses to companies that will support its promotional efforts. A product license with NFLP requires a commitment to market products that support and enhance NFL football, payment of a royalty to NFLP based on a percentage of product sales, an annual payment of an advance against royalties, an annual payment of a minimum royalty of at least $100,000 (unless otherwise determined, on a case-by-case basis, by NFLP) based on actual sales of the products, and maintenance of insurance from a licensed and admitted insurance carrier with a rating not less than A-VIII from an A.M. Best-rated insurance company that must include: comprehensive commercial general liability insurance, on an occurrence form, with a combined single limit for bodily injury and property damage, including products liability (including completed-operations coverage), and including coverage for contractual liability, independent contractors, broad form property damage, personal and advertising injury, in an amount of at least Six Million Dollars ($6,000,000.00) per occurrence and Twelve Million Dollars ($12,000,000.00) in the aggregate. In some instances, these requirements may vary due to the nature of the products and the licensee's business.

Additionally, a product license contains detailed quality control guidelines and other requirements related to a licensee's performance under the license including a requirement that the licensee manufacture units of the licensed product: (i) with the Marks of each of the Member Clubs individually and (ii) in accordance with (x) all applicable laws, rules, and regulations, and (y) appropriate standards regarding fair labor and other human rights.

If you wish to apply for a license, please complete the attached Prospective Licensee Information Form and General Authorization and return them with a product sample and letter of credit from a financial institution to the following address:

New Products Division
NFL Properties LLC
280 Park Avenue
New York, New York 10017
newproducts@NFL.com

NFLP will then review these items and provide you with a decision on your license request as quickly as possible. **Please note that we do not have any obligation to grant you a license by sending you this information package or reviewing your completed Prospective Licensee Information Form and product sample.**
Thank you for your interest in NFL Properties LLC.

Notes

1. Steve Olenski, "The Power of Global Sports Brand Merchandising," *Forbes*, February 6, 2013, http://www.forbes.com/sites/marketshare/2013/02/06/the-power-of-global-sports-brand-merchandising/.
2. Pete Williams, *Card Sharks: How Upper Deck Turned a Child's Hobby into a High-Stakes, Billion-Dollar Business* (New York: Macmillan, 1995).

3. "Types of Licenses," Licensing Industry Merchandisers' Association, accessed September 15, 2014, https://www.licensing.org/education/intro-to-licensing/types-of-licensing/.

4. "NFL Consumer Products Licensing Pre-Qualification Information, Licensing Pre-Qualification Terms and Conditions," National Football League, accessed September 15, 2014, https://www.nfl.info/NFLConsProd/Welcome/CpPrequalify.htm.

Chapter 3

Properties Groups and Players Unions

CHAPTER OBJECTIVES

- Become acquainted with properties groups and players unions.
- Learn the history of properties groups and players unions.
- Learn how the five Ps affect properties groups and players unions.
- Identify key benefits to properties groups and players unions.
- Review creative league deals.

CHAPTER OVERVIEW

This chapter covers the inner workings of running a major sports league. It discusses how the leagues are structured and how the owners and players interact. The rules and regulations regarding the business of sports are also reviewed.

Voices from the Field: Keith Gordon

Biography

Keith Gordon serves as the President of NFL Players Inc., the licensing, marketing, and strategic partnership subsidiary of the NFL Players Association. NFL Players Inc., is composed of four distinct groups: Licensing, Partner Services, Player Services, and Special Events. Keith is responsible for setting the organization's vision, values, and revenue goals while overseeing all operating business units. In addition to serving on the board of NFL Players Inc., Keith oversees a team of 30 employees who are responsible for representing more than 1,800 active NFL players. He joined NFL Players, Inc., as Vice President of Licensing in January 2009. He assumed the role of President in August of the same year.

Prior to joining NFL Players Inc., Keith was Director of Sports Marketing at the Lavidge Company, an independently owned marketing and communications firm in Scottsdale, Arizona. While at the Lavidge Company, he grew the sports portfolio by developing strategic partnerships with local and national businesses, including the Phoenix Suns, KTAR 620-AM Sports, Arizona State University Athletics, the PGA Tour, World Golf Championships, the Phoenix Mercury, and NBA Entertainment.

Keith also spent 8 years with the National Basketball Association as Director of Global Business Development. While at the NBA, he increased both domestic and international licensing revenues as part of the NBA's Global Merchandising Group. During his time with the NBA's TMBO (Team Marketing and Business Operations) Group, he was instrumental in shaping and sharing best practices among NBA, Women's NBA (WNBA), and NBA Development League (NBDL) teams, which led to increased marketing and ticket sales revenues.

Keith is an active member of the Young Presidents Organization and belongs to the Greater Washington, D.C. chapter. He received his undergraduate degrees (political science, history, economics) from Arizona State University and attended the University of Cambridge, where he continued his studies in economics and political science.

Q&A

Q: *What is your current position?*

President of NFL Players Inc.

Q: *What has been your greatest accomplishment at NFL Players Inc.?*

Changing the culture of the organization; emerging from the lockout to create a modern, exclusive, and highly valuable business-to-business brand for the players. Also, the exclusive licensing deals with EA Sports and Nike from a deal perspective. From an innovation perspective, the creation of proprietary licensing tools and intellectual property (e.g., digital licensing engine, player's shop, and caricature product line).

Q: *What has been your favorite moment with an athlete?*

As a fan—my favorite moment was walking out of the tunnel and seeing my Arizona Cardinals play in (and almost win) the Super Bowl the same year I joined NFL Players Inc.

As a person—it's the moments very few people see. When a player lets you in because they know you, they trust you, and you're able to truly connect with them on a personal level.

Q: *What is the most exciting thing about working with the leagues?*

Being involved and at the top of your game in any industry is exciting. Throughout my career, I've had the good fortune to work with some of the best brands, the most creative people, and the most entertaining properties. The most exciting part for me is the pace at which change occurs, and the fulfillment and reward that comes from playing a meaningful role in that process.

Q: *What advice do you have for students interested in working with properties and unions?*

It's important to realize the difference between a job and a career. A career is your journey toward finding personal and professional fulfillment. Jobs are often stops along the way to serve a particular purpose. Embrace opportunity, don't ever shy away from hard work, and always remember to ask "why?"

Courtesy of Keith Gordon.

Introduction

Not every sport is structured the same, but the big four in the United States have similar types of governing bodies. The National Football League (NFL), National Basketball Association (NBA), Major League Baseball (MLB), and National Hockey League (NHL) all have a **properties group** and a **players union**. Although there are many emerging niche leagues such as Major League Soccer (MLS), Professional Bull Riding (PBR), and Major League Lacrosse (MLL), this text focuses on the structure of the big four because they have the most stringent set of rules for partners.

Most fans are never exposed to the properties groups or players unions unless there is some kind of a contract dispute. When a dispute or perhaps a lockout occurs, fans are subjected to hours of press coverage of the event. This is one of the few times when it becomes obvious that there are two distinct governing bodies running the leagues.

The unions represent players collectively in matters of wages, hours, working conditions, benefits, rights, marketing, and licensing. With only a few exceptions, players join the union upon entering a professional sport. The properties groups are in charge of marketing and promoting the teams, their logos, and trademarks (intellectual property) for marketing, licensing, and media rights. In addition, they represent the owners as a group in contract negotiations.

The big four leagues have been around for many years: the MLB since 1896, NHL since 1917, NFL since 1920, and NBA since 1946. It took a while in each sport for the unions to form: MLB, 1953; NHL, 1957; NFL, 1956; and NBA, 1954. These formations can all be traced to disputes that arose when players asked for increased salaries and benefits. In the case of NFL players, the original dispute was the players requesting clean socks to play in. The formation of a union gave players collective bargaining power with the owners and usually led to better working conditions.[1]

Each of the big four leagues is divided into subsets. Baseball features the American League and National League, which are then further broken into conferences of East, Central, and West. The NBA is simply divided into conferences, the Eastern Conference and the Western Conference. The NHL has an Eastern Conference and a Western Conference; the Eastern Conference is broken into the Atlantic Division, Northeast Division, and the Southeast Division, and the Western Conference is divided into the Central Division, Northwest Division, and Pacific Division. The NFL has two conferences, the American Football Conference and the National Football Conference; each conference has divisions that are separated into North, South, East, and West.

Most of the big four leagues are able to filter their players through the use of minor league systems. The most intricate of them all is in baseball. The hierarchy of baseball begins with a rookie league, followed by Short Season A, Low-A, High-A (also known as Single A), AA, and finally the top tier of AAA. Players can enter the draft to begin moving up the minor league ranks as early as when they complete high school. The NBA uses its Development League model (D-League) as a minor league farm pool. Although players may opt to play overseas instead, the D-League is the true feeder system. The NHL's minor league system consists of the American Hockey League (AHL), which serves both the United States and Canada, whereas the East Coast Hockey League (ECHL) operates solely in the United States. Much like MLB, every NHL team has a minor league team. Last, the NFL on paper does not have a minor league system any longer. NFL-Europe was once a means of allowing players to gain experience before moving back to the States to play. This endeavor proved to be too costly and not as fan-friendly.[2] With the elimination of NFL-Europe, teams draft players from the college and university level.

It is important to understand the many leagues, divisions, and subdivisions in sports because each one presents a sports marketing opportunity. The opportunities are many and varied even within a specific level of sports. Teams such as the Yankees and Lakers may not look at a division championship as a big marketing opportunity. Their fans are conditioned to expect only championships as a reason to celebrate. Fans of the Bobcats or Cubs would be happy to wear hats and apparel proclaiming their team as division champ. In the minor leagues of sports, the opportunities may not be as lucrative, but they still exist. A minor league baseball team may not have much appeal beyond the geographic location of the team. But within that region, there are opportunities to create awareness and excitement through sports marketing. The key is understanding where your team fits in the many leagues, divisions, and subdivisions.

Each major professional sports league has a strong players union. The union represents the players' interests, whereas the owners represent themselves as a united front. Unions were not established at the same time as the leagues. Players may have been taken advantage of in the past because of the lack of representation. Through the action of the unions, each league currently has a collective bargaining agreement, or CBA. These agreements are signed by both the players and owners. Successful labor compacts suggest that each party feels fairly compensated for services rendered. When the terms of the CBA are not agreed upon, either side may choose to interrupt the season. The players may strike, or the owners may institute a lockout. In either case, players are unpaid and do not have access to team facilities, trainers, or medical care, and the owners suffer a nearly complete loss of revenue. Lockouts often occur during the off-season, when financial damage to the owners is minimal. A work stoppage continues until both parties can agree to the terms of a contract.

History of Leagues and Unions

It is important to understand the complete history of each league because that history dictates how the leagues are run today. Sometimes a decision that was made 100 years ago affects the structure and strategies of our modern-day leagues.

MAJOR LEAGUE BASEBALL

Baseball made its debut on the major league level in a short-lived entity known as the National Association. This league lasted from 1871 to 1875. Although Major League Baseball and the Baseball Hall of Fame do not recognize the National Association as a major league, it was composed mostly of the highest-caliber players of that time.[3] Major League Baseball does recognize the Union Association (1884), American Association (1882–1891), the Players League (1890), and the Federal League (1914–1915).

The National Association of Base Ball Players (NABBP) came onto the national scene during the 1860s. By 1867, the NABBP had grown to more than 400 member clubs. After many disputes in regard to professional players and amateurs, the NABBP split into two groups in 1871. The second group called themselves the National Association of Professional Base Ball Players. Five years later, the National League of Professional Base Ball Clubs was created. The emphasis on clubs was important because clubs could enforce player contracts.[4] It was good for the fans because clubs were then required to play their full schedule of games. The first attempt at the World Series occurred in 1882 when the National League met the American Association.

The National Association of Professional Baseball Leagues (NA) was created in 1901 to help end smaller rivals from expanding into territories that would threaten the National League. This was important because the American League began trying to create teams in areas that would promote direct competition against the National League. NA is now known as the minor league system, which acts as talent pool for

MLB. After 1902, the National League, American League, and the Minor League system signed a national agreement. This agreement married players' contracts to the league contracts. Baseball players became property of the teams and unable to switch teams when they felt fit to do so.

The period from 1900 to 1919 was called the "dead-ball era." The game appeared slow and low scoring to fans, and owners were not willing to pour money into their teams for common necessities such as balls. To help pick up the speed of the game, the National League adopted the foul strike rule, and the American League did likewise in 1903.[5]

Baseball became known as "America's pastime" because it grew with the country during its time of need and expansion. During World War II, baseball remained a constant despite men being sent overseas. It allowed the public to escape from their everyday lives. In the 1950s and 1960s, MLB expanded, adding teams from north, south, and west. As people began to move from the East Coast, MLB remained a constant in their lives even outside of their hometowns.

MAJOR LEAGUE BASEBALL PLAYERS ASSOCIATION

Before the Major League Baseball Players Association (1953), there were four prior attempts at creating a players union. In 1885, the Brotherhood of Professional Baseball Players was founded. Next, the Players Protective Association was created in 1900, followed by the Fraternity of Professional Baseball Players of America in 1912, and then the National Baseball Players Association of the United States in 1922.

The MLBPA hired Marvin Miller, a previous United Steelworkers of America leader, to head up the association in 1966. Miller served in this capacity until 1983. During this time, he negotiated the first CBA (1968) with the owners, which resulted in increasing the minimum salary for players. The major leagues experienced their first player strike in 1972 because owners refused to increase player pension funds. Another strike occurred in 1981 during the "Miller era" because of the disagreement over free agent compensation.[6]

A major role the MLBPA has played for players is acting as their advocate regarding steroids. Originally, the MLBPA was opposed to random drug testing for these performance-enhancing drugs. After pushback from the public, coupled with the BALCO scandal, the MLBPA agreed to adhere to a stricter policy that included a 50-game, a 100-game, and a lifetime suspension from the league based on the number of failed drug tests.[7]

NATIONAL BASKETBALL ASSOCIATION

Before the NBA, the league was known as the Basketball Association of America (BAA). It was founded in New York City on June 6, 1946. Three years later, the BAA merged with another league, the National Basketball League (NBL), to form what is now known as the National Basketball Association (NBA). This new league, by way of the merger, boasted 17 franchises that played in large and small markets. The playing venues ranged in size from arenas to armories. In an effort to promote the league, the

NBA downsized until the market reached the smallest it had ever been, eight teams. These eight franchises were all located in large markets.

The league faced an external threat in 1967 when the American Basketball Association (ABA) was formed. The ABA introduced new opportunity, and NBA players began to make the switch to play in the ABA.[8] The ABA is also known for introducing the three-point line to the game, helping the sport grow. It was also within the ABA that the All-Star game and Dunk Contest originated.

In 1976, the ABA and NBA merged, keeping the NBA name. The NBA expanded into Canada in 1995, and in 1996, it developed a women's league, the Women's National Basketball Association (WNBA).

NATIONAL BASKETBALL PLAYERS ASSOCIATION

The players created the National Basketball Players Association (NBPA) in 1954, making it the second oldest trade union among the big four. NBA team owners did not recognize this union until 10 years later, in 1964. In 1983, the players and owners reached a historic agreement, introducing the salary cap era.[9] This agreement set precedent for all future players and potential lockouts.

The first NBA work stoppage occurred in 1995, outside of the normal playing season. It lasted from July 1 through September 12. In 1996, there was a second lockout. It lasted only 3 hours. The next lockout lasted almost 200 days during the 1998–1999 season. In total, 464 regular-season games were lost. The basis of this lockout was the owners wanting to change the salary cap system and the players opposing these plans and instead seeking a higher league minimum salary. The end result was a new maximum salary for players and a pay scale for first-year players.[10] This contract served for 6 years.

At the conclusion of the contract in 2011, the owners and players could not agree on the terms of the CBA. The owners began the lockout process. The NBPA dissembled from a union to a trade association so the players could represent themselves in class action antitrust lawsuits against the league. On December 1, 2011, the players voted to re-form a union. In order to negotiate the CBA, the players had to be represented by a union. The current CBA altered the previous agreement on sending players to the D-League, the age limit for the NBA draft, and, of course, compensation.[11]

NATIONAL HOCKEY LEAGUE

The National Hockey League (NHL) was created after the suspension of its predecessor organization, the National Hockey Association (1909). The NHL was established in Montreal, Canada, on November 26, 1917. What began with 4 teams eventually settled into a set of 30 franchises as a result of geographic expansion, relocation of teams, and team contractions.[12] The first American NHL team was the Boston Bruins, formed in 1924. The first NHL All-Star game was played to help support Ace Bailey, a player whose career ended short as a result of a vicious hit.[13] In 1947, the first All-Star game that did not benefit a specific family was played in Toronto, Canada.

The Great Depression and World War II hit the league hard. Many teams were forced to fold because of a lack of funding. The 1942–1943 season included six teams: Boston Bruins, Chicago Blackhawks, Detroit Red Wings, Montreal Canadiens, New York Rangers, and Toronto Maple Leafs. These teams are referred to as the original six because they made it through the 1967 NHL expansion and are still active today.

During the mid-1960s, the Western Hockey League (WHL) planned to declare itself a major league and issued a challenge to play for the Stanley Cup.[14] The NHL absorbed this plan and instead expanded the league to include the teams in the WHL. Canadians became outraged because the six teams added from the WHL were all American teams. In order to calm the Canadians, the NHL added the Vancouver Canucks along with the Buffalo Sabres, whose hometown bordered the Canada-U.S. line.

In the early 1970s, the World Hockey Association (WHA) emerged and created new teams to rival the NHL. Again, the NHL took over the teams, adding markets in Atlanta, New York, Washington, and Kansas City. The WHA and NHL fought over players until the 1979 merger agreement in which the WHA ceased operations while the NHL took over the remaining teams in the WHA. The last large expansion cycle took place in the 1990s and added nine teams to the league.[13]

NATIONAL HOCKEY LEAGUE PLAYERS ASSOCIATION

The first National Hockey League Players Association (NHLPA) was established in 1957 by Ted Lindsay of the Detroit Red Wings and Doug Harvey of the Montreal Canadiens. The league had refused to release pension plan financial information, and these two players decided there needed to be a platform for the players to voice their thoughts and be heard. The NHLPA essentially was dismantled when owners began trading players who were involved with the association or began sending those players to the minor leagues. The NHLPA was reestablished in 1967 when Bob Pulford met with NHL team owners and demanded they recognize the union. Failure of owners to recognize the union would have resulted in the NHLPA appealing to the Canadian Labour Relations Board to officially seek recognition. Pulford also demanded that no player involved be reprimanded. The NHLPA then would represent two-thirds of the league's players, and the players would in turn not strike for the duration of the agreement as long as the owners upheld their end of the deal.

The first strike initiated by the NHLPA was in April 1992 and lasted a mere 10 days. The players thought that by calling a strike so close to the end of the regular season, they had an advantage since the majority of owners make profits during the playoffs. In order for the remaining 30 regular-season games and the playoffs to continue, both sides reached agreement quickly. As part of the deal, the 80-game season was increased to 84 games and players would earn larger increases in playoff bonuses for each round they won.[13] Players feared that this agreement would be short lived and that the owners would eventually lock the players out.

The players' suspicions came true one season later during the 1994–1995 lockout, which lasted 104 days and reduced the season to 48 games. This meant 468 games were lost during this time along with the All-Star game. The biggest culprit leading up to the lockout was the salary cap. Owners were in favor of this notion, while players opposed it. Both parties did agree that there was another big issue that needed to be dealt with: small-market franchises. The league wanted player salaries to be directly correlated to the revenue that the team brought in.[15] The NHLPA wanted to implement revenue sharing to help the smaller markets. In the end, the larger teams such as the Red Wings and the Rangers sided with the league because they feared that the detrimental effects of an extended lockout would outweigh the benefits of obtaining a salary cap.

The lockout ended in January 1995. The regular season for the first and only time extended through the month of May, and interleague games were limited because of the time constraints. The owners were able to institute a salary cap that applied to rookies. Veteran players were not subject to salary caps.

The 2004–2005 NHL lockout was unique in professional sports. The entire professional season was canceled.[16] The season's cancellation marked the first time since 1919 that the Stanley Cup was not awarded. The dispute lasted 310 days, beginning in September 2004 and lasting until July 2005. In 2004, the NHL approached the NHLPA seeking that player salaries be tied to league revenues, much like the argument that arose during the 1994–1995 lockout. The league pitched its idea by presenting six concepts to achieve this goal, including a hard or inflexible salary cap, a soft salary cap, centralized salary negotiation, and a luxury tax. The union rejected all six of the ideas. This battle went back and forth until February 2005 when the NHL commissioner canceled the season. During the lockout, 388 NHL players went overseas to Europe to play. In July 2005, 87% of the players and 100% of the team owners agreed the salary cap would be adjusted each year to guarantee players 54% of total NHL revenue and that there would not be a salary floor.[17] Player contracts were also guaranteed while the player shares would increase if league revenues would reach certain benchmarks. It was also agreed that a pool of money from the top 10 grossing teams would be split among the bottom 15 teams.

NATIONAL FOOTBALL LEAGUE

The American Professional Football Association was formed in 1920 and consisted of 11 teams. Representatives from several professional American leagues and independent teams joined to create this union. Also in 1920, the annual Thanksgiving Day football games began. Two years later, the association changed its name to the National Football League (NFL).

It was not until 1933 that the first official championship game was played. The championship game was not based on a playoff system, but rather the two teams with the best regular-season records played one another in the finals.

The American Football League was a rival league that actively ran from 1960 to 1969. In 1970, the NFL activated and completed a merger with the American Football League.[18] The NFL renamed the American Football League to create the American Football Conference. It also created the National Football Conference. This merger expanded the league and created the Super Bowl.

The NFL stepped outside of its normal Sunday time frame and introduced Monday Night Football in 1970. Four years later, the NFL started airing games on Saturday nights, and in 1978 teams began playing games on Thursday nights.

NATIONAL FOOTBALL LEAGUE PLAYERS ASSOCIATION

Much like the NBPA, the National Football League Players Association (NFLPA) was not immediately recognized as the bargaining agent for the players of the NFL. It was created in 1956 and recognized in 1968 when a CBA was reached. The same year the CBA was announced, the NFLPA voted to strike while the owners countered by declaring a lockout.[19] The lockout lasted 11 days, but a lot of the players believed the agreement did not entitle them to as many benefits as they would have liked. The 1970 merger brought up many questions. The owners were open to acknowledging the union but did not want lawyers to be present. The players disagreed and went on strike. The strike lasted 48 hours and concluded with a new 4-year agreement.

A month-long strike took place in 1974 as players demanded the elimination of the option clause (which gave teams control over player movement). Then, both sides settled and signed a new CBA that lasted until 1982. In 1982, a 57-day strike took place primarily because the union sought a wage scale based on a percentage of gross revenues.[20] In the end, a new 5-year deal was inked that provided severance packages for players upon retirement, increased salaries, and bonuses based on the number of years of experience in the league. In 1989, the NFLPA renounced its status as a union and the collective bargaining agent for the players in order to pursue antitrust litigation.[21]

From 1989 to 1993, a sequence of lawsuits were filed by the NFLPA against the NFL. These lawsuits pressured the league and resulted in a comprehensive antitrust settlement. In 1993, the NFLPA recertified as a union and negotiated a new CBA that spring. The NFL owners opted out of the extended terms from the 1993 CBA, and they allowed for the CBA to expire at the end of the 2010 season. The NFLPA renounced its bargaining rights again in order to allow the players to actively pursue antitrust litigation. The players and owners were able to come to a new agreement in the summer of 2011. This CBA runs through 2021.[21]

How the Five Ps Affect Properties Groups and Players Unions

PRODUCT   In the cases of both the unions and properties groups, the product really comes down to the game itself. While the unions are promoting the players and properties are promoting the teams, the product for both is the game.

PRICE   When these two groups come together, price usually is discussed in terms of a collective bargaining agreement often referred to as the CBA. The CBA includes the terms and conditions under which the league business is conducted. Everything from revenue shares to free agency is defined in the agreement.

PROMOTION   The union's focus is to collectively represent (promote) its players in a positive manner, whereas properties are focused on promoting the teams. As stated previously, both are promoting the game itself.

PLACE   Unions and properties make many place decisions, such as location of franchises, placement of players, and selection of media outlets to broadcast the games. All of these affect fans and their ability to follow their favorite team or player.

PROGRESS   The place where progress has affected properties and unions the most is with the technical advances in equipment. The players unions are always trying to protect their athletes, while the properties groups are trying to provide the best working conditions. The advances in equipment make great strides each year, which improves the end product.

Key Benefits of Properties Groups and Players Unions

PROPERTIES GROUPS

Promotion: While each team does a great job promoting itself regionally, the leagues collectively focus on promoting the excitement of the game. The NBA has done a masterful job of promoting basketball as a global game by using stars like Yao Ming to reach the Chinese market and Manu Ginóbili to reach South America. It also holds off-season clinics throughout the world to promote the game.

Collective negotiation: Just like the players, the owners benefit by having a united front in negotiations. This also comes into play when they must collectively make decisions regarding revenue sharing and how to handle small-market teams that may not have the financial power of a major-market team.

PLAYERS UNIONS

Collective bargaining: Very simply, there is strength in numbers when negotiating with the owners. Typically, each team has a union representative. These reps represent their teammates in regard to all issues of the collective bargaining agreement.

Group licensing and marketing: Most players sign their union's group licensing authorization (GLA). The GLA allows the union to represent the players in marketing and licensing deals. It also makes it easier for companies to complete endorsement deals because they can deal with one entity instead of each player individually.

Review of Creative League Deals

Over the years, the NBA has been one of the most innovative leagues in sports. It has led the way in digital marketing, moving a sport brand into China, and creating sponsorships and endorsement deals. On a number of occasions, it has created deals where seemingly none were possible. When Keith Gordon was with the NBA, a number of interesting and creative deals took place that have opened the door to new ways of licensing and deal making in sports.

All of the leagues are very protective of their official sponsors. These companies pay large fees to be associated with the league brand and in return expect the leagues to protect their investment. Nestlé was an official sponsor of the NBA.[22] Although it is a major player in the candy business, its goal with the NBA sponsorship was to specifically promote its chocolate business. Knowing this, the NBA looked for other potential sponsors in the confection space that could create interesting products and expand the NBA brand with additional grocery store shelf space while not encroaching on the goals of their official sponsorship with Nestlé. The NBA created a sponsorship with the Franklin Candy Company and developed a gummy bear product featuring NBA stars on the packaging. By featuring the players on the packaging, the product itself became a collectible, further extending its reach far beyond the shelf of the grocery store. By understanding the needs of its partner Nestlé, the NBA was able to extend its brand and increase revenues.

Another interesting marketing deal was created by an NBA team. The Detroit Pistons developed a then-unique way to increase its engagement with its team sponsor, the Meijer grocery store chain.[23] By creating a store within a store, the team was able to sell officially licensed Pistons' merchandise within Detroit-based Meijer's stores. This extended the brand presence to a location that it had never before reached. The team leveraged the store-within-a-store concept by offering player appearances, further promoting the brand and bringing more customers into the sponsor's locations. Before this idea was developed, the usual grocery store sponsorship deal consisted mainly of signage and very little engagement between the team, sponsor, customer, and fan. The new deal structure was truly a win-win situation for all parties.

Another interesting idea was pioneered by the NFLPA. It created a league-sponsored product. Sometimes there are deals in place that prevent a company from becoming an official sponsor of a team or league. Rather than just eliminating the opportunity, the NFLPA has found creative ways to make a situation work. The NFLPA developed and marketed its own line of the popular hot-and-cold therapy pack.[24] Using players and the Pro Line brand to help promote it, the NFLPA was able to create an opportunity and revenue stream where none seemed to exist.

These deals are examples of the power of a sports brand. By being creative, the leagues have generated many new channels of revenue and created presence and visibility in many new markets and demographics.

Case Study

After an incident in an MLB locker room, one player accused a teammate of attacking him and then left the team. The team immediately suspended the accused player. Both players have threatened to sue the team. The first, because the team did not provide a safe working environment. The second, for being falsely accused and suspended.

Conor Smyth of the Players Union is responsible for representing players when they have a grievance with the team.

1. How should the union handle representing both players? A law firm can't ethically represent the accused and the accuser.
2. What obligation does the team have to police the locker room?
3. If you were in charge, how would you handle the investigation? Would you immediately suspend a player?

CRITICAL THINKING ACTIVITY

Based on what you have read about marketing, league development, and strife, develop a simple league plan for an independent professional football minor league. What are the key features you want to include? How should ownership be structured? Should the teams be individually owned or league owned? How should pay be structured? Do you think that a minor league can have a successful licensing program?

CHAPTER QUESTIONS

1. When were each of the big four players unions formed?
2. What does *CBA* stand for? What does it do?
3. When was the last lockout in a big four league? What were the issues?
4. Search online and find out who are the leaders of each of the big four properties groups and players unions.
5. Who is the players association team representative for your favorite team?
6. What is the GLA? If you were a professional athlete, would you sign it?
7. Find an example online of a league advertisement. What is the focus?
8. Search the Web and find an example of a league-branded product. In your opinion, is the product a good brand extension for the league?
9. Find an example of a league or team that has sponsors in similar categories. What do you think differentiates the sponsors? Why do you think there are competing brands as sponsors?
10. In your opinion, which league is the most creative from a marketing perspective? Why?

Notes

1. List of links to sports unions and leagues, Rutgers University Libraries, accessed September 15, 2014, http://libguides.rutgers.edu/content.php?pid=148775&sid=1276918.
2. AP News, "NFL Europa to Cease Operations," NFL.com, June 29, 2007, http://web.archive.org/web/20070703064828/www.nfl.com/news/story/10240829.
3. David Pietrusza, *Major Leagues: The Formation Sometimes Absorption and Mostly Inevitable Demise of 18 Professional Baseball Organizations, 1871 to Present* (Jefferson, NC: McFarland & Company, 1991).

4. Warren Goldstein, *Playing for Keeps: A History of Early Baseball* (Ithaca, NY: Cornell University Press, 1991).

5. Daniel Okrent and Harris Lewine, *The Ultimate Baseball Book* (New York: Houghton Mifflin, 2000).

6. "Top 10 Work Stoppages in Sports: 4. 1981 MLB Strike," Real Clear Sports, May 17, 2013, http://www.realclearsports.com/lists/work_stoppages_in_sports/1981_mlb_strike.html.

7. Major League Baseball Players Association/Major League Baseball, "MLB, MLBPA Announce New Drug Agreement," MLBPlayers.com, November 15, 2005, http://newyork.mets.mlb.com/pa/releases/releases.jsp?content=111505.

8. Jan Hubbard and David Stern, *The Official NBA Basketball Encyclopedia,* 2nd ed. (New York: Villard Books, 1994).

9. Larry Koon, "NBA Salary Cap FAQ: 2011 Collective Bargaining Agreement," CBAFaq.com, accessed September 15, 2014, http://www.cbafaq.com/salary-cap.htm.

10. "NBA: Let the Games Begin!" CBS News, January 6, 1999, http://www.cbsnews.com/2100-500609_162-27218.html.

11. Marc Stein, "Billy Hunter Sends Players Memo on BRI," ESPN NBA, November 27, 2011, http://espn.go.com/nba/story/_/id/7285446/billy-hunter-tells-players-get-512-percent-bri-2011-12.

12. National Hockey League, *NHL Official Guide & Record Book 2008–2009* (New York: Triumph Books, 2009).

13. Arthur Pincus, *The Official Illustrated NHL History: The Story of the Coolest Game on Earth* (New York: Readers Digest Association, 2006).

14. T. Price, "NHL Team Guides: Teams, Stadiums, and Players," The Free Resource, accessed September 15, 2014, http://www.thefreeresource.com/nhl-team-guides-teams-stadiums-and-players.

15. Edward Dolan, *In Sports, Money Talks* (New York: Twenty-First Century Books, 1996).

16. Thomas Heath and Tarik El-Bashir, "Cold Reality: NHL Cancels the Season," *Washington Post*, February 17, 2005, http://www.washingtonpost.com/wp-dyn/articles/A28922-2005Feb16.html.

17. Jamie Fitzpatrick, "2005 NHL Collective Bargaining Agreement Main Points in the NHL CBA That Was in Effect from 2005 to 2012," About.com Hockey. http://proicehockey.about.com/od/nhlnewsscoresstats/a/2005-Nhl-Collective-Bargaining-Agreement.htm.

18. "History: 1961–1970," NFL Enterprises, accessed September 15, 2014, http://www.nfl.com/history/chronology/1961-1970.

19. William Wallace, "N.F.L. Players Reject Owners' Offer; Strike Favored by a 377-17 Vote Players Likely to Refuse to Report to Camp -- Pension Issue is Unresolved." *New York Times*, July 3, 1968.

20. Gordon Forbes, "'82 Strike Changed Salary Dealings Forever," *USA Today Sports*, June 8, 2001, http://usatoday30.usatoday.com/sports/comment/forbes/2001-06-08-forbes.htm.

21. Associated Press, "NFL Labor History Since 1968," ESPN NFL, March 3, 2011, http://sports.espn.go.com/nfl/news/story?page=nfl_labor_history.

22. Andy Bernstein, "Nestlé USA Renews Its Deal with the NBA," *Sports Business Journal*, July 2, 2001, http://www.sportsbusinessdaily.com/Journal/Issues/2001/07/20010702/This-Weeks-Issue/Nestle-USA-Renews-Its-Deal-With-The-NBA.aspx?hl=This%20Weeks%20Issue&sc=0.

23. Geoff Mott, "Meijer Signs Three-Year Deal as Team Presenting Sponsor of the Saginaw Spirit," *Saginaw News*, December 22, 2010.

24. NFLPA Communications, "NFL PLAYERS and Thera-Pearl Announce Partnership," NFL Players Association, June 19, 2012, https://www.nflplayers.com/articles/Press-Releases/NFL-PLAYERS-and-TheraPearl-Announce-Partnership/.

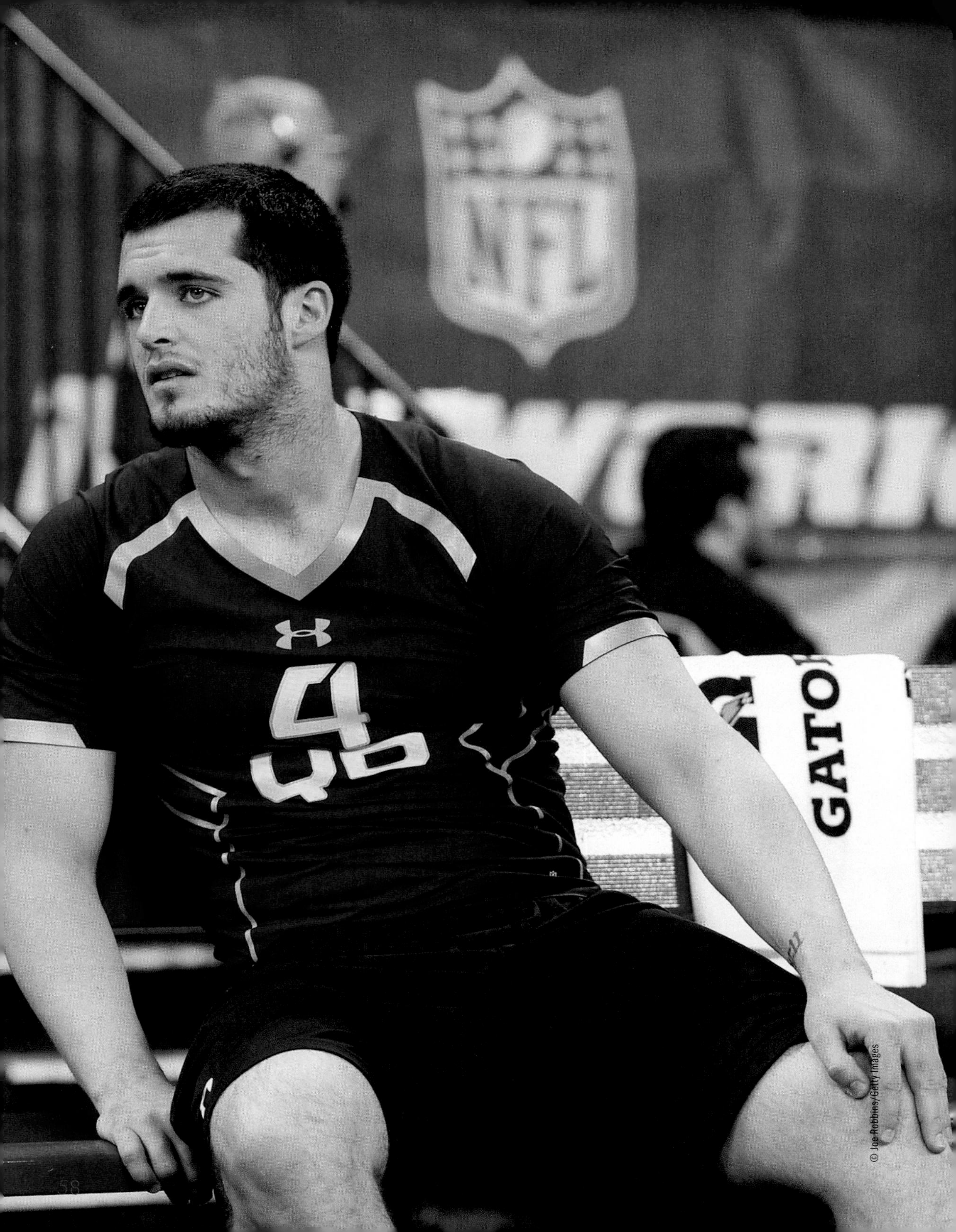

© Joe Robbins/Getty Images

Chapter 4

Athlete Marketing

CHAPTER OBJECTIVES

- Learn about athlete marketing.
- Learn the history of athlete marketing.
- Understand how the five Ps affect athlete marketing.
- Identify key benefits of athlete marketing to both marketer and athlete.
- Learn key components of an athlete marketing plan.
- Review athlete marketing endorsement deals.
- Review an athlete marketing contract.

CHAPTER OVERVIEW

This chapter discusses how the top athletes in the world are marketed. It gives a behind-the-scenes look at how one sports marketing expert positions his athletes to maximize their value in the endorsement game. A sports marketing endorsement contract is reviewed and analyzed.

Voices from the Field: Bill Sanders
Biography

Bill Sanders, Senior Vice President, Personal Brand Management, PMK-BNC, is considered one of the gurus of athlete marketing. Bill brings experience from the entertainment industry to help athletes project and maintain a polished image, which helps maximize endorsement opportunities. Bill believes the key to effective player marketing is the formulation of a long-term player/brand strategy. The plan includes a substantial commitment to community involvement, a proactive media relations plan, and the pursuit of appropriate corporate partners. Bill and his staff are dedicated to the development of individual marketing strategies that highlight each player's strengths, talents, and interests. Bill is also author of the popular sports marketing blog, An Athlete Marketing Guy.

Bill earned his MBA, with an emphasis in marketing and entertainment studies, from UCLA in 1998. He earned his Bachelor of Arts in political science from Loyola Marymount University (LMU) in 1988. Bill teaches sports marketing at LMU each fall semester.

Q&A

Q: *What is your current position?*

I am currently the Senior Vice President of Personal Brand Management at PMK-BNC. Prior to that I was the Chief Marketing Officer at BDA Sports Management, where I oversaw the marketing department. Other agencies focus on sales, but our group focuses on brand building. Our staff includes full-time public relations, community relations, and digital marketing experts.

Q: *What was your career path?*

After graduating from Loyola Marymount University with a degree in political science, I went to work in the film industry. I began at Trimark Pictures in the theatrical distribution department. Our job was to build awareness of low-budget films and place them in theaters nationwide. I was at Trimark for 8 years and was eventually promoted to General Sales Manager and VP of Theatrical Sales. I then went to Lionsgate and served the same role. At that time, I realized that I wanted to focus full time on marketing. I enrolled in the fully employed MBA program at UCLA and earned my MBA in 1998. Shortly thereafter, I was introduced to Bill Duffy by his head of European Basketball, Rade Filipovic. I was immediately impressed by Bill's vision for the company. At that time, NBA agencies were going in one of two directions. Some were part of a consolidation trend. Others were scaling back and providing only contract services. Bill Duffy wanted to split the difference: provide full service to clients and become large enough to yield power and influence in the industry, yet remain small enough to provide personal service to his clients and their families. Duffy also believed that basketball was poised to explode internationally, especially in Europe and China. He wanted me to join the group and help players evolve off the court as businessmen and as spokesmen.

Q: *How did you become an expert in your field?*

I put in my "10,000 hours"! I think I was a good fit because of my belief in the ability of a good marketer to help develop brands. My philosophy was (and is) that the ultimate brand loyalty is between a fan and a team. Focusing on building and rewarding loyal fans increases an athlete's marketability, making them more valuable to sponsors. This approach has worked. In addition, I was given the support of the company and was allowed to build a great team of marketers to help fulfill our vision.

Q: *Tell me about your department. Who works with you?*

I oversee a group of five. Our staff includes a Senior Director of PR and Marketing, a Director of PR and Special Events, a Community Relations Manager, a Digital Marketing Coordinator, and a Marketing Sales Coordinator.

Q: *How is it structured?*

The marketing team reports directly to me, but we encourage a team environment. At BDA, each client had a "brand team" that focuses on that player's own marketing goals.

Q: *Each draft brings you a new crop of athletes. How does that affect your business?*

In our business, a great deal of your current success is measured by your rookie draft class. It's kind of an insane way to measure company success, as each company has strong and soft years. But it is critical, and we are usually at or near the top each year.

Q: *What was your greatest accomplishment at BDA?*

Contributing to the change in attitudes toward player marketing. I think we were among the first to view athletes as brands. We were also among the first to engage athletes in social media. We are usually pioneers when it comes to player marketing, and I really enjoy that.

Q: *What has been your favorite moment with an athlete?*

My favorite moment was during a conversation with Yao Ming. I was telling him that he probably underestimated his skill set as a businessman. He said, "By the time you bring me an opportunity, it is always a shiny apple. If you give me two choices, it is between one shiny apple and another. You don't bring me bad apples." Yao conveyed his trust in me. That means more to me than any magazine cover or TV ad ever will.

Q: What is the most exciting thing about the field of athlete marketing?

It is constantly changing. When I first started, sponsors were spending a ton of money and getting little in return. Now, sponsors demand much more. This results in athletes necessarily becoming better spokespeople. Sponsors need to justify their decisions, so we are now much more involved in the activation process, which helps sponsors get their money's worth. It's much more collaborative than it used to be.

Q: What advice do you have for students interested in athlete marketing?

It is critical to understand the consumer. **Fan loyalty** is the single most important goal for any marketer. We have lifelong loyalty toward our sports teams. We aren't nearly that loyal to anything else. Sponsors want to borrow that loyalty, which is why they sponsor teams and athletes. If you understand how to increase fan loyalty, you have the keys to the kingdom.

Introduction

Athlete marketing occurs when a brand owner contracts with an athlete in exchange for that athlete's endorsement of the brand. These contracts typically include an exchange of **fees**, **product**, **equity**, or some combination and may include the use of **image**, **likeness**, and **appearances** by the athlete.

An **endorsement** by definition is an athlete's support of a company or product in exchange for compensation from that company. For an endorsement to be highly effective, there must be a match between the athlete's fan base and the company's target market. When the fan base and target market match, the athlete has the opportunity to influence the buying patterns of that fan base.

History of Athlete Marketing

Athlete marketing has a long history. The use of baseball cards to help promote the sale of tobacco products dates back to the 1870s. As early as 1905, Honus Wagner had his autograph emblazoned on a Louisville Slugger bat.[1] Ironically, Wagner also is the face of arguably the most famous baseball card of all time. (See **FIGURE 4-1**.) The T-206 Honus Wagner card has been sold a number of times over the last 20 years. It was supplied by the American Tobacco Company (ATC) from 1909 to 1911 as part of a series of cards used to promote the company's tobacco products. This early example of using athletes as endorsers led to some controversy that has made this particular card sought after. There is much speculation about why Honus Wagner eventually denied ATC the right to use his image. Some say that he didn't want kids to buy tobacco products to get his card. Others say that he didn't think that he was being paid enough. Regardless, he asked ATC to stop including his card in the set. Only about 50 cards actually made it into the cigarette packs.[2] The most famous of these sold in 2011 for $2.8 million. Recently, it was determined that the card was trimmed to create better consistency. This led to much controversy in the marketplace and jail time for the culprit.

FIGURE 4-1 Honus Wagner T-206 trading card.
© Bloomberg/Getty Images.

In the 1930s, Lou Gehrig became the first athlete to appear on a Wheaties box. In what may be the first use of an amateur athlete to promote a brand, Jesse Owens was given free Adidas shoes while competing in the Olympic Games. In their heyday, heroes like Babe Ruth and Joe DiMaggio earned off-the-field income by pitching

FIGURE 4-2 Louisville Slugger player-endorsed bat.
© Tony Freeman/PhotoEdit Inc.

products. However, many agree that the start of the modern era of sports marketing began in 1960 with Mark McCormack, who went on to found International Management Group (IMG). He started by signing Arnold Palmer, Jack Nicklaus, and Gary Player as his first clients. IMG helped each icon build very successful endorsements that reached far beyond sports brands.[3] By building these athletes' reputations as spokesmen, he created the model for athletes as endorsers.

How the Five Ps Affect Athlete Marketing

PRODUCT Your first thought may be that the athlete is the product. That's almost correct. The athlete's image is actually the product. The player may not be the nicest person in the world. But if the agent has worked to create a positive image, that image will sell.

PRICE The price of endorsement contracts can take many forms. Traditionally, a fee is paid in exchange for an athlete representing a brand. In some cases, payment may take the form of free product or equity in a company. The price of the contract is negotiated by the athlete marketer.

PLACE In the context of athletes and endorsements, place implies matching the player with the right company. A good endorser has a distinct personality. That personal style may be a natural fit with some products more than with others. Michael Jordan selling Nike basketball shoes is a natural. What about Tiger Woods as a Buick spokesman? Do you think that Tiger's first choice of a vehicle would be a Buick? But that ad relationship lasted several years, so GM must have been happy.

PROMOTION Promotion of the athlete takes many forms. A strategic marketing plan developed by an athlete marketer includes combinations of public relations, cause marketing, media training, and social media.

PROGRESS In the past, the personal relationships between athlete marketers and companies determined how many endorsement deals were completed. There were often multiple phone calls and face-to-face meetings for the marketer to pitch the company on the attributes of the athlete. Now, most athletes have a Twitter account, Facebook page, and personal website. Companies can take an intimate look at potential endorsers by following the social media output of those athletes. It is a key challenge of an athlete marketer to try and craft and control such messages.

Why Are Endorsements Popular?

Endorsements are popular for the simple fact that consumers are influenced by celebrity. There are thousands of magazines, TV shows, blogs, and websites dedicated to celebrity lifestyles. We know what these famous and influential people wear, eat, drink, drive, and just about every other detail of their lives. Knowing that a celebrity uses a particular brand can create a perception of that brand based on the celebrity's image. If a professional athlete is seen using a product, the automatic assumption is that the product must be a high-end or high-quality brand because people assume that celebrities, who can afford just about anything, would use only the best brands. Of course, these assumptions could be wrong, but often they are what the athlete marketers and brands wish to create.

Brands are willing to invest great amounts of their marketing budgets to quickly create an image with their consumer base. Attaching their brand to a celebrity with an endorsement deal is an easy way to create an image.

Weight Watchers has had several celebrity endorsers but may have hit gold when it signed Charles Barkley. The Round Mound of Rebound has famously large appetites, one of which is for food. During his college days at Auburn, rival fans used to throw pizza boxes on the court during games. Barkley thrived with his Weight Watchers endorsement, steadily and visibly shedding weight. Unfortunately, a live microphone picked up this inadvertent quotation from Barkley:

> "I've been on Weight Watchers three months. I have to lose two pounds a week. I'm at 38 pounds now. They come and weigh me every two weeks. I ain't never missed a weigh-in. Never going to. . . . I'm feeling much better. But I ain't giving away no money. I'm not giving away no free money. I thought this was the greatest scam going—getting paid for watching sports—this Weight Watchers thing is a bigger scam."

Smart celebrities spend a great amount of their time creating an image. A carefully crafted image can lead to endorsement deals that far exceed the athlete's earning potential on the field or court. It is the job of the marketing agent to help shape and project that image. The athlete and agent must then select companies consistent with the created image. Carefully chosen endorsements may provide years of revenue stream.

Key Benefits of Endorsement Agreements

Companies hire athletes to endorse their products for many reasons. The bottom line is that the company is hoping that the endorsement will drive sales.

Benefits to a Company

Connect to an athlete: Creating a connection with an athlete is an easy way to project an image about a brand. Athletes have a personal brand and image—excellence at their sport, integrity, or even the rebel/bad boy image. There are many examples of athlete brands. For example, when you think of excellence, maybe Michael Jordan comes to mind. The names Derek Jeter or Peyton Manning may suggest integrity. A bad boy image could be associated with Ron Artest or Bryce Harper. On the basis of these perceptions, a brand can quickly establish its message by attaching a product to an athlete.

FIGURE 4-3 Godaddy.com advertisement.
© HOEP/Go Daddy/AP Images

Connect to an athlete's fan base: The most popular athletes often have millions of fans who closely monitor everything that the athlete does. A brand can quickly introduce itself to a wide demographic by simply being introduced to an athlete's fan base. For example, GoDaddy went from being a complete unknown to one of the top Web hosting companies in the industry by using sports marketing and athlete endorsements as a brand recognition strategy. Using Super Bowl ads and athlete endorsements, it quickly became the most recognizable name in the industry.[4] (See **FIGURE 4-3.**)

Build brand recognition: A consumer has so many choices and so much information, it is difficult for brands to differentiate themselves. One way is to obtain an endorsement from an athlete who fits in a similar demographic as the consumers the brand is trying to attract.

Attach to an athlete's brand image: Every athlete projects some kind of image. Although consumers' perception of that image is subjective, there are ways to measure athletes' popularity and how recognizable they are. One popular way is through marketing evaluation companies. One of the most used is the New York–based company **Q Scores.**[5] A Q Score measures familiarity and appeal of an athlete's brand image.

Reach a new demographic: An athlete's fan base is usually diverse. By entering into an endorsement agreement, a company can reach new demographics without advertising in many different niche industries. The athlete provides the exposure needed to reach this diverse audience.

Dangers to a Company

Athlete's personal brand: Although the positives of an athlete's personal brand attract companies, there are also risks involved. There have been many high-profile negative cases involving athletes—everything from legal issues and domestic disputes to arguments with coaches or teammates can create front-page news. When an athlete is tainted by negative publicity, it can seriously affect a company's brand.

Although it is impossible to anticipate many issues, it is important for a company in an endorsement agreement to have a plan in place to deal with unforeseen circumstances. Most contracts now include a morals clause that clearly states that a company can cancel the contract if the athlete is involved in a serious transgression.

Benefits to Athletes

New revenue source: Even though most marketable athletes are paid well, endorsement deals can add a significant amount of revenue to their income. When an endorsement deal is structured correctly, the athlete's time commitment is minimal in relation to the money received.

Showcase personality: Endorsement deals, particularly those that include commercials, can be a great way for athletes to expose their personality. Athletes need to stay focused and serious during games and rarely have the opportunity to reveal their true personality. NFL players wearing helmets are not recognizable to the average fan. Being a part of an advertising campaign gives the athlete the chance to project an image that may not be practical to do on the field or court.

Personal branding: A company can find it beneficial to attach itself to an athlete's brand, and there is also a reciprocal relationship: An athlete can also build his or her brand by attaching to a company. For example, a golfer who represents a business consulting company projects the image of a smart businessman. If developed correctly, his marketing agent could try to create endorsement deals with other high-end business partners.

The Athlete as a Product

When you think about sports marketing or brand building, companies like Nike or Reebok might spring to mind. But consider the professional athlete as a brand as well. An athlete's brand begins with success on the field or court, and it does not end there. Athletic performance is the most critical factor in determining athlete marketability. Fans, the media, and sponsors love winners who dominate the game. Eyeballs and dollars follow success. But marketability also depends greatly on away-from-the-game factors such as integrity, charisma, and good looks. It is the marketing agent's job to build that brand in the eyes of the corporate world using every available resource. Proactive marketing leads to increased marketability, which leads to the ever elusive endorsement contract. Finding the right product fit is often crucial to having a successful marketing campaign.

In the past, many endorsement deals didn't require the athlete to have much participation with the product or brand. In today's tough economic times, words like engagement and activation are almost always discussed during the negotiations of an endorsement agreement. Engagement is how an athlete interacts with the customers of the brand being endorsed, such as through appearances, advertising, public relations (PR), and social media. Activation is how the terms of the agreement are executed. I have seen many endorsement contracts that require the company to pay an athlete for multiple appearances. Often, that section of the contract is not activated and the company pays the athlete for doing nothing.

Savvy marketing agents actively participate in the activation of an endorsement contract. They know that if their athlete does a good job with engagement and activation, then the odds of receiving a future deal increase. Unfortunately, the norm in the industry is for the endorser to do as little as possible.

Endorsements

TYPES OF ENDORSEMENTS

Sports-Related Products

Endorsement of sports-related products is what typically comes to mind when athlete endorsements are considered. Many companies have successfully used an endorsement strategy to market their sports products. The most notable example of using an athlete endorser to build a brand is Nike. Early in the company history, Nike decided to attach its brand to a rising star named Michael Jordan. This decision helped Nike expand beyond the running community and launch a global sports brand that dominates the industry.

Non-Sports-Related Products

Many companies that produce non-sports-related items realize the power of celebrity and want to attach their brands to that power. Athletes have endorsed everything from watches, computers, hotdogs, and underwear to cereal and cars. The list is almost endless. Often, the idea *if an athlete likes it, I might like it too* is enough to get a consumer to try a product. Brands bank on this connection and spend significant amounts of their marketing budgets on this strategy.

Services

Especially in recent years, industries such as financial services, credit services, and consulting services have used athlete endorsers to build their reputations and brands. Visa and American Express have spent millions on commercials featuring athletes to help build trust and brand recognition for their credit cards. Major consulting companies have often used golfers to promote their brands. Golf is often called the gentlemen's game, and it has an air of integrity and trustworthiness. The trust factor is exactly the image that these institutions look to promote.

QUALITIES OF A GOOD ENDORSER

Although no one knows for sure what attracts fans to a celebrity, certain attributes are usually present. Most successful endorsers exhibit one or more of the following characteristics:

Winner

Large fan base

Likeability

Best-in-class image

Good looks

Easily recognizable

Class

Integrity

Even though athlete marketers can't control whether an athlete wins, they can help develop many of the other traits needed for success.

Key Components of an Athlete Marketing Plan

One of the biggest challenges of an athlete marketer is managing client expectations. Most professional athletes assume that making the pros means instant endorsement deals. That is simply not the case. Especially in the post–"Tiger Recession" era, endorsement deals are extremely hard to come by. To help athletes understand and measure their own marketability, BDA Sports Management came up with the Athlete Marketability formula:

$$\text{athlete marketability} = (\text{talent} + \text{success}) + (\text{integrity} + \text{charisma})$$

The equation has four components, which are not equally weighted. On-field/on-court performance is always the most important factor. But talent and success are not enough. Any athlete possessing all four components will be in high demand. An athlete missing any of the components will not.

Talent: Talent, in the equation, means the kind of highlight-reel talent that ends up shown repeatedly on ESPN SportsCenter. Viewership for regular-season games is quite low outside of local markets. But sports fans worldwide watch ESPN SportsCenter. Athletes with show-stopping talent get the coverage.

Success: Sponsors and fans show very limited interest in losing teams. Winning drives interest, and championships lead to fan support and sponsor interest.

Integrity: We live in the "Age of Transparency." Thanks to the proliferation of cell phones, cameras are ubiquitous. Regardless of the image that celebrity handlers want to portray, who their clients really are will eventually be revealed. Sponsors want to align with spokespeople who are genuine and who have integrity in the eyes of consumers. Reputation is more critical than ever.

Charisma: In Hollywood, they call it "star quality." Marketable athletes possess it, and it can't be manufactured. For years, marketers tried to turn the San Antonio Spur's Tim Duncan into a marketing icon, but the public never embraced his mild-mannered demeanor.

Since the first endorsement deals, contract terms have been structured in a similar manner. Typically, the athlete gets a fixed amount of money for providing a list of agreed-on services, such as making appearances, signing autographs, and granting image and likeness rights for use in advertisements, promotions, and commercial shoots. Today, deals are very likely to contain social media components, including required Facebook posts and Twitter tweets.

Athlete marketing agents have a saying that describes their payment structure: "If you don't eat, I don't eat." Most marketing agents are not paid a retainer or hourly fee but instead earn a commission on the deals they produce for the athlete. The agent's share is typically 10–20%. Some marketing agents provide only endorsement services, whereas others also offer PR, cause marketing, and social media services.

There has been a recent trend toward owner/equity deals. In these deals, the athlete forgoes the typical endorsement payment and instead accepts ownership in a company. For companies, this can be an attractive option because they don't have to make an upfront payment to the athlete. Money can go toward building the brand and increasing sales. For athletes, there is the potential to make significantly more money on the back end than a typical endorsement deal offers and there may also be a tax advantage in delaying payment until after the player's peak earning years. Savvy agents know something about tax planning for highly paid athletes.

In 2007, David Wright of the New York Mets cashed in on such a deal. According to many published reports, his endorsement deal with Vitamin Water called for him to get a 0.5% stake in the company. After the success of the brand increased, Coca-Cola purchased the company for $4.1 billion. This made Wright's deal worth somewhere in the neighborhood of $20 million.[6] (See **FIGURE 4-4**.) I estimate that his take was 200 times greater than the take from a normal deal as a result of the unconventional structure of the contract. The lesson here is that every deal is negotiable and an opportunity to be creative.

There are several challenges with equity deals, however. Unlike typical endorsement deals, equity deals are extremely speculative. If the start-up succeeds (like Vitamin Water did), the athlete can make much more money than can be made with a traditional-fee deal. However, more often than not, start-ups fail. In these cases, the athlete might provide services and never receive any compensation. It is up to the marketing agent to determine the strength of the potential sponsor and the likelihood of its success before recommending an equity opportunity to the athlete.

FIGURE 4-4 David Wright attends Vitamin Water event.
© Mark Von Holden/Stringer/WireImage/Getty Images

PR, Cause Marketing, and Social Media

Public relations (PR) can be defined as athletes' use of free media to help them become more marketable. It is arguably the most powerful tool at an athlete market-er's disposal. The media are the athlete's conduit to fans. As mentioned earlier, game viewership outside a local area is relatively low. Yet the number of people reading print media and watching news programming such as ESPN is much larger. In sports, the media has constant access to athletes through mandatory "media availability" times after practices, after games, during training camps, and at other times. Some athletes dismiss the media as a necessary evil. Savvy athletes realize that the media can help them build their brands and increase their engagement with the general public. The main benefit of using PR as part of an athlete's marketing plan is that it doesn't appear to be marketing. Convincing a third party to report on what an athlete is doing makes the fan base feel that they are receiving a behind-the-scenes look at the athlete. This only increases interest and loyalty.

Athlete-related cause marketing generally refers to an athlete's involvement with a charity. (See **FIGURE 4-5**.) As mentioned, integrity is crucial to athlete market-ability. In the wake of the Tiger Woods crisis, sponsors put more emphasis than ever

FIGURE 4-5 Athlete at a charity event.
© Steve Parsons/Press Association/AP Images.

on the character of their spokespeople. Athletes who want endorsement deals must engage in charity work. Photo opportunities with sick children are not enough, and often come across as insincere. Athletes today must engage with causes that matter to them.

As traditional advertising dollars diminish, sponsors are spending more money on cause marketing (cooperation between a for-profit company and a nonprofit entity). Athletes who are seen as philanthropic are often considered as spokespeople for sponsor cause-marketing efforts.

Social media has changed how athlete endorsement contracts are structured. (See **FIGURE 4-6**.) Almost every contract has some kind of a social media element attached to it. In the early days of sports marketing, athletes and fans had little direct interaction. Traditional fan clubs would allow fans to demonstrate their enthusiasm via a membership card or a signed 8-by-10 photo. Today, social media enables enthusiastic fans to develop a deeper connection with their favorite athletes. Athletes who have embraced the power of Facebook and Twitter reward their most loyal fans by giving them a more personal connection than has ever been available before. These

FIGURE 4-6 Social media buttons: Facebook, Twitter, YouTube.
© Twin Design/Shutterstock, Inc.

fans spread the word through "likes" and retweets. This in turn increases the athlete's following. Today, many players have Facebook and Twitter followings in excess of 1 million fans, creating their own network with which to share news, thoughts, and personal insights.

Sponsors today expect spokespeople to offer them access to broad fan bases. Athletes with large followings are much more likely to attract sponsor interest and endorsement deals than are less-connected athletes. Social media has become one of the most critical components of any athlete marketing strategy.

Spotlight on Yao Ming

When Yao Ming was selected by the Houston Rockets as the number 1 pick in the 2002 NBA Draft, many sports columnists said he would never be marketable. Yao Ming was pegged as a tall, awkward, non-English-speaking foreigner. No one believed he would ever become a marketing icon. Those critics were dead wrong. They underestimated the importance of integrity and charisma, which Yao has plenty of.

Yao assembled a management group to help him with his transition into the NBA. Dubbed "Team Yao," the group included a brilliant young businessman (Erik Zhang), a university professor and respected econo-

mist (John Huizinga), a highly regarded NBA agent (Bill Duffy), and an experienced athlete marketer (Bill Sanders). The team knew that Yao's potential was tremendous. In an unprecedented move, the team worked with the University of Chicago's MBA program to create a fully developed marketing plan. The plan defined key brand pillars and identified potential sponsors that would fit with Yao's brand. (See **FIGURE 4-7**.)

When Yao arrived in Houston, he quickly captured the world's attention. Not only did he work hard and excel on the court but also his personality and sense of humor immediately shone through. Press conferences followed almost every game during Yao's rookie season, and his performances quickly became legendary. Yao's charm and hard work led to national TV ad campaigns with some of the best brands in the world: Apple, Visa, Gatorade, and McDonalds. These ads further demonstrated his charisma, and before long Yao was no longer thought of as a strange foreigner.

In later years, Yao became a heroic figure in his homeland. Yao's emergence coincided with the enormous economic boom in China. Yao came to represent modern China: a blend of traditional values and individual achievement. He carried the Chinese flag into the opening ceremo-

FIGURE 4-7 Yao Ming trading card.
© Mayskyphoto/Shutterstock

nies of the Athens and Beijing Olympic Games, claiming his place as one of China's most beloved icons.

Presently, Yao has transitioned from typical athlete endorsements into more entrepreneurial ventures. He owns the Shanghai Sharks (the team he played for prior to his NBA career) and is also involved in several other business ventures. Yao is building a business legacy that is likely to last for many years to come.

Falls from Grace

There has always been controversy in the field of athlete endorsements. In recent years, we have seen some of the biggest falls from grace in the history of professional sports: Tiger Woods, Michael Vick, and LeBron James, three icons, experienced almost complete destruction of their once spotless images. Tiger Woods was arguably the most trusted spokesperson in sports marketing history when scandal brought that empire crashing down. Michael Vick was the most exciting player in the NFL when his involvement with dog fighting was exposed. LeBron James's handling of his move to Miami instantly sidetracked his image as the loyal hometown athlete. (His decision to hold a live press conference on ESPN—called "The Decision"—was met with almost universal dislike outside of Miami, where he decided to "take his talents.") This section looks at these events from an athlete endorsement angle.

Just after the news on Tiger was reported, my class asked me what I thought would happen. I predicted that the companies that had products that weren't performing well would take this as an opportunity to get out of those deals and drop him as a celebrity endorser. The companies that had deals that were based on Tiger's integrity would also drop him. Finally, the companies that had based entire product lines on Tiger (Nike, Upper Deck) would have to keep him.

If you were Tiger's marketing agent, what would you have done the morning after the news broke that he was allegedly involved in multiple affairs?

I have been very close to the Michael Vick saga. I worked directly with him before and after his controversy. I even visited him in Leavenworth Penitentiary to discuss his image strategy upon release. It is apparent that a marketing agent can only do so much. In the end, it is up to the athlete to make the right decision for his or her life. Because these decisions affect a marketing agent's ability to make a living, they can be frustrating.

If you were Vick's agent, what would have been your marketing strategy for the initial months after he was released from prison?

In the case of LeBron James and "The Decision," it is important for the marketing agent to see events from the fan's perspective. (See **FIGURE 4-8**.) Did LeBron have the right to switch teams? Of course he did. Was it a good decision to raise money for a charity? Of course it was. But to announce it on national television without regard to his loyal hometown fans created a firestorm around his brand. It didn't matter that he did nothing wrong or even that he raised a lot of money. The perception was that he didn't care about his fans. Consumers are fickle, and arrogance is a killer for an athlete's image.

If you were LeBron's agent, how would you have handled his departure from the Cleveland Cavaliers to the Miami Heat, and now back again to the Cavaliers?

It is difficult to be the marketing agent for an athlete embroiled in a crisis. It quickly becomes obvious that you have little control over your product. As a brand manager

FIGURE 4-8 LeBron James.
© Ari Edlin/Shutterstock

for a company, you can create and control your product. Managing and promoting a human being can be difficult—one misstep on the athlete's part, and all of your hard work is shattered.

The moments right after the controversy is reported can be the most critical in terms of an athlete's future marketability. For example, Tiger chose to hold a press conference well after the event, and it was reported to have come off as staged: Cameras kept their distance, Tiger's mother sat awkwardly in the front row as he read prepared statements. The media in attendance was hand selected, which led to brutal criticism from media that were not invited. This only further disappointed his fans.

In the era of baseball and steroids, Mark McGuire, Roger Clemens, and others denied usage but have been linked for years to almost every story regarding MLB and steroids. Andy Pettitte immediately admitted usage and is rarely mentioned. How the athlete reacts to a controversy molds the athlete's future marketability.

RECOVERY MARKETING STRATEGY

Although every situation is different, often these simple rules can help an athlete recover from a crisis:

- Be truthful.
- Admit failure. This will help fans relate to the athlete.
- Apologize and be sincere.
- Share a recovery plan.
- Follow through on the plan.

Although fans often look at athletes as icons, they also realize that these people are human and can make mistakes.

Example Endorsement Contract

Many endorsement contracts will be similar to this one. As you become familiar with typical content, it will be easier to negotiate a favorable deal.

ENDORSEMENT AGREEMENT

SAMPLE LANGUAGE THIS ENDORSEMENT AGREEMENT is entered into between ("Athlete") and ("Company").

The Athlete is a former collegiate football player, and Company wants to license Athlete's name, signature, likeness (collectively, the "Athlete") for use in connection with trading cards, collectibles, and memorabilia ("Product").

MEANING This is standard contract language that spells out what intellectual property or properties the athlete is licensing for exactly which products.

INSIDER TIP This is an example of a trading card contract. It is important that the player's marketing representative recognizes that a company may try to include other products beyond trading cards. Notice the paragraph mentions *collectibles* and *memorabilia*. This may seem insignificant at first, but the company will sell collectibles and autographed products for a premium, and therefore autographs should command a higher price than standard trading cards, which are given away free in packs of cards. These are the types of add-ons that the marketing agent can easily miss. To avoid problems later, it is critical for the agent to understand the exact intent of the agreement.

A. GRANT OF LICENSE

SAMPLE LANGUAGE Athlete grants to Company nonexclusive rights to Properties as listed above. Company will use Properties to promote and sell Product as defined above. Company does not have the rights to use NFL or collegiate marks or logos in Product unless it receives written permission from the holder of those rights.

MEANING The contract is clearly stating that this is a nonexclusive agreement. The athlete has the right to seek other endorsement agreements in this category. In some niches of the sports industry, agreements will be exclusive to a category. For instance, an athlete would not be allowed to endorse both Nike and Reebok.

INSIDER TIP Two aspects of this paragraph are significant. First, this is a nonexclusive agreement. Unlike the shoe and beverage categories, where agreements are almost always exclusive to a single company, the trading card industry often uses the same players in competing sets. If a player is exclusive to one company, that company will be paying a significant contract premium.

Second, in this particular case, the company does not hold NFL or collegiate licenses. Stating that it does not have the rights to use trademarks or logos signifies that the players will not be shown in uniform. Most likely, they will be shown working out in generic gear. By not showing them in uniform, the company avoids having to pay a league licensing royalty. The downside is that the cards are typically less valuable to the collector because they are not officially licensed. These nonlicensed deals are typically less lucrative than are officially licensed deals because they drive less revenue.

B. REPRESENTATIONS AND WARRANTIES

SAMPLE LANGUAGE Athlete warrants that he is owner of the Properties listed above. Athlete warrants that he has full legal rights to enter into this agreement.

Athlete warrants that he has no other contract that will interfere with his obligation to perform the duties listed above.

MEANING The athlete is letting the company know that he does not have any competing agreements in place.

INSIDER TIP This is the section that causes many disputes. There are numerous cases of athletes being sued for breach of contract because they have a competing deal in place with another company. Often, it is an innocent mistake on the part of the athlete and marketing agent.

As an example, say that an athlete signs a deal with a collectibles company to manufacture limited edition product using his image. Then, a year later he signs a deal with a toy company that wants to create product using his image. The toy company then manufactures and sells a bobblehead doll of the athlete. The collectibles company considers that a breach of their rights, and a dispute arises. The athlete and his marketing agent never considered that a collectible and a toy would overlap when they signed each agreement. However, the dispute puts the athlete right in the middle of a legal mess. This is why the Product descriptions must be clearly defined.

C. TERRITORY

SAMPLE LANGUAGE Company will have worldwide distribution rights, the ("Territory").

MEANING The company is requesting the ability to sell its product anywhere in the world.

INSIDER TIP Athletes should not give away territory rights unless the company can deliver product to those territories. By limiting territories, the athlete retains the ability to have multiple contracts in different territories.

D. LICENSE PERIOD

SAMPLE LANGUAGE The rights are granted on the date above and terminated on May 31, 2014 (the "License Period"), unless as set forth in termination section ("Termination").

MEANING This section determines the length of the agreement.

INSIDER TIP This is another seemingly innocent paragraph with a hidden agenda. The NFL draft is in the middle of May. By ending the contract on May 31 of the following year, the company has the rights to use the player's image again next year in a draft set. Say that your player is paid $5 per signature this year. Then, let's say he goes on to be the NFL Rookie of the Year and by the end of the season is commanding $40 per signature. The company can make cards using last year's rate on signatures without paying the athlete the new going rate. You must pay attention to these seemingly simple details or you could cost the athlete significant amounts of endorsement income.

E. COMPENSATION

SAMPLE LANGUAGE Company agrees to pay Athlete in accordance, as set forth below:

Terms: 1250 autographs @ $5 per, with the following bonuses:
- Additional $2.50 per autograph if drafted from pick numbers 1–5
- $1500 if supplied a game-worn jersey

MEANING This section determines what the athlete will be paid for the rights granted.

INSIDER TIP Understanding the market and where your player ranks among peers is critical to negotiating a favorable agreement for the athlete. There are many creative ways to build a compensation plan. In this example, a bonus is paid based on draft position. It is very common for a shoe company endorsement contract to include product as part of the compensation package. For a less marketable player, a shoe deal may be structured to provide on-field shoes, a $3000 credit in off-field shoes and apparel, and no cash. It is up to the marketing agent to create a plan that is favorable to the company and athlete.

Each rate is negotiated. It is the job of the athlete marketing agent to maximize the athlete's rate. On the flip side, it is the job of the company to keep the rates as low as possible. The economy often affects these negotiations. In a recession, companies are more apt to dictate rates and give a take-it-or-leave-it ultimatum to a marketing agent.

F. AUTOGRAPHS AND UNDERTAKINGS BY ATHLETE

SAMPLE LANGUAGE Athlete shall provide to Company the quantity of autographs listed above. Athlete shall also sign an additional 5% of quantity, at no additional cost to Company, to compensate for damaged Product.

MEANING This section determines the number of signatures that the athlete must sign.

INSIDER TIP An additional 5% may not seem like a lot, but if the contract is for 8000 signatures, this can become a ridiculous number. It would be better to negotiate a fixed number. Also, contracts usually call for additional signatures based on product damaged in shipping and handling. Although it is reasonable to ask an athlete to redo signatures that are smudged or illegible, the athlete should not be responsible for companies mishandling product.

Michael Jordan has one of the best signatures in the business. This doesn't happen by accident. He takes pride in his signature and wants to give his fans a good product. Not many athletes have signed more product than he has, and yet he has been very meticulous with each signature.

G. SIGNING SESSION

SAMPLE LANGUAGE Company can request, within a reasonable time frame (fifteen [15] days), that Company be present when athlete signs Product ("Signing Session"). Company shall pay all reasonable expenses of athlete for Signing Session.

MEANING For authenticity reasons, some companies witness athlete signings.

INSIDER TIP Some companies want to witness the signatures. An athlete should do everything possible to accommodate such a request. It is good for the industry and protects the athlete signature's authenticity.

H. SIGNATURES

SAMPLE LANGUAGE Athlete will sign full name or agreed upon variation. No initials, nicknames, or variations will be accepted unless requested by Company. At the request of Company, Athlete will add acronyms such as ROY, HOF, or Champion when appropriate.

MEANING The company is being very specific in exactly what it wants from the athlete.

INSIDER TIP Most negotiations are focused on the dollar figure. It is critical the marketing agent pay close attention to the details. In this section, the company has added a broad clause to include acronyms along with the athlete's signature. If your athlete wins the Rookie of the Year award, you should be able to command a premium for that callout on an autograph product. If you give those rights away in a contract, you are not maximizing the athlete's endorsement revenue.

I. AUTHENTICITY

SAMPLE LANGUAGE Athlete will sign a sworn affidavit (provided by Company) verifying that he alone signed each autograph. Athlete will return affidavit along with Product in Company-supplied mailing envelopes.

MEANING The athlete must sign the product. The integrity of the industry depends on it. In this case, the company is asking the athlete to swear that it is his signature.

INSIDER TIP The authenticity of a product, whether it is autographed or officially licensed, is a huge issue for the sports industry. Anything that an athlete can do to help a company protect the image and authenticity of a product should be reasonably accommodated.

J. TIMING

SAMPLE LANGUAGE Autographs must be returned to Company within thirty (30) days of Athlete's receipt (the "Due Date") of Product. Company will deduct 20% from agreed upon compensation for each fifteen (15)-day period past Due Date.

MEANING The company should be very specific about the timing of agreed-on services, such as commercial photo shoots, autograph sessions, and appearances, among other things.

INSIDER TIP This can be one of the most trying aspects of being an athlete marketing agent. The management of the athlete's time and obligations can be difficult. Everyone is happy signing the contract, but sometimes executing the particulars of the deal becomes a chore. Educating the athlete on the importance and obligation of each deal can make execution of the deal a little easier.

From the company's standpoint, not having one of the key ingredients of a product, the athlete's signature, can cause delays and even loss of sales.

I've been on both sides of this problem. Once as a company executive, I signed a top NBA player to a lucrative autograph deal. When it came time for the items to be signed, my company representative flew to meet the athlete, unpacked hundreds of jerseys, balls, and pictures, and waited for the athlete in the hotel ballroom. On two separate occasions, the athlete failed to show. After many excuses and apologies, the athlete's marketing agent agreed to personally fly to the athlete's hometown and be with him at the signing session. So, for a third time my rep flew across country and set everything up. As agreed, the marketing agent was there and was in constant communication with his client, who was sorry for being late but was caught in traffic. After a while, the athlete stopped answering his phone, and the representative and agent finally gave up and packed up. That evening, in his hotel room, my company representative saw a clip on ESPN of the athlete at the opening of his new restaurant, which was about a thousand miles away. Dealing with personalities can be the most trying aspect of an athlete marketer's job.

K. INDEMNIFICATION

SAMPLE LANGUAGE Company will indemnify and hold Athlete harmless from any and all loss or damage resulting from suits against Athlete arising from use of Product. This obligation survives the expiration or termination of this Contract.

MEANING If there are issues with licensing or rights to trademarks or copyrights, it is the responsibility of the company, and not the athlete, to defend those rights.

INSIDER TIP It is the marketing agent's responsibility to protect the athlete in business dealings. There can be many unforeseen circumstances involving companies. The agent must keep the athlete out of any potential litigation.

L. SAMPLES

SAMPLE LANGUAGE Athlete may request up to 25 of his individual cards. Specialty and autograph cards are excluded from samples.

MEANING Most companies are happy to provide samples, unless the product is expensive.

INSIDER TIP Although many athletes are multimillionaires, they still get excited to see their first rookie cards. Companies are typically happy to provide an agreed-on quantity. It is always beneficial to include the request in the contract.

M. MORALS CLAUSE

SAMPLE LANGUAGE Athlete shall refrain from conduct that would offend the public and that may create negative publicity. Athlete shall avoid any criminal activity. Activities of Athlete deemed by Company to be morally indecent may result in termination of the contract.

MEANING The company can employ this out clause in the contract if the athlete does something that will affect the company's brand and the athlete's marketability.

INSIDER TIP I have been on both sides of this issue as well. As a company executive, I once had to deal with a famous football player who was under contract with my company. The player was arrested for drug possession. Fortunately, we had included a morals clause in the agreement. We decided to exercise that clause, automatically terminating the contract.

Working on the athlete side, I've seen firsthand how quickly brands can jump ship when public perception turns negative. As a marketing agent, you are part business representative, mentor, coach, and psychologist. But at the end of the day, the athlete has to make the right choices.

N. SELL-OFF PERIOD

SAMPLE LANGUAGE Upon expiration or termination of Contract, Company shall stop manufacturing Product featuring Athlete's image and likeness as described in this agreement. Company can continue to sell remaining inventory for six (6) months.

MEANING Although the contract may be over, the company can still sell what is has produced for a period of 6 months.

INSIDER TIP Many contracts miss this simple stipulation. Once while I negotiated a seven-figure, exclusive deal with an NBA player, it was revealed that another company had more than 10,000 of his autographs in inventory, and there was no sell-off period in the contract. That one small clause excluded from the original contract changed our deal from a seven-figure exclusive to a much smaller nonexclusive deal; it cost the athlete hundreds of thousands of dollars. Six months is a reasonable sell-off period for most product categories.

IN WITNESS WHEREOF, the parties hereto have executed this License Agreement as of the date first above written.

Athlete: _____
(Signature)
SS#: _____

Case Study

Elizabeth Patrick represents one of the top players in the NBA. For the past 6 months, she has been working on an endorsement deal with American Express for the player. The details of the deal have been finalized, and all that is left to do is to develop the contract and get all parties to sign the document. Everyone is happy with the deal and is looking forward to a long-term, successful relationship.

At this point, Elizabeth gets a call from Visa. Visa offers a similar deal with one major difference: It will develop a Super Bowl commercial featuring this NBA star.

1. If you were Elizabeth, what would you do?
2. If Elizabeth switches to Visa this late in the game, do you think that she jeopardizes doing any deals with American Express in the future?
3. Does Elizabeth have an obligation to her other clients to keep the American Express relationship in good standing, or is her only obligation to maximize the opportunity for this single client?

CRITICAL THINKING ACTIVITY

Choose a league—NFL, MLB, NBA, NHL—and then choose one athlete in the league and create a marketing pitch for that athlete. This pitch is what the athlete's agent will use to convince a company to choose the athlete to represent the company's brand. In addition to the pitch pieces, include a list of target companies and reasons why the chosen companies are good fits for the athlete.

CHAPTER QUESTIONS

1. Give an example of an endorsement.
2. Why would an athlete engage in cause marketing?
3. What are the main benefits of using PR as part of a marketing plan?
4. Why is it important to include a morals clause in an endorsement contract?
5. Describe an example of an athlete losing an endorsement contract because of off-field, off-court activities that is different from the ones mentioned in this chapter.
6. Provide an example of an endorsement deal where the company and the athlete are a good fit.

7. Provide an example of an endorsement deal where the company and athlete are not a good fit.
8. Find an example of cause marketing on your favorite team's website.
9. How does your favorite athlete promote his or her endorsements on a Facebook page? If your favorite athlete doesn't have a Facebook page, find one who does and check for endorsements.
10. Give an example of an athlete using PR to help build his or her brand image.
11. Shaquille O'Neal is often shown in ads wearing a plain jersey. Why is there no team name included?

KEY ATHLETE MARKETING COMPANIES

Athletes First: Founded by David Dunn and focusing primarily on football, this agency is located in Laguna Hills, California. The Web address is www.athletesfirst.net.

BDA Sports Management: BDA is an agency based in Walnut Creek, California, that was founded and is run by Bill Duffy. BDA represents basketball players and has had many number one picks in the NBA draft. The Web address is www.bdasports.com.

Creative Artist Agency (CAA): This agency originally focused on representing entertainers but has become a major player in the athlete management business. The Web address is www.caa.com.

IMG: IMG was created by Mark McCormick and is considered the first athlete representation agency. It has developed into a major sports marketing and event agency. The Web address is www.img.com.

Octagon: Octagon is one of the biggest sports agencies in the field. It has a diverse clientele in most major sports and is active in events and entertainment. The Web address is www.octagon.com.

Rosenhaus Sports Representation: This agency was founded by Drew Rosenhaus and has a large client base. The company is located in Miami, Florida, and the Web address is www.rosenhausesports.com.

Scott Boras Corporation: This agency focuses primarily on representing baseball players. It is located in Newport Beach, California, and its Web address is www.borascorp.com.

WMG Management: Wasserman Media Group is a global sports, entertainment, marketing, and management company. The Web address is www.wmgllc.com.

Notes

1. "Timeline," Louisville Slugger Museum and Factory, accessed September 16, 2014, http://www.sluggermuseum.com/timeline/.
2. Michael O'Keeffe and Teri Thompson, *The Card: Collectors, Con Men, and the True Story of History's Most Desired Baseball Card* (New York: HarperCollins, 2007).

3. Mark McCormack, *What They Don't Teach You at the Harvard Business School* (New York: Bantam Books, 1984).

4. "About Us," GoDaddy, accessed September 16, 2014, http://www.godaddy.com/NewsCenter/about-godaddy.aspx?ci=9079.

5. "The Value of Q Scores," Q Scores, accessed September 16, 2014, http://www.qscores.com/Web/value.aspx.

6. "David Wright Cashes in on Vitamin Water Deal," Boxden.com, May 31, 2007, http://slumz.boxden.com/f5/may-31-david-wright-cashes-in-on-vitamin-water-deal-50-cent-info-too-919014/.

Chapter 5

Sports Agents

CHAPTER OBJECTIVES

- Understand what it takes to be a sports agent.
- Learn the history of the sports agent business.
- Learn how the five Ps affect agents.
- Identify key benefits of the sports agent role.
- Learn key components of an athlete business plan.
- Review a team contract.

CHAPTER OVERVIEW

This chapter reviews the business of being a sports agent. It looks at the rules and regulations that govern sports agents and the pros and cons of the career. It presents a team contract for analysis and reviews strategies for maximizing the athlete's revenues.

Voices from the Field: Bill Duffy
Biography

With more than 25 years of experience representing professional athletes, Bill Duffy is one of the most successful and respected agents in professional sports. In 1998, Bill founded BDA Sports Management, a full-service firm that provides clients with high-quality career management advice and the tools necessary to enhance personal growth and achievement. With each client, Bill focuses on individual needs and long-term career planning. He assembled a knowledgeable staff so that each client receives unmatched personal attention and guidance.

BDA currently represents more than 35 NBA players, including 20-plus first-round picks and more than 45 professional basketball players who play overseas. BDA clients include Andrew Wiggins, Joakim Noah, Tayshaun Prince, Brandon Jennings, Rajon Rondo, Steve Nash, and Greg Oden. BDA has delivered global, national, and local deals to its iconic clients with the world's best marketing partners. The clients are among the highest endorsements earners in the NBA. BDA's network includes key decision makers at most major sponsors, including Nike, Adidas, Reebok, McDonalds, Coca Cola, Pepsi, Vitamin Water, Red Bull, T-Mobile, and many others.

BDA is also highly focused on business partnership opportunities for clients. More than ever, athletes with strong brand equity have opportunities to participate in long-term business partnerships that can generate income far beyond their playing careers.

A basketball player himself, Bill competed at the collegiate level at the University of Minnesota and Santa Clara University and was selected by the Denver Nuggets in the 1982 NBA Draft. Bill graduated from Santa Clara University in 1982 with a Bachelor of Arts degree in General Humanities and was a District Eight Academic All-American and Santa Clara's 1982 Scholar/ Athlete of the Year.

Q&A

Q: *What is your current position?*

I am the President and CEO of BDA Sports Management, which I founded in 1998.

Q: *What was your career path?*

I played college basketball at the University of Minnesota before transferring to Santa Clara University. Following my college career, I was drafted by the Denver Nuggets. After college, I worked for an agent and learned the business. Soon after, I started seeking clients on my own, and BDA was born.

Q: Tell me about your company. Who works with you? How is it structured?

We have five divisions at BDA: Management, Agents, Marketing, Player Relations, and International. I have six agents who work with me. We are one of the few agencies in the business to have a dedicated marketing department to develop endorsement opportunities for our players. Also, our International department supports dozens of clients playing overseas.

Q: What has been your greatest accomplishment at BDA?

The greatest accomplishment has to be bringing Yao Ming to the NBA. (See **FIGURE 5-1**.) There were so many hurdles to overcome. To see him drafted number one overall was the culmination of years' worth of perseverance and brought a great feeling of accomplishment. I'm thankful that he chose me as his agent.

FIGURE 5-1 Yao Ming.
© Alexandra Wyman/WireImage/iStock.

Q: What has been your favorite moment with an athlete?

That's such a hard question to answer. I've had so many great moments with my guys. Very early in my career I remember going with Antonio Davis to buy his mother a 735i BMW for her birthday. We bought it and wrapped it up. He was so proud to be able to give his mom such a special present that it made me feel great. This was the first time one of my clients had the ability to do something so special and give back to someone who was always there for him. I still remember that day.

Q: What is the most exciting thing about being an agent?

Every day is exciting. Helping players get drafted and traded and placed with certain teams is incredibly complex and exhilarating. I feel like I have a real-life fantasy sports team. These moves influence organizations. To be a part of that is incredibly exciting.

Q: What advice do you have for students interested in being an agent?

This is not your typical nine-to-five job, and your hard work is not always rewarded. This business is about access, relationships, and sustainability. You must be constantly building your network. The person with the best network is usually the winner. Start early and never stop building.

Introduction

A **sports agent** is a person who represents an athlete in negotiations for team contracts and endorsements. In return, the agent receives a percentage of that athlete's earnings. Agents may also manage personal finance for their client athletes, which requires expertise in financial planning, investing, and taxes. It has been said that agents can play the role of parent, counselor, advisor, and friend, all wrapped up into one. As portrayed in movies and on television, the job seems fun and glamorous. Of course, at times it is. NBA agents' job is to secure a spot on an NBA team for their clients. To put that into perspective, let's compare some numbers. The U.S. Congress has 535 members.[1] The National Basketball Association has 360 active members. There aren't too many job markets that are more competitive. Although being an agent can be fun and glamorous, it can also be extremely difficult and stressful.

History of Sports Agent Business

The beginning of the sports agent business is often attributed to Mark McCormack, who formed International Management Group (IMG), one of the most famous agencies in the business. He successfully represented golfers Jack Nicklaus, Arnold Palmer, and Gary Player in the early 1960s, but well into the 1970s most athletes still did not have an agent.[2] The role's responsibility often fell to the player's parents or even to the player. Unfortunately, this often resulted in players receiving less-than-equitable contracts with their teams.

In the early days of sports contracts, there simply wasn't that much money to negotiate over. However, with the rise in popularity of modern sports, the dollars being negotiated became significant for TV network deals, free agency, and multi-million-dollar endorsement deals. Athletes felt the need to be represented by an expert. Many agents are lawyers and have great experience writing and understanding contracts. Today, only a few professional athletes are not represented by agents.

How the Five Ps Affect Sports Agents

PRODUCT   An agent like Bill Duffy has two products. First, he is selling himself and his company to potential clients. Second, he is selling his client's services to coaches and general managers and marketing his client to potential sponsors. Highly successful agents can represent multiple players. If two client-athletes play the same position, can the agent represent both equitably in free agency? Multiple clients may be candidates for one sponsorship. How does the agent ethically represent these competing interests? Although this doesn't happen very often, it does happen. Agents should discuss this with their clients in advance and develop some ground rules, and then none of the parties will be caught off guard by a difficult situation.

PRICE   Price comes into play for an agent when negotiating salaries, bonuses, and endorsement deals. Because athletes typically have such short careers, it is critical for agents to maximize the worth of each contract. Price also factors into agent reimbursement, a negotiable item.

FIGURE 5-2 Dodger Stadium.
Courtesy of Fathead L.L.C. Used with permission.

PLACE   Although the average fan probably never thinks that distribution is part of an agent's job, it can be a critical step in sports agent work. Defining the best location for the client is very important. (See **FIGURE 5-2**.) Finding the right fit with a team and city could make all the difference with an athlete having long-term success or a short career.

PROMOTION   The agent must self-promote to sign the client. Then, the agent must promote the player to teams, sponsors, the media, and fans. Potential clients are first shown brochures and a website. An agent will sit down face to face with an athlete and possibly the athlete's parents, coaches, and advisors to try and convince the athlete to sign with the agency. Once signed, the agent first promotes the new client to organizations to try and convince them to draft, sign, or trade for the athlete.

PROGRESS   Many of an agent's clients are young millionaires. Often they are tech savvy and own the latest and greatest devices. To stay connected and relevant with clients, agents must stay informed of all the newest social media trends. Agents offer clients guidance. If agents don't appear hip and savvy, they will find it hard to impress and communicate with sophisticated young players.

Key Benefits of the Sports Agent to the Athlete

Contract expertise: An athlete typically is not an expert in contract language. Many agents are lawyers or at least have a good knowledge of contracts and their intricacies. Providing contract guidance is an important part of an agent's job.

Skilled negotiator: Because many agents have multiple clients, they are almost always negotiating some kind of a deal—with a team or company for a position or endorsements and advertising. This constant practice in the art of negotiation helps agents become skilled negotiators.

Experience: Professional athletes are amazing at their sport. This does not make them amazing at business. They have focused their attention on perfecting their athletic ability, sometimes to the exclusion of all else, including business. Hiring an experienced agent who is an expert at business allows the athlete to continue to focus on the sport.

Market understanding: Because most agents represent multiple athletes, they have firsthand knowledge of the market. When they negotiate team contracts, bonuses, and endorsement deals, they know what other athletes with similar skills have been paid. By understanding comparable market values, agents can make sure their clients' contracts are equitable. A thorough understanding of each league's salary cap structure is also essential for agents to evaluate options for clients.

Draft prep: For an athlete coming out of high school or college, the days leading up to the draft can feel like a circus. Draft prep includes both physical and mental exercises. In the time between leaving school and the draft (typically 1–2 months), the athlete will be interviewed by the media, tested in many different ways by teams, and poked and prodded by doctors. For a young and inexperienced athlete, this can be overwhelming. It is up to the agent to prepare the athlete both physically and mentally for the incredibly important time leading up to the draft. (See **FIGURE 5-3**.) Many agents bring all of their rookies together and house them in the same place. This way they can monitor the athletes' training, diet, and education process all together.

Peace of mind: Hiring a competent agent allows athletes to focus on their job—which is playing their chosen sport. Hours of preparation go into each game. Knowing that the business piece of their job is being handled properly allows athletes to focus on honing athletic skills.

Career advice: A unique thing about a career as a professional athlete is that it is short compared to careers in other industries. The average career span is only a few years. The best agents help athletes prepare for life after their sports careers. Many times, athletes are still in their twenties when their playing days are over. Good agents help athletes take that next step to be successful in a second career—possibly in business, coaching, or broadcasting. Regardless of the profession, good agents try to facilitate athletes' transition.

FIGURE 5-3 2012 NFL Combine.
© Joe Robbins/Getty Images.

Agent Compensation

Agent compensation is typically controlled by the league, but commissions generally fall into the 2% to 5% range. Often, different structures are used for rookie and veteran deals. Most people think that agents are paid huge amounts of money, but it is important to look at the complete picture. If a player's contract is for $500,000, an agent's commission may be $10,000. Although this is a nice commission, agents often spend tens of thousands of dollars recruiting each player. Compound this with the fact that some players switch agents, and it's easy to see that agents might find it difficult to be profitable. Most agents bank on having a long-term relationship with a client. Although the agent may not make a lot of money upfront, a player's contract often grows exponentially as the athlete becomes a veteran in the sport, and the corresponding agent commissions grow as well. This is why it is so disappointing for agents when a player leaves for another agency.

For marketing deals, agents are typically paid between 10% and 20% of the athlete's income. Again, these may seem like great commissions, but the reality is that very few players obtain lucrative endorsement deals. Agents often need to agree to the lower end of the commission scale in order to land a highly marketable client. Marketing commissions are not monitored by the leagues.

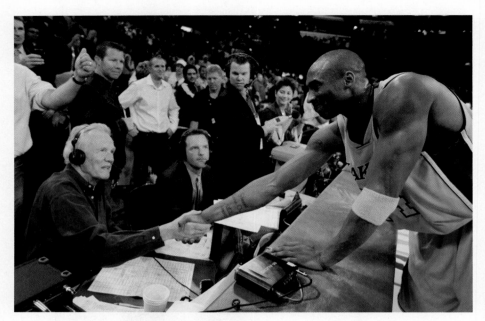

FIGURE 5-4 NBA announcers.
© Matt Sayles/AP Images

Agent Business Plan

Top agents like Bill Duffy always have a strategic plan for their athletes. Duffy uses a three-part formula when trying to place an athlete in the right situation. He looks at three variables:

- *Fit*: By *fit*, Duffy means he looks at the situation on the team to determine the atmosphere of the organization, style of play, and environment in the locker room. His product is a living, breathing person, with a distinct personality. The fit of that personality to the organization may determine how long a client stays in the league. It is critical that agents do their homework and know the pulse of each team.
- *Economics*: Although the salary cap determines the extent of some sports opportunities, an agent's ability to negotiate affects a player's contract value. Even though not every decision is based on price, money is very important. Short careers require maximum short-term return.
- *City*: When drafted, athletes have little choice but to go to the city that picked them. For free agents, the players' choice of location definitely comes into the equation. Being in a comfortable living situation can help an athlete focus on performance. The city also becomes a big factor if the athlete is married and

FIGURE 5-5 Bill Duffy with Recruit.
Courtesy of BDA Sports Management.

has kids. Understanding the needs and desires of clients helps an agent create successful opportunities.

For rookie clients, the marketing plan includes more detail. Below are the main steps that an agent will take to help develop a successful career path for a new professional athlete:

Recruiting: Regardless of the sport, an agent's work begins with recruiting. (See **FIGURE 5-5**.) Recruiting is the process of convincing an athlete to hire the agent as his or her representative. Much like prospecting and business development in other industries, recruiting is what keeps the agent's business fresh and growing.

Player development: Once an athlete agrees to a representation contract, the sports agent must create a player development plan. Each player is a unique individual with different needs. The agent must assess those needs and clearly lay out a plan for the athlete. Having a structured plan in place can control the expectations of the client and avoid misunderstandings later.

Recruiting Example

Bill Duffy, BDA Sports Management

"While not my most famous client at BDA, the recruitment of Speedy Claxton is a classic example of how the process works. Speedy played for Hofstra University where he led them to the NCAA Tournament. (See **FIGURE 5-6**.) While Hofstra isn't known as a basketball power, the play of Speedy caught my eye. I decided that I would try and recruit him as a client.

Access is often the key to landing a client. I had a friend who could make an introduction to Speedy's brother and I asked him introduce me at one of Hofstra's games. Speedy's brother then introduced me to his parents. They agreed to meet with me and listen to my pitch. I did my homework and laid out a plan for Speedy's future. I remember leaving the meeting and thinking that they seemed cautious and not that interested. I can't blame any parents for being cautious, but I had really become a fan of Speedy while watching him play and felt a little disappointed. Soon, however, his parents called me and asked if I would come back and meet with Coach Jay Wright. I did so, and the meeting went great. I must have passed the test because a few weeks later I met with Speedy and his Mom and Dad. They chose me as his agent and we got to work preparing him for the draft.

He was chosen in the first round of the 2000 NBA draft by the Philadelphia 76ers. In 2003, he was traded to the San Antonio Spurs where he was a valuable member of their championship team.

Speedy played for 4 teams over his 10-year career. He now works for the Golden State Warriors as a college scout.

His recruitment is a classic case of a family and coaching staff being involved in the selection of an agent. As an agent, it is important to determine early on who the decision makers are and to understand their needs."

FIGURE 5-6 Speedy Claxton.
© Kent Horner/Getty Images.

Pre-draft testing: All leagues have some kind of pre-draft testing. The NBA has a pre-draft camp in Chicago every year, and the NFL has its combine in Indianapolis. The NFL Draft Combine is the most visible testing ground in sports. The entire weekend is broadcast on television. As in other sports, the players are put through a battery of tests, including physical and mental tests. The NFL is famous for using the Wonderlic test, which is a cognitive ability test that assesses the athlete's mental skills.[3] The first use of the Woderlic test has been credited to Paul Brown of the Cincinnati Bengals. Tom Landry, the coach of the Dallas Cowboys, made it a big part of the team's athlete evaluation in the 1970s.[4] On the physical side, the players are tested in various running, jumping, and weightlifting drills. The tests that get the most attention are the 40-yard dash and the bench press. If athletes can excel at those tests, they can usually increase their draft status significantly. There is much debate about the validity of many of these tests. A player who had a great 4-year college career may not run the 40-yard dash well on a particular day and, because of that, may slip in the draft. On the flip side, a player may run a great time, mesmerizing teams with speed, and the player may move up in the draft. How much weight to put on one day of testing versus 4 years of playing is debated each year. Fair or not, the agent must prepare the athlete for these pre-draft workouts to ensure draft status is maintained or improved.

Team workouts: Teams in all sports bring athletes in to assess their skills. It is the agent's job to schedule these workouts for clients. The agent's relationship with the teams and understanding of team needs are critical to an athlete's success. Placing an athlete with a team that is a good fit for the athlete's skill set and personality increases that athlete's chance of being successful. This is where an experienced agent with good team contacts can be critical for providing an athlete the chance to perform.

Draft positioning: When it comes to draft positioning, the agent has to act as a salesperson for the athlete. (See **FIGURE 5-7**.) It's the agent's job to convince a team that it should draft the player. Again, the agent's relationship with a team can be a driving force in whether the athlete gets a chance to perform.

Team contracts: Contracts in each league are structured differently. Some have salary caps and rookie pay scales, and some don't. It is the agent's duty to become an expert in clients' sports leagues where negotiation will take place. In the NBA, the pay scale for rookies and veterans is well structured. In other leagues, much is left open to negotiation.

Shoe deals: Often, an athlete's first endorsement deal will be for shoes. Although highly marketable athletes can negotiate seven-figure shoe deals, those deals are very rare. Many athletes receive no cash for their deals, and instead the compensation is

FIGURE 5-7 NBA Draft.
© Pat Greenhouse/The Boston Globe/Getty Images.

made up of free on-field/on-court gear and an agreed-on amount of free shoes and apparel for personal use. Even as most fans assume that athletes make hundreds of thousands if not millions on their shoe deals, only a few athletes get big money. Many of the deals are for as little as $3000 in free gear.

Finances: Many agents establish financial plans for their clients by partnering with a financial advisor. A financial plan should give the player a clear picture of where all of the money is going. Sadly, many young athletes are financially naïve and undisciplined. Some players are bankrupt on the last day of their career. The financial plan is in part a simple budget. Sums are allotted for taxes, agent commissions, family support, living expenses, and investments. Good planners can create a diversified set of investments to provide long-term income.

Trades: Being traded can be one of the most complicated situations in sports. Imagine coming to class today and having your professor tell you that from now on, your class will be held in a city 2000 miles away. You must be there and be prepared by tomorrow afternoon—you have 24 hours to pack up your dorm room and move across the country. At times, that's the life of an athlete. Factor in a spouse, kids in school, friends, and home ownership, and it can be a very trying position. Much of the organization of such a move can fall to the agent. The athlete may start playing for the new team and depend on the agent to take care of everything else.

Most fans think a life in professional sports must be very glamorous. Many aspects are, but trades can be difficult for athletes and their families. A few "franchise athletes" cannot be traded without their consent. But, for most, the lack of stability and ability to be grounded and rooted in a community can be wearing. The agent should prepare the athlete long before a trade happens so that a plan can be ready to ease the shock of the move.

Athlete education: Athlete education takes many forms. Many players have not completed their formal education by the time they apply for the draft. An agent can act as a mentor and help implement an education plan for the athlete.

In a less formal, but no less important, setting the role of teaching life lessons can fall to the agent. Many athletes are young and on their own for the first time. Couple that with millions of dollars at their disposal, and it can be a recipe for disaster. A good agent takes on the responsibilities of parent and mentor when needed.

Finally, agents should educate clients about their options for the time after their playing days are done. Many athletes' careers are over while the athletes are still in their twenties. A good agent makes sure that clients are set financially or have options in business, broadcasting, or coaching when they are ready to start their second career.

Negative Aspects of Being an Agent

Like many jobs, being an agent can have its difficulties.

Agent hopping: Unfortunately, many players show very little loyalty to their agents. Athletes can hire and fire agents whenever they please. Many times, athletes are young and impressionable, which can lead to people constantly trying to influence them with promises that they can do a better job than their current agent is doing. A number of agents in the industry have the reputation of client "stealing." It's a difficult part of the business. Even the best agents occasionally lose a client for various reasons.

Although athletes can fire agents any time that they want to, contracts usually cover an agent's previous work. If an agent closes a shoe deal for an athlete while under contract with that athlete, the agent will continue to receive a commission on that deal even if the agent has been terminated by the athlete.

Payoffs: Many college teams have been sabotaged by collusion between undergraduate players and agents. High-profile players can prove to be a bonanza for whoever represents them. Unscrupulous agents have sometimes paid players before the athletes' college sports eligibility has ended, hoping players will retain them when they turn professional. This arrangement violates National Collegiate Athletic Association (NCAA) rules and may bring harsh penalties down on the college program. But, with a potentially large amount of money at stake, this problem won't disappear anytime soon.

Bad agents: It's tough recruiting against bad agents. Many agents promise the world to young players and have no intention of delivering on those promises. Players and families might not realize that they are comparing apples to oranges when evaluating some competing agents. Every industry has its issues about quality of products, but it is particularly difficult in the agent industry.

Personal issues: When an athlete gets into trouble publicly, often the agent first addresses the issue with the team, media, and even law enforcement. This can be the most difficult part of an agent's job: being in the awkward position of needing to publicly stand by the client when all of the attention about an issue is negative. Because agents have no control over clients' personal lives, the best they can do is educate athletes about being good citizens, and then hope for the best.

Mark Steinberg, the agent for Tiger Woods, was thrust into the spotlight and forced to perform damage control after Tiger's scandal became public. Steinberg had to handle all of the sponsors and media to protect the golfer's formerly spotless image. Some corporate sponsors used a morals clause to end their endorsement contracts with Tiger. But Steinberg was able to salvage a few of Tiger's deals.

The inner circle: Often, an athlete is surrounded by an inner circle—family members, friends, girlfriends or boyfriends, coaches. Sometimes these advisors offer advice in areas where they have no expertise. Agents might find it difficult to navigate these waters. It is important for the agent to stay on good terms with these people because they may control access to the athlete. If an agent loses access to a client, it is very difficult for the agent to do an effective job. It's possible that the agent may have very little in common with the people that surround an athlete. Sometimes the agent wants nothing to do with them. But figuring out how to have a workable relationship with the posse may determine whether an agent can build a long-term relationship with a client.

Spotlight on Michael Vick

I was asked to help handle Michael Vick's marketing. (See **FIGURE 5-8**.) Our first meeting occurred at his home in Atlanta. He introduced me to his marketing team, which consisted of five guys who lived in his house. It took me about 30 seconds to realize that this setup could never work. The plan was for me to create endorsement deals for Vick and then to pass them to the marketing team for review and execution.

This posse had been with him for around 5 years. At the time he had two small deals with major companies. It was very apparent that the marketing team wasn't doing any marketing. The reality was that they were living the high life, leaching off of Vick. They had no incentive to work or produce marketing deals. Also, if I started creating opportunities for Vick, it would make them look bad. I immediately started putting endorsement offers in front of the group, most of which they immediately declined. Our relationship lasted only a few months, and I stopped being a part of the madness surrounding Vick.

This is a classic example of the inner circle controlling the athlete. As an agent, you must decide whether you want to deal with an athlete who has an inner circle whose values don't match your own. If you were in a situation similar to the one described here, would you turn a blind eye to the workings of the athlete's inner circle of influencers and collect a lucrative paycheck or would you exit the situation with your reputation intact? The answer may seem like an easy choice, but many very famous sports industry executives have chosen to profit from Vick before, during, and after his incarceration for dog fighting.

FIGURE 5-8 Michael Vick.
© Brian Cleary/Getty Image/Thinkstock.

Agents and the Law

Whenever large sums of money and celebrity are combined, legal trouble won't be far behind. In such a competitive business, famous agents such as Jay Z, Scott Boras, Lee Steinberg, and Drew Rosenhaus always seem to be going after each other. Numerous lawsuits for tortious interference have been filed when one agent accuses another of recruiting an athlete already under contract with another agent. Agents are often reprimanded by the leagues for ethical and league rule violations. With large sums of money at stake, agents might bend the rules to acquire an athlete as a client.

Agent Rules and Regulations

Most professional leagues have some sort of agent certification program. They are all structured differently. The NFL has one of the most thorough systems. A potential candidate must complete the agent application and pay a $2500 fee. Next, the candidate must attend one of three new-agent seminars. The candidate must carry insurance and have an advanced degree. Once accepted, the agent must pay a yearly fee of $1200–$1700 (depending on the total number of clients) to the league.[5]

Some leagues have strict guidelines regarding contact with amateur athletes, whereas others have no rules. States and the NCAA have imposed rules on agent–athlete contact, but most rules are simply ignored.[6] With few resources directed to policing, overseeing contact is almost impossible.

Example Team Contract

Understanding the ins and outs of an athlete contract can help you to become a successful agent. The example contract below will help you create the best situation for your client.

This contract made on _____ [Date] is between _____ ("Team"), a member of League ("League"), and _____, an Athlete ("Athlete"). The parties agree as follows:

A. TERM

SAMPLE LANGUAGE The Team employs the Athlete as a skilled player for a term of _____ year(s), starting on April 15.

MEANING The term is the length of time the athlete will be under contract with the team.

INSIDER TIP Every league is structured differently. A team contract can cover a term that spans a few days to a number of years. Some NBA contracts, such as rookie first-round deals, are pretty standard. Other leagues don't have such structured salary guidelines. Some contracts are guaranteed, whereas others are not.

B. SERVICES

SAMPLE LANGUAGE Services defined in this contract will include: any spring training or training camp, team practices, meetings, training and conditioning workouts, and position training requested by Team. Also included are all preseason, regular season, and playoff games (if any) and any league all-star game and the events surrounding the game, if Athlete is invited. In addition, services include any Team or League marketing initiatives that are covered in the Player's Union contract.

MEANING The team or league will be very clear on all the duties expected of the player.

INSIDER TIP The more that the agent can educate the player on all that is expected, the easier it will be for the agent to get the player to execute the required tasks. There is much more to being a professional athlete than playing the games. Beside the workouts and games, there are agreed-on marketing and community service efforts that the team requires its players to perform. If players understand expectations when they sign the contract, they are less likely to balk when the team's marketing person requests help with an initiative.

C. COMPENSATION AND EXPENSES

SAMPLE LANGUAGE   Team agrees to pay the Athlete for services described above at the agreed upon rate in this contract (less applicable government withholdings). In addition, Athlete will be paid compensation from team-earned Playoff money. Athlete will be paid in twelve (12) equal payments. Athlete will receive an additional $2000 per week (less applicable government withholdings) for each week of preseason practice or training camp.

Team will pay all necessary expenses of Athlete while Athlete is traveling for a team function or game. Expenses include lodging, transportation, and meals.

MEANING   Exactly what the player will be paid and reimbursed for is covered in this section.

INSIDER TIP   Players are well compensated, and most of their expenses are covered while they are traveling on team business. Notice also that the athlete will receive additional compensation if the team makes the playoffs.

D. CONDUCT/BANNED SUBSTANACES/PROHIBITED ACTIVITIES

SAMPLE LANGUAGE   The Athlete will comply with all Team and League rules, as outlined in this contract and Players Union agreement. This includes both time on and off the field/court. The Athlete agrees to adhere to the League dress code when involved in Team activities. The Athlete agrees to conduct himself with the highest integrity and not to do anything to bring negative publicity to himself, the Team, or the League.

The Athlete agrees that the League Commissioner can deliver a fine and/or suspension at his sole discretion.

Gambling of any kind is strictly prohibited and may result in a fine, suspension, or permanent ban from the League. The ruling of the commissioner will be binding and unappealable.

When an Athlete is fined or suspended, he and the Players Union will be notified in writing with the exact details of the fine or suspension.

Athlete agrees that this contract can be terminated for breaching the League's anti-drug policy. If contract is terminated, Team has no obligation to pay Athlete beyond date of termination.

MEANING   The leagues and teams are very specific about what is required of their employees when it comes to player conduct. As for any large company, a great deal of work has gone into the development of its brand. The leagues are very protective of the brand equity they have built. The players, as representatives of the leagues, must agree to a certain level of moral conduct to enhance, protect, and build that brand.

INSIDER TIP   It is critical that the agent makes certain the player completely understands what is required by the contract. There are many examples of players losing their high-paying jobs as a result of off-the-field/court conduct. The agent can only do so much, but that education must be done when the contract is signed.

The agent must also educate the player on banned substances. Not only illegal drugs are included on the list. The leagues ban many over-the-counter substances. On occasion, players test positive for banned substances after they consume a common product. They assume that if it is sold to the public, it must be OK. As hard as it can be to monitor the ingredients in everything players put into their bodies, it must be done or athletes risk suspension.

E. PHYSICAL CONDITION

SAMPLE LANGUAGE   Athlete agrees to keep himself in good physical condition during the season. Athlete agrees that at the start and end of each season he will submit to a physical given by Team doctor and trainers. If Team determines that Athlete is not in good enough physical condition to play, the Team can suspend Athlete without pay.

Athlete will notify Team immediately if he is injured. If an Athlete is injured during a team-sanctioned event, all reasonable medical expenses will be paid by Team provided that Team approves hospital and doctors used to treat injury. If Athlete chooses to use his own physician, Athlete agrees to make available all information deemed necessary to Team physicians.

MEANING   The team depends on the player to be able to perform at the highest level possible. It is up to athletes to keep themselves in shape. Injuries happen, and this section of the contract spells out how such injuries will be handled.

INSIDER TIP   Sometimes players don't want to disclose when they are injured. Some think that they can show how tough they are by ignoring and playing through pain. Although that is bound to happen, it is important for athletes to be honest with the team training staff. First, they are charged with helping players recover. Second, if the injury becomes worse and the player can't play, it is important from a contractual standpoint that the team was aware of when and how the injury occurred. It is in the agent's and player's best interests to avoid any dispute about who is responsible for medical coverage and expenses.

F. ASSIGNMENT

SAMPLE LANGUAGE   Team can assign this agreement to any other Team in the League. Athlete acknowledges such rights and agrees to report and perform for new Team. If agreement is assigned, all reasonable expenses involved with moving Athlete and family to the new Team will be paid by new Team. If the Athlete does not report to new Team, Athlete will be subject to fines in accordance with League rules.

MEANING   In the assignment section, the team will delineate its rights to trade a player.

INSIDER TIP   One of the most difficult parts of being a professional athlete is being traded. Imagine showing up to work and being told that you now work in another city thousands of miles away. As players get more experienced, some have enough leverage to demand a no-trade clause in their contracts.

G. PROHIBITED ACTIVITIES

SAMPLE LANGUAGE Athlete acknowledges that the participation in certain activities can result in injury that could impair his ability to perform his job at the level required to be a professional athlete. Athlete agrees that he will not participate in any game not sanctioned by Team, without written consent from Team. Also, he will refrain from participation in activities that would reasonably be considered having the potential risk of bodily injury unless written consent is received by the Team. Activities include but are not limited to driving a motorcycle or moped, piloting an aircraft, bungee jumping, sky diving, and snow skiing. Athlete does not need to receive Team consent for participating in hiking, golf, swimming, volleyball, tennis, snowboarding, or other amateur, noncontact sports.

MEANING The team will be very specific about what it will allow the athlete to do off the field/court.

INSIDER TIP One of the biggest worries of any team is that the athlete will lose his ability to perform. If an injury occurs during a team-sanctioned activity, the team is liable for paying the athlete's contract. Teams realize they can't control athletes' personal lives, but they don't want to be responsible for paying athletes if they can't perform as the result of injuries that could have been avoided. These activities clauses are added to the contract to protect the team's investment.

Spotlight on Jay Williams

Jay Williams was a prize client of BDA Sports Management. A star at Duke University, Williams was chosen by the Chicago Bulls with the second pick in the 2002 NBA Draft. Ironically, this was one spot behind another BDA client, Yao Ming. Though prohibited by his contract, the summer after his rookie season, Williams was riding a motorcycle in Chicago when he crashed into a streetlight. He was severely injured and never played in the NBA again. Although he was in violation of his team contract, the Bulls graciously gave him a lucrative settlement when they decided to waive him from the team. It didn't hurt that Williams had a well-respected agent who had worked with the organization in the past and would most likely work with it in the future.

H. GROUP LICENSE/PROMOTIONS

SAMPLE LANGUAGE Athlete grants to League the exclusive rights to use the Athlete's image and likeness (Attributes) as defined in the Group Licensing Agreement (GLA) between League Properties and League Players Union. League has exclusive rights to use Attributes for the purpose of League advertising, marketing, and promotion. League may use attributes of a single player and is not required to use Attributes in a group. League is not required to seek approval for use of such Attributes.

The Athlete agrees not to make appearances, write a newspaper or magazine column, host a TV or radio show, or enter into product endorsement deals without consent from the Team. Team agrees that consent will not be withheld unless there is a direct conflict with Team or League.

MEANING   The league will use its players to promote and market its product. Under the rules of the GLA, the league can use attributes as it sees fit to market the league.

INSIDER TIP   Once a player signs the GLA, he has given most of his marketing rights to the league. The league will use those rights to promote its brand and games. Notice that the league does not need to seek approval and can use individual players in its promotions. Companies who are officially licensed by the league have a different set of rules to follow. All products and marketing must be approved. The use of individual players is not allowed without consent of that player. Most licenses have a rule of six, meaning that any marketing must feature at least six players and not feature any one player more prominently.

The player also is agreeing that he will get approval from the team for all outside marketing. Although teams generally don't withhold consent, they do want to make sure that any outside marketing does not conflict with their sponsorships and programs.

I. PERFORMANCE AND TRAINING INCENTIVES

SAMPLE LANGUAGE   Team agrees to pay Athlete a bonus of $50,000 if Athlete attends 90% of team off-season workouts. In addition, Team agrees to pay Athlete a bonus of $100,000 if he reports to the 2014 preseason training camp below the weight of 265 pounds.

MEANING   When a clause attached to performance is added to a contract, often the team is concerned about the work ethic of a particular player. Monetary incentives are given to encourage the player to work hard in the off-season.

INSIDER TIP   In these cases, it often falls on the shoulders of the agent to monitor the player and make sure that he is taking care of his business off the court or field. This is one of the situations where the agent plays the role of parent, psychologist, and motivator all wrapped up into one. Although not in the job description, it is critical to the success of the player, and thus the success of the agent.

AGENT CERTIFICATION

I, _____ am the agent for _____.
I swear, to the best of my knowledge, that the terms of this contract are correct.

_____

Player Agent Certification Number: _____

Case Study

Nick Meriggioli is an agent for a college basketball player from the University of Wisconsin. He hoped that the player would be picked in the second round of the NBA Draft. Unfortunately, the player went undrafted. Three NBA teams have invited the player to their camps and have shown great interest. He has a decent shot at getting a nonguaranteed contract for the upcoming season. Nick has received an offer from a team in Poland. It's a guaranteed 1-year deal for $400,000 tax free, with a condo and car provided.

1. What should Nick recommend to the player?
2. Is it better to take the guaranteed contract or follow the NBA dream?
3. Should Nick make any special requests of the team in Poland if the player decides to sign the contract?

Critical Thinking Activity

Choose two athletes and do a complete review of their endorsement portfolios. Compare an athlete who has a well-thought-out and strategic portfolio to one who has endorsements that do not fit the perceived image of the athlete.

For both athletes, prepare a future plan that shows a clear and strategic group of endorsement deals that would maximize the athlete's earnings.

CHAPTER QUESTIONS

1. Why do most athletes have an agent?
2. Why is it important for an athlete to understand the demands of a team contract?
3. Why is it important for agents to understand the salary cap structure of a league?
4. Provide an example of an athlete who has a discipline problem with a league. What was the situation and consequences? How did the athlete's agent handle the problem?
5. What role can an athlete's family play in choosing an agent?
6. What is the typical agent commission for team contracts? Endorsements deals?
7. Research online and find the top salary paid in the NFL, NHL, NBA, and MLB. Approximately how much is the agent's commission in each case?
8. Choose your favorite athlete. What can you tell about the athlete's endorsement deals?
9. Why do teams prohibit certain off-the-field/court activities?
10. Find the results for the latest NFL Combine. Where did the top performers in the 40-yard dash, bench press, and shuttle run get drafted?

Notes

1. "The United States Congress Quick Facts," ThisNation.com, August 28, 2011, http://thisnation.com/congress-facts.html.http://thisnation.com/congress-facts.html.

2. Mark McCormack, *What They Don't Teach You at the Harvard Business School* (New York: Bantam Books, 1984).

3. "Wonderlic Cognitive Ability Tests," Wonderlic, accessed September 16, 2014, http://www.wonderlic.com/assessments/cognitive-ability.

4. "Cowboys History," Everything Dallas Cowboys, accessed September 16, 2014, http://www.everything-dallascowboys.com/cowboys-history.

5. "Agent Certification FAQs," NFL Players Association, accessed September 16, 2014, https://www.nflplayers.com/About-us/FAQs/Agent-Certification-FAQs/.

6. "State Agent Laws Unenforced," ESPN College Sports, August 17, 2010, http://sports.espn.go.com/ncaa/news/story?id=5470067.

Chapter 6

Team Marketing

CHAPTER OBJECTIVES

- Understand team marketing.
- Learn the history of team marketing.
- Explore how the five Ps affect team marketing.
- Identify key benefits to the team of team marketing.
- Learn the key components of a team marketing plan.
- Review a team marketing plan.
- Review minor league team marketing.
- Learn how teams manage a crisis.

CHAPTER OVERVIEW

This chapter discusses how teams market their products to their fan base. It reviews the marketing strategies that teams use to sell tickets and create rabid and loyal customers. It also presents a team marketing plan and promotions strategy as an example and discusses the rising use of social media in team marketing.

Voices from the Field: Ken Derrett
Biography

To excel in sports marketing, you must excel at selling.

Ken Derrett, CMO San Diego Chargers

Ken Derrett has followed an interesting career path to his current role as Head of Marketing for the San Diego Chargers. His football career with the Canadian Football League (CFL) spanned from 1978 to 1988. Among his accomplishments is developing the annual business and operations plan for the Grey Cup Championship. Moving from the CFL, Derrett was the Manager of Sport and Entertainment Properties at Labatt Breweries of Canada from 1988 to 1995. He managed Labatt's interests with the NFL, Toronto Blue Jays, Canadian Olympic Association, Hockey Canada, Canadian Curling Association, and the Commonwealth Games. In addition, he managed several strategic relationships for the company, including SkyDome, TSN, and the Canadian Country Music Association. He joined the NBA in 1995 and was named Managing Director of NBA Canada in 1996. He was the Senior Vice President of Global Marketing Partnerships for the NBA from 1999 to 2001.

Ken joined the San Diego Chargers in 2001 and is responsible for all of the team's marketing and sales functions. During his tenure, the team has experienced significant growth in premium seat sales, sponsorships, and broadcast revenue and merchandise sales. Ken was elevated to Senior Vice President and Chief Marketing Officer in 2010.

Ken currently serves on the board of directors and marketing committee for the San Diego Convention and Visitor's Bureau. He is on the marketing committee for the partnership council of the American Cancer Society and held a similar post for the 2008 U.S. Open Golf Championship.

A native of Winnipeg, Manitoba, Ken earned his Bachelor of Commerce in Sports Administration from Laurentian University in Sudbury, Ontario. In 2008, he received an honorary doctorate in sports administration from the school, and in 2010, he was acknowledged by Laurentian as one of 50 Distinguished Graduates of the University.

Q&A

Q: *What is your current position?*

Senior Vice President/Chief Marketing Officer.

Q: *What was your career path?*

Graduated from Laurentian University in Sudbury, Ontario, with a Bachelor of Commerce in Sports Administration in 1978; worked at the Canadian Football League from 1978 to 1988; worked at Labatt Breweries of Canada from 1988 to 1995; worked at NBA Canada in Toronto from 1995 to 1999; moved to NBA headquarters in New York City in 1999 and stayed until 2001; have been with the San Diego Chargers since 2001.

Q: Tell me about your department? Who works with you? How is it structured?

There are four major areas I am responsible for:
  Premium seating
  Ticket sales, service, and operations
  Sponsorship, which includes all partnerships, broadcasting, and events
  Media buying and creative, which works with creative and buying agencies

Q: What has been your greatest accomplishment at the San Diego Chargers?

To be part of a group that was able to generate tremendous revenue growth over the course of less than 3 years in all facets of the business.

Q: What has been your favorite moment with an athlete?

While I have been in San Diego, it was watching several athletes compete at an extremely high level when we defeated the Indianapolis Colts in their stadium. That allowed us to go on to the AFC Championship game the next weekend.

Before coming to San Diego, it was probably at the 2000 Olympics in Sydney, Australia, when Steve Nash helped lead Canada to a win over host Australia—I was on the board of Canada Basketball, and with fellow board members we were in a small minority in the loud and noisy host arena as the underdogs came through.

Q: What is the most exciting thing about the field of team marketing?

The opportunity to be part of a winning organization—and to compete for a World Championship. While we can't affect the outcome on the field, everyone in the organization is focused on winning and each week the entire organization has a singular focus—to win!

Q: What advice do you have for students interested in team marketing?

It's an extremely exciting space to work in—the change in aspects like technology, the quality of the athlete, and level of competition has never been higher. The one thing I believe students need to learn is the importance of sales across all parts of the business. Students should be thinking about new ways in which sales can help an organization.

Courtesy of Ken Derrett.

Introduction

Professional sports are big business. College ("amateur") sports are often big business as well. The purpose of any business is to generate revenue and earnings. Winning is not necessarily what the owner cares about most, but it is the means to an end, and the end is profit. But you will never hear the team say that!

Although all sports and teams are different, the ultimate goal of all team sports marketers is to create brand loyalty. Some teams do it better than others. Teams such as the Chicago Cubs, Boston Red Sox, Pittsburgh Steelers, Oakland Raiders, and Dallas Cowboys have created followings not based solely on wins and losses. Each team has created a fan base that has a rabid passion for its team. As in any other business, achieving brand loyalty helps create a sustainable customer base even when things may not be going so well. Although winning certainly brings attention to and helps build excitement around a brand, it can't be the driving force behind a team's marketing plan because only one team can win the championship. Teams must figure out a way to create passion and loyalty, even when they don't win it all or even make the playoffs.

History of Sports Team Marketing

As long as there have been professional sports, teams have sought brand loyalty and ticket sales. **Team marketing** is the promotion of a sports team. Modern elements of promotions include events and games, player appearances, community service and outreach, and branded merchandise.

Many of the events that teams stage to draw attention today can be traced to baseball owner and promoter extraordinaire Bill Veeck. (See **FIGURE 6-1**.) Crazy fan promotions, exploding scoreboards, the singing of "Take Me Out to the Ballgame" during the seventh inning stretch, and even names on the back of uniforms were all Veeck's ideas. One might even attribute to Veeck the first use of social media in sports marketing: Long before Facebook, Twitter, or even personal computers, Veeck figured out a way to engage his fan base. In 1951, as owner of the St. Louis Browns, he held "Grandstand Manager's Day." Fans held up placards to vote on strategic in-game decisions, leading the team to a 5-3 win. Earlier that season,

FIGURE 6-1 Bill Veeck.
© Francis Miller/Time Life Pictures/Getty Images.

in maybe his most famous stunt, he sent Eddie Gaedel, who stood at 3'7" and was the shortest player in history, to the plate wearing the number $\frac{1}{8}$ to draw a walk.[1]

Sports marketing is highly visible and continues to develop and grow through advertising, events, and promotions. Marketing revenue is important to the success of the team. The money is developed through sponsorships, broadcast contracts, ticket sales, and the sale of licensed products. Profits will, to a large degree, determine the funds available to sign players and win games. Although most fans don't think of the effect of marketing dollars on their team's record, it does play a major role.

Venue naming rights consist of a company paying a fee to have its name associated with a team's stadium. Venue naming rights have played an important role in the history of team sports marketing. One of the first examples is when the Buffalo Bills sold the rights to their stadium to Rich Foods. The $1.25 million, 25-year deal created a new revenue stream for team marketers.[2] Now commonplace, teams sell naming rights to stadiums, fields, entrances, concourses, and just about any part of a stadium.

In 2013, Levi Strauss & Co. purchased naming rights for the new San Francisco 49ers stadium for $220 million. For this breathtaking sum, the team will play in Levi's Stadium for the next 20 years. It's not a bad fit, since Levi's has been part of the West since gold rush days.

Whereas fun promotions get most of the press in team marketing, this niche goes much deeper. Venue naming rights, sponsorships, public relations, and community relations all play major roles in any team marketing plan.

How the Five Ps Affect Team Marketing

PRODUCT   For a team, the product has many dimensions. The team, live and broadcast games, promotions, events, and licensed goods are all products developed by a team marketer.

PRICE   There are many pricing decisions in team marketing. Tickets, sponsorships, and licensed goods must all be effectively priced to ensure a successful marketing campaign.

PROMOTION   Advertising (TV, radio, Internet), public relations (PR), community outreach, and social media are all used to promote the marketing message of a team.

PLACE   The key to fan support is the development of a loyal fan base. The location of the team and its venue are key components to success. On the professional level, there are many examples of teams moving to other markets (Oakland Raiders, Cleveland Browns, St. Louis Rams, and San Diego Clippers) because of the lack of fan support or venue issues. Developing excitement around a team is much easier if the team is located in an area with a rabid fan base.

Some teams and cities have cooperated in capitalizing on fan enthusiasm. New stadiums are often built in deteriorating neighborhoods. Coors Field is a good example. Built in an old Denver warehouse district, the Rockies stadium has transformed the neighborhood. Derelict buildings were torn down. Many others were renovated into popular restaurants, offices, and retail spaces.[3] Such projects are multi-billion-dollar investments. The team typically makes a large investment in the site. The city then floats a bond for its investment, pays for infrastructure improvements, and often offers tax incentives.

Place is also important in marketing the venue itself. The home viewing experience is better than ever. TV sports broadcasting is very sophisticated, with high production values. Fans can drink and snack in front of their widescreen, high-definition television for a fraction of the cost of attending a game. This has led to reduced ticket sales and local broadcast blackouts. Teams have responded by making the stadium part of the experience. New venues are beautiful with excellent seating and bathrooms. The lethal "stadium dogs" are now supplemented by a wide variety of food choices. Instant replay (and ads) are available on gigantic high-definition displays. Wi-Fi is standard. Meeting rooms and stadium tours are available. These innovations have improved game day and make venues attractive for off-season events.

In college athletics, place also comes into play. Schools with off-campus venues (San Diego State football, DePaul basketball) often struggle to attract the student body to attend games. Convenience and atmosphere around the venue play a part in attracting fans. University gyms and stadiums usually are located on campus. Attending games is a natural part of the college experience. Loyalty to the team is almost automatic. Many universities directly depend on sports marketing to boost their endowments. Alumni reunions are timed to correspond with home football games. Nostalgic alumni, meeting up with old friends at the game, may be generous in giving to their alma mater. Sports work. Alumni parties are seldom held in libraries or chemistry labs!

PROGRESS Social media has dramatically changed how teams interact with their customers. Simple radio and newspaper advertising campaigns are no longer the sole method of communication with a fan base. All teams now use Facebook, Twitter, and many other forms of social media to engage their customers. In addition, teams are starting to use social analytics as a way to get almost instant feedback on marketing initiatives.

Key Benefits of Team Marketing

As with any business, the goal of marketing is to drive sales. In this case, sales include tickets, sponsorships, and licensed merchandise.

> *Ticket sales:* The most important piece of any marketing plan is the return on investment (ROI). In most cases, a team's marketing plan is focused on selling tickets. This is done in a number of ways. Unlike many consumer brands, much of the marketing and selling of the team's product (season tickets) is done by the sales department on a one-to-one basis. The team sales department spends hours each day executing the marketing plan by calling individuals and companies for suite, premium seats, and season ticket sales. This personal selling position is the first job most employees get when joining a team.

If you want to succeed in this business, you must be able to sell. The financial success of a team is driven by individual and premium ticket sales, suite sales, and sponsorship sales. The ability to sell those products is critical to a team's survival. If the team is winning championships, the job of selling tickets is usually an easy one. But if the team is not successful on the field or court, the job can be very difficult. Most teams start out with a crop of new hires in this sales position. That crop is quickly whittled down in a survival-of-the-fittest fashion. A few survive and become part of the organization. Most realize that their glamorous vision of what it is like to work for a team does not match the reality of that first team job.

Brand building: Just like any consumer products company, a team's brand is at the heart of its marketing campaign. The Oakland Raiders have Raider Nation, a rough-and-tumble group of fans who reflect the attitude built by former owner Al Davis. The team and the NFL have done a masterful marketing job. Raider Nation appears to be a spontaneous creation of the fans that represents a large, working-class fan base. In fact, the term was created by owner Al Davis. The Raider Nation trademark is owned by the team, and infringements have been litigated.

The Dallas Cowboys promote themselves as America's Team. Their clean-cut image is quite the opposite of the Raiders' and their fans'. Each team has chosen a style that it thinks its fan demographic can relate to. America's Team is a cleverly chosen title to attract fans from cities and states that have no NFL team. Some brands form themselves. Cubs fans rally around the lovable loser theme that stems from a 100-year-plus World Series drought. The brand focuses on enjoyment at a historic ballpark, and not the team's record. It is one of the few losing franchises in sports that has a formula to consistently fill a stadium despite a poor product on the field. Beyond ticket sales, great brand building can lead to better TV contract, sponsorship, and licensed goods sales revenues.

Player development: Teams know that if their fans love their players, they are more likely to support the team through ticket sales and merchandise. Because of this, many teams feature players in their advertising campaigns. When an athlete's playing style matches the style of a city's identity, the marketing opportunities can be plentiful. Walter Payton's tough running style endeared him to the hardworking population of Chicago. Even during his many losing seasons, Payton's fans continued to show their support by buying tickets and merchandise. The downside of featuring a player occurs when injuries or trades happen. These can be devastating to a campaign. Imagine being on the Cleveland Cavalier marketing team when LeBron James decided to "take his talents" to Miami. Almost all of the team's marketing was based on LeBron and his hometown appeal.

Community relations: Most teams have foundations, participate in cause marketing, and hold youth camps as part of their overall marketing program. Charity work is important, and it sends a distinct marketing message that the team cares about its fans and community. The Chargers have youth and breast cancer initiatives as well as

FIGURE 6-2 San Diego Chargers Community Foundation.

Courtesy of the San Diego Chargers Community Foundation.

the Chargers Champions Foundation. (See **FIGURE 6-2**.) The program provides educational institutions with funding for nutrition, physical fitness, and athletic programs.[4] Programs like these may not lead directly to ticket sales, but in the long run promoting good feeling in the community is a big part of any team's marketing plan.

Sponsorships: Like ticket sales, sponsorships are a key revenue generator for teams. Organizations at every level of sports sell sponsorship packages to companies that want to connect with a loyal fan base. Each sponsorship package is unique. Financially, they may consist of cash, trade, or a combination of both. Engagement may take the form of signage, food and beverage rights, advertising, events, giveaways, and many others.

Licensed goods: The sale of licensed goods not only drives revenue for a team but also creates a walking billboard for the team's brand. (See **FIGURE 6-3**.) In general, the more passion and loyalty that the marketing team can create, the more licensed goods will be sold. Branded merchandise, once sold, can be worn or used even in the off-season. This helps to drive ticket sales the following year. Amazingly, branded team merchandise has worldwide appeal. For example, colorful NBA and NFL apparel is often worn by youth in China, Japan, and Southeast Asia. Wearers may not know the actual team, or even the sport. But those colors are a visible way of buying into the American experience.

FIGURE 6-3 San Diego Chargers jersey.

© Norm Hall/Getty Images.

MLB Team Strategic Marketing Plan

Every company, in every business involved in the sale of products, should begin its year with a strategic marketing plan. Teams are no different. They spend the off-season planning for the upcoming year and trying to figure out ways to increase their brand loyalty and the excitement around the teams and players. This section presents a sample marketing plan for a Major League Baseball team. Although all major sports teams have marketing plans, baseball team marketing plans are often more complex because of the number of games involved in a season. An NFL team must engage its fans 16 times per year, and only 8 times at home. An MLB franchise must create that same excitement 162 times, and 81 times at home. Whereas this is more work, it also creates more opportunity and dictates that they become more creative in their offerings to sponsors and fans.

As you review the plan, you will see my notes interspersed. The entire plan is not presented here; however, the main parts are included to give you a good overview as to what a team finds important.

Example Team Marketing Plan Summary

SAMPLE LANGUAGE   Baseball is our Passion. Fun is good. Laughter is our Business.

No matter what happens—strikes, steroids, trades—we must not forget that baseball is a kid's game played by men having fun! Almost every kid has played Little League or has at least played catch with their mom or dad. Those fond memories help them relate to a day at the ballpark. Every marketing decision that we make should rekindle those wonderful feelings when fans spend the day with us at the stadium.

MARKETING PLAN

SAMPLE LANGUAGE   MLB Baseball Club
February 9, 2013

MEANING   Marketing plans are typically finalized around this date, just before spring starts. The winter meetings are over and spring training has not yet begun.

A. MISSION STATEMENT

SAMPLE LANGUAGE   Our mission is to be an organization of fans that create an exceptional and fun experience for our partners, customers, and fans. We will provide outstanding customer service in everything that we do. This year will be the year of the fan!

MEANING   A mission statement is a formal written declaration that clearly states the company's purpose. All major decisions should be made in consideration of the mission statement. Notice that this plan mentions partners (sponsors), customers (people who attend games), and fans (fans could be anywhere in the world). The goal is to engage each group.

B. MARKETING OBJECTIVES

SAMPLE LANGUAGE

> Have fun in everything that we do. If we do not love what we do, how can we expect the fans to love our team?
>
> Increase attendance an average of 5% per game. Season attendance goal: 3.05 million fans.
>
> Increase the number of season ticket customers by 12%.
>
> Create flexible ticket packages to increase advance ticket sales.
>
> Create more group-targeted events.
>
> Increase sponsorship sales by 15%.
>
> Improve quality and variety of licensed goods.
>
> Increase involvement with chambers of commerce and civic organizations.
>
> Increase use of social analytic activities to create an atmosphere of responsiveness and caring.

MEANING   This list of objectives covers many aspects of business. The marketing department is involved with many groups, both internal and external to the organization. Every decision should be made keeping these marketing objectives in mind.

C. CUSTOMER SERVICE

SAMPLE LANGUAGE   Our goal is to become a customer service–driven organization. Each decision should be made in consideration of our customers' wants and needs. It is the job of the marketing department to clearly communicate our message to each member of our organization. Everyone from the players and coaches to the ushers should understand the brand message that we are trying to communicate to our fans.

MEANING   Customer service takes two forms: guest relations and client services. Guest relations focus on the satisfaction of the ticket buyer, which encompasses the entire experience from purchasing the ticket and getting to and from the game to the time spent at the stadium. Client services take care of the team sponsors. Getting a company to commit to purchasing a sponsorship is just the beginning of the partnership. Most client services managers attend every home game and personally see that the sponsor's needs are met each game.

D. ADVERTISING

SAMPLE LANGUAGE   This year's advertising plan should have an equal balance of player, game, promotions, and team attitude. The season plan will be to focus on families and civic/business groups. Both groups have been underdeveloped in the past.

Families: The advertising strategy for families will be to focus on a safe and affordable entertainment value. The goal will be to develop repeat purchases during the season. It has been determined that the decision maker the majority of the time is the mother.

Civic/business groups: The advertising strategy for the civic/business community will be to focus on the ease of accommodating large groups and offering discounts. Making it easy and affordable for companies to reward their employees will result in an increase in our corporate business.

MEANING   It is important for advertising campaigns to have a specific focus. In this case, both the message and the target are clearly stated.

E. TICKET SALES PROMOTIONS

SAMPLE LANGUAGE   Our goal for 2013 is to increase attendance an average of 5% per game. The season attendance goal is 3.05 million fans. This would put us at an elite level and in the top 10 in MLB attendance. Currently, we average 35,914 fans per game, or 74.5% of capacity. Our new plan is to develop ticket packages that range from 10 games to a full season. Game day promotions will have a particular emphasis on attracting families.

Every attempt should be made to avoid discounting ticket prices. Our sales focus should start with the 30–35 dates when we can emphasize a key opponent or promotion. Selling these tickets using a "must have" sales strategy will give us a head start on achieving our sales goal for the season.

MEANING   As with any business, the goal is to grow revenues and increase and strengthen a loyal brand following. Notice the particular emphasis on families. Creating affordable options for families is a great way to introduce the team to kids and create brand loyalty and fans for life. A recent *USA Today* article discussed many ways that teams are using promotions to attract fans. The Orioles have more than 20,000 fans signed up to receive a free ticket on their birthday. The Twins have tickets tied to the stock market so that if the market has a bad day at least that means Twins fans can get cheaper tickets. Finally, the Braves and Astros have tickets for as little as $1 for certain games. Even with inexpensive entry, holders will pay full price for refreshments and parking.[5]

Although teams aren't going to get rich selling $1 tickets, they have a chance to get new customers. The idea is to create a great experience for the new fan, who may later return as a happy regular-price customer.

F. SPONSORSHIP

SAMPLE LANGUAGE   Our goal for the 2013 season is to increase sponsorship by 15% using 3- to 5-year deals. Sponsorship packages can include signage, hospitality, pouring rights, premiums, and vendor sales.

The first step to achieving this goal is to create a centralized and current list of all sponsors with details of contract terms and renewal dates. Maximizing current sponsorship opportunities is our first priority.

Every attempt should be made to bundle the most desirable inventory with harder-to-sell options. When possible, subdividing the most desirable inventory into multiple opportunities should be attempted. We must maximize every opportunity to achieve our revenue goals.

We will make a commitment to personally communicate with each of our sponsors no less than twice each month. On April 15, we will hold our first Sponsorship Forum. This will be a chance to gather all current sponsors to discuss our plans and opportunities for the coming season. In addition, it will be an opportunity for our sponsors to meet and brainstorm with us.

The following category target list is meant as a starting point for our sponsorship sales campaign. This list should be updated continually.

MEANING   Team sponsorships take many forms. By definition, a sponsorship is a paid form of marketing between a brand and a property, where the brand is given access to the attributes of the property. The creation of a sponsorship forum is a great way to help the sponsors feel that they are a part of the organization. Hopefully, this will help the organization create long-term relationships.

The first step in securing a sponsorship is to create a target list of potential customers. You will see from the following list that many categories are considered targets. Categories can be broken down even further to include national and local companies and manufacturers and retailers of particular products.

Teams need to be as creative as possible with their sponsorship packages. In today's economy, brands are very careful with their spending. One creative package was recently delivered by the Chicago White Sox. To persuade 7-Eleven to become a team sponsor, the Sox received approval from Major League Baseball to change the time of their 46 night games from 7:07 to 7:11. This 4-minute difference in throwing out the first pitch was enough to create a major sponsorship opportunity for the team. For 7-Eleven, the PR buzz created by the change gave the brand huge exposure in the media.[6]

Do you have an instinct for sports marketing? **FIGURE 6-4** shows a number of products and services with advertising dollars to spend. Pick three from the list. For each, think of a fresh marketing campaign linking that product to a local team or player. Imagine that you will go to that potential sponsor with a storyboard illustrating the idea. Your marketing job depends on making that sale!

Figure 6-4 Example Sponsorship Category Prospect List

Accounting firms
Apparel/clothing
Automotive manufacturers
Automotive products
Boating/fishing
Builders/developers
Business services
Business/office equipment
Candy
Car rental
Cellular communications hardware
Communities
Computer hardware
Consumer electronics/cameras
Cookies/crackers/cereal/snacks
Dairy/ice cream
Department stores
Directories
Dot coms, Internet service providers, Web hosting services

Entertainment attractions
Female-oriented
Gaming/casino/lottery
Hairstylists
Health/beauty aids
Home security
Insurance and related
Internet services
Jewelers
Legal
Liquor manufacturers/importers
Movie theaters
Moving companies
Outdoor power equipment/tools
Paint
Personal care/nutritional supplements
Pest control/lawn care
Pharmaceuticals (especially ones focusing on products/sports, e.g., Lamasil, Claritin, Viagra)

Quick Service Restaurants
Real estate services
Residential homes
Restaurants
Retail/entertainment complexes
Sellers/listing agents
Sporting goods stores/apparel manufacturers
State agencies/lottery
Telecommunications
Telephones
Temporary services/staffing
Tires
Trade organizations
Uniforms
Video/audio

G. VENUE NAMING RIGHTS

SAMPLE LANGUAGE   Our current venue naming rights sponsorship package expires on 12/31. Our goal is to secure a 20-year contract with a nationally known major brand. Our target date for finalizing this contract is 5/1. Our marketing materials will be completed by 6/1.

MEANING   There are three items to note in the plan. First, the timeline for securing this deal is more than a year in length. Although most plans are focused a few months in advanced, for a major item like venue naming rights it may take a long time to work out all of the details. Second, the team is looking for at least a 20-year commitment from a brand. With this length of commitment, it is essential that there is a good match. Finally, the team is searching for a major, nationally known brand. A number of deals have been made with Internet startup companies that have not lasted because of the company having financial hardships. Venue naming rights agreements are often long and arduous deals to structure and complete. The team wants to make sure that it is attaching its stadium to a stable brand that can make a long-term commitment.

H. PUBLIC RELATIONS

SAMPLE LANGUAGE   Press releases should be offered for all game day information, promotions, community service, and important sponsorship information. In addition, any player movement should be followed by a press release. All employees should receive an internal press release just before release to the public.

MEANING   Note that all employees also receive a copy of each press release. This is done so that all departments are on the same page and speaking the same brand message. Things that relate to advertising and sales are not typically covered in press releases. PR is not the venue to solicit business.

I. COMMUNITY RELATIONS

SAMPLE LANGUAGE   Our goal is to be visible in the community all year long. To do this we will focus on the promotion of our foundation and its ongoing events. In addition, we must maximize the use of all of our human assets. Players, coaches, mascots, and front office staff should all be a consistent part of our community outreach.

When possible, the sponsorships sales staff should be included in all events where potential sales can be developed.

MEANING   Community relations is an important part of any team's marketing plan. Even though no direct return on investment is realized, long-term good will, the main goal, is built. Notice that the inclusion of the sponsorship sales staff shows that the team always has an eye open to potential new clients.

J. BROADCASTING

SAMPLE LANGUAGE   This season, for the first time, our TV and radio broadcast rights will be produced in-house. Our partners broadcasting the games will be Interstate Cable channel 4 and AM 1080 The Game. In addition to the game broadcasts, we will be responsible for pregame, postgame, and one weekly team feature show. Our sales group will sell the sponsorship and commercial inventory for the broadcasts.

MEANING   Teams have flexibility with their local radio media rights. Some teams sell those rights to a network that then acts as a broadcast partner. Others keep those rights in-house and produce their own shows. Teams producing their own shows can then sell the shows to a network or buy time on a network and sell the advertising and sponsorship inventory rights themselves.

Many teams produce weekly shows and even create their own content to be shown on the Jumbotron during games.

K. MEDIA RELATIONS

SAMPLE LANGUAGE   We operate in one of the largest media markets in the country. This gives us an almost unmatched opportunity to promote the team. Consistent, engaging stories about the team are the best and most cost-effective way to spread our brand message.

We must make best efforts to enhance relationships with all reporters. This can be done by creating unique and interesting stories for reporters that include both on- and off-field dynamics. Marketing and PR staffs should work together on all media relation initiatives.

MEANING   Reporters can set the tone for a team. A good relationship with the media can help that tone be a positive one. When fans read stories or listen to sports radio and always hear how great the players and management are, they will more likely keep their loyalties to the team. When a radio host is constantly telling listeners that the management and players are not competent, that erodes fan enjoyment and loyalty.

L. INTERNET

SAMPLE LANGUAGE   Our goal for next season is to be the leader in sports for online fan engagement. When possible, all of our marketing initiatives should have an online component. Our events, fan clubs, advertisements, and promotions should all have a way for fans to interact online as part of the participation. We will employ the best-in-class social analytics tools to monitor fan reactions to our initiatives. We must be a nimble organization that can react to our fans' likes and dislikes.

Although multiple departments use the Internet and social media as a way to communicate with our customers, it is our job as the marketing department to manage the brand message of the team. Constant internal communication is necessary so that all departments are on the same page with our new marketing plan.

Facebook: Our goal is to increase our fans on Facebook to 250,000 from its current total of 197,000. We will implement a fan gate to capture e-mail addresses. All fans that agree to like us through our fan gate will get a 20% off coupon for two game tickets.

Twitter: The marketing department will control the team's Twitter account. The plan is to tweet a minimum of four times per day. Tweets should have a behind-the-scenes tone and feel whenever possible.

Blogs: We will expand our fan blogger program from four to six bloggers. Fan bloggers will continue to receive limited access to team functions.

MEANING   Like businesses, some teams are more progressive in their use of social media. Teams like the San Francisco Giants have developed cutting-edge programs that use social listening to monitor fan preferences.[7] In the NHL, the New York Rangers have created a group of fan bloggers and have given them the same access to the team and its players that the traditional media has.[8]

As with all social media, new opportunities to promote a product on Facebook develop every day. It is up to the marketing department to stay on the cutting edge of these new opportunities. This is often done by watching the trends develop in industries that use social media as their main method of communication. It is also a good idea to monitor the communication of other teams in sports.

Most teams use Twitter as a way to connect and inform their fan base. Most of the time, it is handled by the head marketing person at the team. The use of Twitter by players usually has the team's marketing department on constant patrol. Although a player has the right to free speech, it's usually the marketing team that has to clean up the mess if a player tweets something controversial.

Blogs are a great way to create brand loyalty at a grassroots level. Loyal and positive bloggers can spread the team's message. These blogs can help reinforce the marketing message without the use of traditional advertising.

Note the mention of internal communication. It is often overlooked in a marketing plan. Especially with social media, where multiple departments may be tweeting or updating Facebook pages, it is critical to manage the message. When all departments are aware and have ownership of the marketing plan, it is easier to create a cohesive brand message. Don't create the marketing plan in a vacuum. Get all departments involved.

M. PROMOTIONS

SAMPLE LANGUAGE   The team will host 45 promotions during the new season. Each must be attached to an appropriate sponsor. Organization is the key to a successful promotion. All media outlets will receive a sample of the promotion 14 days in advance. All involved employees will meet 3–5 days in advance to receive a one-sheet on the upcoming promotion. Staff handing out the items will be trained on how to interact with fans.

MEANING   Most teams will host promotions for bobbleheads, fireworks night, hats, shirts, and kids run the bases. Some will be creative with ideas, such as "bring your pet to the ballpark" or "mullet night." Sometimes teams catch on to a developing trend such as the Beanie Babies craze and pack the house with collectors trying to get their hands on a collectible. Successful promotions help a team meet its attendance goals.

Minor League Team Marketing

Minor league baseball is the leading edge of sports promotion. For years, hundreds of smaller teams have existed, sometimes thrived, in the hinterlands. Thirty years ago, advertisements on the outfield walls or dasher boards were considered "bush league." Twenty years ago, allowing fans—kids, especially—onto a baseball field was taboo and forbidden. Serious, "real" organizations relied on the on-field success of their team as their "product." Promotion? That was the province of a desperate Bill Veeck or Charley Finley. Fast-forward: Kids run the bases routinely after Sunday games in Major League parks, and seats to see Paul McCartney in center field at Wrigley command top dollar.

Minor leagues figured out early that fans and sponsors pay to be close to the action. Going to a minor league game has always been more of a 360° experience. Minor league operators are not necessarily smarter or more creative. Those teams promoted to survive and were not under a microscope or subjected to the conventions of Major League teams or larger markets. They had freedom to experiment. They were close to their fans and sponsors, knew what these groups wanted, and had the ability to deliver it quickly, free of restriction. Though the innovation gap has narrowed as larger, slower Major League organizations begin to "get it," the minor leagues continue to be a great source of sports promotional innovation.

Tom Whaley knows as well as anyone that minor league baseball is one of the few sports that doesn't rely on wins and losses for a large part of its marketing success. Whaley is the Executive Vice President and minority owner of the St. Paul Saints. An informal survey conducted by the Saints revealed that the majority of people attending a game didn't know who the team was playing, what the final score was, or even who won or lost. Unlike Major League Baseball, where loyal fans live and die by every pitch, the majority of the minor league fans are there for the entertainment. Creating the fan experience is critical to success.

Marketing on the minor league level takes many forms. Budget constraints create the need to be incredibly creative. It's been said that nothing will surprise a St. Paul Saints fan. Known for creating fun and over-the-top promotions, the Saints always seem to keep it interesting. One of the marketing department's biggest challenges is topping the last crazy promotion—and this should come as no surprise because two members of the ownership group are comedian Bill Murray and Mike Veeck, son of legendary Bill.

TOM WHALEY'S KEYS TO MARKETING SUCCESS

Promotion is a lifeline of any club, particularly a minor league club. A few rules of thumb that maximize the time spent on promotion are as follows:

Brainstorming: Brainstorming is the lifeline of promotion, the "fun part." So, to the extent practical, include everyone in the process. It boosts morale, lifts spirits. That guy in Finance or that gal in Operations may hold some of your organization's best promotional ideas. At a minimum, their perspectives likely will force everyone to think differently or consider more alternatives.

Plan spontaneity: It takes time to be creative! Make the time! Schedule it! Since it is the fun part, brainstorming may feel like goofing off. It's not. You take time to plan budgets, create employee handbooks, and draft emergency exit plans. Those are important. Why wouldn't you plan around a lifeline for your business?

Get out of the office! Place has a significant impact on perspective. You can get just as much solid promotional brainstorming in at a bowling alley or at the beach. Minds are freer when they're not occupied with all the stuff they see every single, solitary day.

Be willing to make a mistake: Fail faster! Take risks. The good news is your team plays games for a living. No one is going to die on your operating table. No one's financial fortune is in your hands. They're not relying on you to educate their children. You can screw it up once in a while.

No idea is a bad idea: You can slag someone else's, but you have to have one of your own to replace it.

Read the news every day, and not just Sports Business Journal: If you're going to entertain them, you've got to know what concerns them, what they're doing. The news is a great source of inspiration for promotion.

Keep a promotions idea file in the office: When you have a promotional idea, no matter how slight or silly, no matter when it comes to you (even when you are not planning the coming season's promotions), be in the habit of writing it down and throwing it in the idea file. Most are crap, but you run into a great one once in a while and, at a minimum, that collection of ideas—good and bad—is great fodder for discussion when you go to plan.

Team Crisis Management

Not all of Bill Veeck's promotions were successful. One of the biggest public relation disasters in the history of sports was the Disco Demolition promotion by the Chicago White Sox. (See **FIGURE 6-5**.) On July 12, 1979, the Sox ran a promotion with a local rock radio station that had an anti-disco disc jockey named Steve Dahl. The idea was that the team would blow up disco albums between games of a doubleheader against the Detroit Tigers. Any fan that brought a disco album to the game received a ticket for $0.98 (the radio station was FM 97.9). The DJ had a huge following at the time, and from an attendance perspective, the night was a great success. The stadium was sold out, and thousands of fans were outside the stadium trying to get in.

Between games, the DJ arrived and blew up the albums. Soon after, fans stormed the field and basically tore it apart. Fires were started and turf was torn up. The Sox were forced to forfeit the second game. On the surface, this looks like a disaster. But

FIGURE 6-5 Disco Demolition.
© Fred Jewell/AP Images.

was it really? The incident is legendary, and the team and owner learned a lot about publicity.

Other events are far more serious. Accidents will happen. Sometimes fans are injured. Recently, the Los Angeles Clippers found themselves in a unique crisis management situation when their owner, Donald Sterling, was caught on tape saying racist remarks. Both the team and the NBA found themselves reeling in the aftermath. Each crisis management situation is different and requires unique actions; however, for most, teams can follow basic guidelines that include the following:

- State the problem.
- Speak directly to the fan base.
- Offer regret and apologize.
- Communicate a clear plan of action to alleviate the problem.
- Give fans a way to communicate their concerns.
- Follow up.

Jobs in Team Marketing

Because many students' first opportunity to start a career in sports is with a team, **FIGURE 6-6** is an example of a team organizational chart. As discussed, the initial available positions are often in ticket sales. Although not always glamorous, they do offer a great chance to get experience within a professional sports organization. As you can see on the chart, there are other opportunities within the team beyond cold calling and trying to sell season tickets.

In client services positions, you take care of high-profile sponsors. In partnerships and broadcasting, you help build the media and advertising relationships for the team.

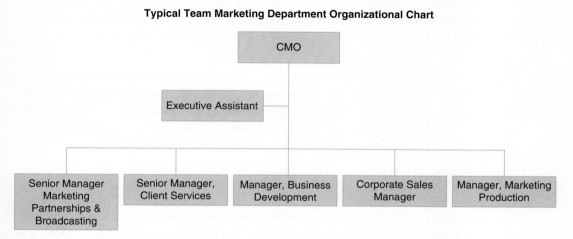

Typical Team Marketing Department Organizational Chart

FIGURE 6-6 Team organizational chart.

In marketing production, you help craft both the internal and external marketing messages for the organization. Whereas many of the first jobs with teams are similar, diverse opportunities in team marketing become available to those who survive and move up.

The San Diego Padres may be the most progressive team when it comes to developing new talent for the business side of their organization. They have two programs that are recognized as best in class by the industry. The first is their internship program. They have a rotating system that develops three classes of four to eight interns at a time. The three classes are spread out over the year so there is always an influx of new talent into the organization every few months. With the rotating staff of 20 interns, fresh ideas are always developing. Six different departments in the organization can bid on the use of the interns for their various projects. This is a great way to develop talent and give the interns real-world experience.

The second program is their inside sales program. The trainees work closely with the sales team to develop the skills to become a productive member of the team. The Padres look at this program as their in-house AAA team, which builds the foundation for their next generation of managers. To date, more than 50 members of the program are working in sports for the Padres or another organization.

With thousands of applicants for these positions, choosing the interns can be a difficult task. The Padres look for certain characteristics in their new hires that they believe are key indicators of success. The top three are attitude, effort, and competitiveness. It is important that your résumé demonstrates these qualities.

Case Study

Julie Porucznik is the Chief Marketing Officer for a Major League Baseball team. The team has finished in the lower half of its division for the past five seasons. Attendance has been on the decline during this time, with an average attendance of 63% during the past season. There is an internal debate regarding ticket pricing. One group advocates keeping the prices at their current level, arguing that once the team starts discounting it is difficult to increase prices. Another group wants to offer deep discounts and even to give away many of the extra tickets to ensure a full stadium.

1. What should Julie do?
2. If the team starts discounting and giving away tickets, should the marketing department be worried that their current fans, who buy tickets at full price, will stop buying tickets at full price and wait to see if discounted tickets are available?
3. Is it worth discounting the tickets and the inherent risks that go along with that to create an exciting, sold-out atmosphere at the stadium?

Critical Thinking Activity

A drunken brawl erupted in your stadium last night. Some innocent fans were hurt, and the police had to intervene. Media coverage is widespread. Fans wonder whether it is safe for their families to attend a game. You hold a press conference at 10 a.m. It is your job to formulate the plan to help guide the team through this PR disaster. What course of action will you take?

CHAPTER QUESTIONS

1. Why is it important to excel at sales if you want to work for a professional sports team?

2. Review the website for your favorite team and see if you can find its mission statement. If there isn't one, what would you recommend it say?

3. Who are the key sponsors of your favorite team? How are they promoting their association with the team?

4. With so much focus on ROI, why would a team engage in community service?

5. Have you attended an event that had a premium giveaway? If so, how did it make you feel? What giveaway would make you consider buying a ticket to an event?

6. What is the difference between guest relations and client services?

7. Find a promotional schedule for a professional team. What unique items did you find? What sponsors were attached to those items?

8. Find a city with multiple sports teams. What type of marketing strategies does each team use to compete for the fan base in that city?

9. Compare and contrast the marketing efforts of a team that won the most recent championship in its sport and the team that finished in last place.

10. Which team in professional sports does the best job of marketing its product?

Notes

1. Brendan Macgranachan, "Grandstand Managers Day," Seamheads.com, February 27, 2009, http://seamheads.com/2009/02/27/grandstand-managers-day/.

2. Matt Warren, "On the Naming Rights to Ralph Wilson Stadium," SB Nation, May 9, 2009, http://www.buffalorumblings.com/2009/5/9/868618/on-the-naming-rights-to-ralph.

3. "ULI Case Studies: Coors Field," Urban Land Institute, accessed September 18, 2014, http://casestudies.uli.org/Profile.aspx?j=8216&p=5&c=8.

4. "Chargers Community Foundation," San Diego Chargers, accessed September 18, 2014, http://www.chargers.com/community/foundation.html.

5. Candice Choi, "Bargain Baseball: Teams Offer Deals to Draw Fans," *USA Today*, April 3, 2011, http://www.usatoday.com/money/industries/2011-03-30-Baseball-Bargins.htm.

6. Jon Greenberg, "Sox Lose 7-Eleven; Eye New Start Times," ESPNChicago.com, January 20, 2010, http://sports.espn.go.com/chicago/mlb/news/story?id=4843174.

7. Adam Helweh, "How the Champion San Francisco Giants Scored with Social Media," Social Media Explorer, December 16, 2010, http://www.socialmediaexplorer.com/social-media-marketing/how-the-champion-san-francisco-giants-scored-with-social-media/.

8. List of bloggers on the New York Islanders Blob Box, NewYorkIslanders.com, accessed September 18, 2014, http://islanders.nhl.com/club/page.htm?id=43149.

Chapter 7

Sports Advertising

CHAPTER OBJECTIVES

- Learn about sports advertising.
- Review the history of sports advertising.
- Identify key benefits of sports advertising to the advertiser.
- Learn key components of an advertising plan.
- Review a sports advertising campaign brief.
- Review an advertising campaign.

CHAPTER OVERVIEW

This chapter looks at the use of sports advertising as a means for the world's largest brands to spread their message. It explores how companies try to harness the passion and loyalty of the sports fan to promote their products and services. Also, it analyzes a number of sports advertising campaigns and discusses the strategies behind the campaigns.

Voices from the Field: Chris Raih

Biography

Hailing from Minnesota, Chris spent his early advertising days at Fallon, in Minneapolis, and Weiden + Kennedy working on nationally recognized advertising campaigns for United Airlines, BMW, and Nike. He is cofounder of the Venice-based creative agency Zambezi, which now is one of the most successful agencies in the business.

Q&A

Q: *What is your current position?*

Founder, Managing Director of Zambezi.

Q: *What was your career path?*

While working at Weiden + Kennedy in Portland, I was a key account player for Nike and met my Zambezi cofounder, Brian Ford.

I was 28 when Brian and I started Zambezi. Just 5 years later, the agency has blossomed into an internationally recognized creative hot shop with 50+ employees. We've also recently opened an office in Shanghai. The agency was named *Advertising Age*'s 2011 Small Agency of the Year—West Region and made it onto the *Inc.* 500 | 5000 list of fastest growing companies in the United States in 2011.

Q: *Tell me about your department. Who works with you? How is it structured?*

As Managing Director, I am responsible for all the departments in the company. This includes Account Services, Creative, Brand Strategy, Production, and Design.

Q: *What has been your greatest accomplishment in sports advertising?*

The wonderful wife and business partner I somehow convinced to marry me, our two beautiful, happy kids, and running an agency to which our employees invite their friends to come work.

Q: *What has been your favorite moment with an athlete or sports company?*

There are many. We have been blessed. One moment when I feel like my pilot light was lit was the very first Nike shoot I managed. It doubled as LeBron James's first advertising shoot ever. It was a "pinch me" moment, where all my skills and interests collided, and I knew I'd found my place in the universe.

Q: *What is the most exciting thing about the field of sports advertising?*

In the age of DVR and ad-skipping devices, sports are the last live, unscripted drama in modern society. A team and its athletes write the story as they go—nothing is promised, nothing is guaranteed. We meet new heroes each season, and as creative people, we get to help tell their stories and "build their brands" in innovative ways.

Courtesy of Chris Raih/Zambezi.

Introduction

The word advertising is becoming more difficult to define every day. Most definitions describe it as some form of paid communication through mass media. At its core, however, the objectives remain the same no matter what form it takes: building a brand, creating loyalty, and influencing spending. An ad can be moving, funny, or silly, but if it doesn't influence spending, it cannot be deemed successful.

At one time, the delivery options or medium for an ad were easy to define. TV commercials, print ads in magazines and newspapers, and billboards accounted for most of the options. Today, it seems that the number of paths to reach the consumer is infinite. These days, many very successful ad campaigns are never aired on television, never published in print or on billboards. Google, Facebook, YouTube, Twitter, and many other social media options have created the opportunity to reach very targeted demographics in very nontraditional ways. With new forms of advertising, companies must also analyze the frequency of their campaign. Frequency means the appropriate number of times a consumer must see a message before responding.

Although sports advertising takes many forms, a common link is that brands want to tap into the passion of the sports fan. Sports advertising can be broken into two categories: sports and nonsports.

Sports advertising is when the product, company, or brand is in the sports industry, such as equipment or apparel manufacturers, leagues or teams, or perhaps sports-related video game makers, among others. (See **FIGURE 7-1**.) Sports brands such as Nike and ESPN have done a masterful job creating brand equity for their offerings through sports advertising.

Nonsports advertising is when the product or company has no apparent connection to the sport but uses sports to reach the desired demographic. Companies such as Anheuser-Busch and Visa spend significant amounts of their advertising budgets on sports-related programming.

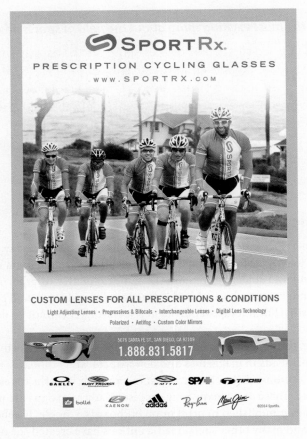

FIGURE 7-1 SportRx advertisement.
Used with permission from SportRx.

History of Sports Advertising

One might argue that an ancient Native American petroglyph could be construed as one of the earliest forms of outdoor advertising. Even before the majority of the population could read, symbols were used to communicate messages—of the blacksmith, doctor, trading post. As society developed and radio, television, and billboards became prevalent, companies saw the benefit of using these media to communicate their message.

Sports and advertising were really brought together with the advent of television. The first televised sporting event in the United States was a baseball game between Columbia University and Princeton in 1939.[1] In 1948, nearly 200,000 homes had a television.[2] By 1951, that number had exploded to more than 15 million.[3] Much of the early prime-time programming was based around sporting events. In 2011, $10.9 billion was spent on advertising during sporting events, and more than 42,500 hours of live sporting events were broadcast on television.[4] The industry has continued to develop into billion-dollar league deals and multi-million-dollar ads during the Super Bowl. The Super Bowl can now command upward of $4 million per 30-second spot.

It is clear that many brands see the power of sports and want to be close to the loyal and passionate fan. Many companies have dedicated the majority of their ad spend to sports-related opportunities. Companies that spend the majority of their ad budget on sports include Anheuser-Busch (80%), Nike (91%), MillerCoors (75%), and Southwest Airlines (72%). All of these top 50 advertising spenders believe in the power of sports.[5] According to Nielsen, the top overall sports advertising spenders include AT&T, Bud Light, Verizon Wireless, McDonalds, and DIRECTV.[6]

The Bleacher Report published its list of the 50 most iconic sports ads of the last 25 years. Both sports and nonsports companies are on the list. Nike and Michael Jordan own a number of the spots. While Jordan was creating his legend on the court, Nike was helping build it on the airwaves. Their partnership helped build Jordan's public persona and make him the most sought after spokesman in the business. Nonsports companies such as McDonalds, Miller Light, Budweiser, MasterCard, and Coca-Cola also hold a number of spots on the list. Coke's commercial with Pittsburgh Steelers great Mean Joe Green giving his jersey to a young fan after a tough game, and receiving a Coke in return, is one of the all-time greats. Starting in the 1970s, Miller Light used famous older players to help launch and build its brand. Retired athletes such as Dick Butkus, Yogi Berra, Bob Uecker, and Bubba Smith became fixtures on prime-time television.[7] The creativity and longevity of these ads show that the excitement around sports makes sports a perfect match for brands trying to promote their business. Super Bowl ads have become so popular that many people watch to see the ads as much as the game itself.

How the Five Ps Affect Sports Advertising

PRODUCT In this case, the product is an intangible message. The advertisement, or **spot**, creates an image used to influence a consumer. The agency that creates the spot sells its services to companies trying to promote a brand.

PLACE Where advertising is placed is critical in reaching the target audience. The ad may be shown on television, in print, or online. Each medium offers many options. For example, for a print campaign that tries to reach basketball fans, many decisions must be made: Should it use newspapers or magazines? If magazines, should it use general sports options such as *Sports Illustrated* and *ESPN The Magazine* or refine the scope even more with a publication like *SLAM*? Decisions like these may determine whether the target customer ever sees the campaign.

PRICE Price comes into play at a number of levels in sports advertising. First, the agency must price its work for the client and secure the business. Next, the client must determine the amount of money it will spend on the campaign. Finally, the agency must negotiate the **media buy** with the appropriate media. A media buy is the purchasing of space for an advertisement.

PROMOTION   It is the sole job of an agency to promote its clients. Effective campaigns lead to increased sales, which hopefully lead to more business for the agency. Many brands choose to promote their products through sports. They are banking on the idea that fan loyalty translates to loyalty to their company's products.

PROGRESS   Sports advertising may be the niche of the sports industry most affected by progress. Just a few years ago there was almost no Internet advertising. Now many agencies specialize or only work in the digital world. Agencies must consider whether their expensive TV ads will translate well to the computer screen. Will computer advertising work on a tablet or smartphone? The survival of every company in the industry depends on the company's ability to adapt to the digital advertising age.

Identify Key Benefits to the Sports Advertiser

Advertisers love to tap into the passion of the sports fan. The following key benefits have led to companies paying millions of dollars a year to be a part of the sports advertising.

Reach: Reach is the number of people an advertiser will meet with its message. Reaching a committed, passionate, and loyal fan base is the main reason companies choose sports-related advertising. Some companies may have the resources and benefit from the broad demographic offered by major sporting events such as the Super Bowl or the Olympics. Others may be trying to reach a more specific demographic and may choose to advertise in a specific sport or part of the country.

Customer retention: Keeping customers is almost as hard as securing new customers. By building a customer base that is loyal to a team, player, or league, a company increases its chance at retention. Companies making hotdogs, soda, automobiles, cell phones, and many other products bank on the notion that associating with a sport, team, or athlete helps keep a customer loyal to their brand.

Less selling: The more persuasive the advertising campaign, the less of a sales job the company has to do. Nike has created a near fanatical fan base with its Brand Jordan line. Loyal customers line up to be one of the first to purchase a pair of shoes when a new type is released. The sales people at the store selling those shoes are not trying to convince the buyer to purchase the item based on a discussion of new features and benefits. Because of the advertising campaign and time spent building the brand, the consumer almost automatically purchases the new launch of product.

Increased sales: Tapping into the passionate sports fan base with the right message can quickly increase sales of a brand. Having a good product isn't always enough to ensure great sales. Marketing books are full of case studies about companies that failed despite having a good idea or product. Using sports to advertise a product almost guarantees that a large base of consumers is exposed to the message.

Brand building: Attaching a consumer brand to that of a sports brand with a rabid following can quickly send the consumer a brand message. Brands that advertise at the Masters Golf Tournament are more than likely trying to communicate a high-end advertising message. A brand that may sponsor the X Games is probably communicating a more hip message. Companies can spend millions of dollars creating a brand message. Associating with sports can help speed up the introduction of that image.

Key Components of an Advertising Campaign

Advertising is no different from any other aspect of business. Either business finds you or you find business. A hot agency may have clients reaching out to it to solicit business. Typically, this happens when an agency creates a great campaign that is moving the sales needle for a company. Other companies see it, like it, want that to happen to their business, so they seek out the agency responsible. When an agency gets hot like this, it must be disciplined and select clients that fit its strengths and company culture.

Although it's nice to have companies chasing you for business, this rarely happens. Agencies must prospect for business. **Prospecting** means identifying potential business opportunities. Once an opportunity has been identified a strategy must be built to turn that opportunity into a client. This usually falls to a person with a job title of Business Development Manager. This person's job is to constantly develop relationships that lead to new clients. Sometimes companies that are planning to conduct an advertising campaign put the work out to bid. Interested agencies develop a strategy and make a pitch to the company. Companies typically allow only two to three agencies to bid on a particular project. Part of prospecting is identifying projects that are put out to bid and building the relationship needed to be one of the agencies allowed to pitch. Other projects are developed in a partnership between an agency and a company. Prospecting in this case is needed to identify potential companies and make them aware of the agency's capabilities.

Once a client is secured, a budget must be determined. Every situation is different, and many factors dictate a project's advertising budget. The budget could be as simple as an agreed-on percentage of revenue each year or a reaction to an advertising strategy of a competitor. The stage of a product's life cycle also can influence the amount spent on a campaign. A new product or company may need to spend more to get its message across to a consumer. A mature product, whose message has been established, may be able to maintain its position without a significant ad spend. From the agency side, the budget determines what type of campaign it can develop.

Each campaign starts with an **advertising brief**. The advertising brief is the bible of an advertising campaign. It outlines all the key components of the plan and gives direction to all departments involved with executing the plan. The brief ensures that the client and agency are on the same page at the start of the project.

Although each brief is unique, and agencies have different styles, most cover these main points:

Background: The background section should start with an overview of the client. Besides the company background, the reason for advertising and the goal of the communication should be clearly stated. Any specific history or current situation that would affect the campaign should be discussed in this section. Also, any challenges standing in the way of the campaign should be mentioned.

When an agency starts working with a new company, understanding the company's background, vibe, mission, goal, and history is a key piece to developing a campaign. One important component of many campaigns is athlete endorsement. In some cases, the company has athletes under contract and the campaign must be built around them. Other times, the agency is charged with picking the best possible endorser for the project. It is critical that the agency has its finger on the pulse of the ever-changing world of sports.

Role of communication: An explanation of the specific assignment is included here. Also covered is the reason why the client is advertising and what the desired outcome is.

Target audience: Who are the ads talking to? An overview of the audience is included here. Demographics, psychographics, and geographics should all be discussed. In addition, what role does the product play in the lives of the target audience?

Key idea: What is the most important thing the ad campaign should convey? The entire campaign should be able to be communicated in 10 seconds. What concise message can be given to clearly state what the campaign is all about? This message can help every department in the agency make the right tactical decisions for the client.

Reason to believe: Why should the consumer believe in this campaign? This section includes any claim-based statements that are at the heart of the campaign. A sports drink ad may claim that it has 10% more Vitamin C than its competitor does. That type of claim and research are discussed in this section. Also included are specific copy points and product details that the client wants to feature in the campaign.

Tone: This section discusses the brand voice. What does it represent? What image is it trying to promote? It will also discuss what the brand is not. If there are distinct characteristics that the brand would like to avoid, it will be listed here. Some brand messages are loud and in your face, while others are quiet and classy. The tone affects the message and style of the campaign.

Deliverables: The first things mentioned will be the type of ads that will be produced. Whether the campaign will be digital, 30- or 60-second TV spots, radio, print, or some combination affects the creative process. In addition, the creative team needs to know whether specific themes or taglines must be used or developed.

Timing: All of the deliverables will be on a schedule, typically starting with the brief and ending with the launch of the campaign. It is critical to the success of the program that all groups are on the same page with the timing of each step of the campaign. The client must also be in the loop with the timing so all expectations are clear, managed, and met.

Sample Advertising Campaign

Below is an example of a sports advertising campaign that uses both a sports-based product and a popular athlete to lead the way.[8]

Additional Types of Sports Advertising

Viral advertising is ads placed only online with the hopes that they will catch on and be spread person to person over the Internet. With minimal investment, a company can run a successful advertising campaign if it can get its ad to "go viral." Whereas some ads go viral naturally, many ad agencies use Web video seeding companies. Seeding companies help make content available in as many places as possible. They also make sure that the content is easily shared. Sometimes an ad that appears to have become an overnight Internet sensation has had a little help getting started.

San Francisco–based advertising agency Pereira & O'Dell created the second most watched viral video of 2009. The "Sexy Pilgrim" campaign for Muscle Milk seemingly had nothing to do with sports or, for that matter, Muscle Milk. (See **FIGURE 7-2.**) By design, the agency created a video that brought together two things that seem to have no connection: Thanksgiving dinner and the thought of that somehow being sexy. The funny rap video ended with a simple mention of Muscle Milk. This quirky spot spread like wildfire over the Internet and gave Muscle Milk huge exposure with a diverse demographic of potential customers.[9]

Grassroots Advertising

Grassroots marketing often uses small groups or key influencers to spread the brand message. The Active Network has done an incredible job of creating grassroots marketing campaigns for many sports brands. It provides technology applications and marketing services to more than 75,000 community service organizations worldwide.[10] Providing the technology piece to organizations and races puts Active directly in front of hundreds of thousands of sports-minded individuals.

Zambezi Fantasy Football Advertising Campaign

Client Category: Beverage

Project Theme: Fantasy Football

BACKGROUND

A beverage company seeking to connect to the participants in Fantasy Football chose Adrian Peterson as their spokesman. The company wants to create a campaign around Peterson using viral videos, Facebook/Twitter, mobile, OOH (out-of-home advertising; billboards and street furniture), as well as PR. The idea is to have a presence online where Fantasy Football owners live, as well as to leverage Peterson's existing fan base. The campaign will be grounded in a 2-minute viral film.

ROLE OF COMMUNICATION

Connect with male audience in an insightful, on-brand way. Hit them where they live, using Fantasy Football as a strategic + media platform.

AUDIENCE

Males 18 to 34 years old. Sports fans. Computer savvy. Owners of multiple communication devices.

CREATIVE CONCEPT

Adrian Peterson is the first overall pick in millions of fantasy leagues around the country. His "owners" collect money, trophies, and bragging rights. They get the glory, but who does all the work? Who takes the pounding on Sundays? Adrian Peterson does. And as the fantasy season heats up, it only makes sense that Adrian Peterson would want to collect his "cut."

REASONS TO BELIEVE

The beverage is packed with things that are good for you. There are flavors and formulas to meet many different needs.

TONE

The tone of the ad will be fun and hard hitting. We will back the craziness of actor Gary Busey with the intensity of Adrian Peterson.

DELIVERABLES

One 2-minute viral video featuring Adrian Peterson and Gary Busey.

TIMING

March 10, contract signed

April 1, brief distributed

May 5, initial concepts delivered to client

May 15, concepts finalized

June 15, video shot

July 1, video editing completed

August 1, project launch

Courtesy of Chris Raih/Zambezi.

This kind of access is very appealing to sports brands for activities such as sampling and surveying. Active has created a network that many brands have used to reach a sports-minded demographic. Because it has access to many events and participants, the network often creates teams of participants to help spread the word, such as a group of runners wearing or using a product during a marathon or a triathlon. These groups are of course noticed by the other participants and create awareness for the brand.

Cross-Promotional Advertising

Often, noncompeting companies can benefit from working together to reach each other's loyal consumer base. Cross-promotional advertising happens when two or more companies share an advertising campaign. This works best when both companies are seeking a similar consumer demographic.

One such situation that I created brought together Fathead and Topps. The companies produce noncompeting sports-related products and share a very similar consumer base. The shared target group consists of predominantly male, loyal, and sometimes fanatical sports fans. In sports terms they can be defined as "the man cave guy": sports fanatics in the medium to high financial demographic.

FIGURE 7-2 Muscle Milk. Check out YouTube to see Muscle Milk's "Sexy Pilgrim" commercial.
© Robert Beck/Sports Illustrated/Getty Images.

Topps has been a leading brand in the trading card industry for more than 50 years. Its distribution model is driven by sales of cards in thousands of mom-and-pop trading card stores and big box retail stores such as Walmart and Target. It has a fanatical sports consumer base.

Fathead is a newer company on the sports licensing scene. Its life-sized wall graphics became an instant hit among sports fans when the products hit the market in 2005. Fathead's distribution model is dominated by direct-to-consumer advertising on television and online. By definition, **direct-to-consumer advertising** is an ad with a call to action guiding the viewer on how to immediately buy the product. Fathead's sometimes over-the-top TV ads prompt the viewers to call an 800 number or go online to purchase a life-size wall graphic of their favorite player or team. The initial ads featured Pittsburgh Steelers quarterback Ben Roethlisberger joking around with NFL fans, encouraging them to buy a Fathead.

The reason that this cross-promotional advertising opportunity worked was because both companies coveted the other's distribution model and loyal consumer base. Fathead wanted to expand its distribution model into the retail space. Topps wanted to tap into the growing sports consumer base that Fathead built online.

Fathead agreed to advertise the promotion on its website and drive consumers to the Topps website for details. In return, Topps included an **advertising burst** on its packaging alerting consumers of the joint promotion with Fathead. A burst is typically some type of an additional callout on packaging to catch the eye of the consumer. In this case, it was in the form of a gold star with promotional details inside.

The details of the promotion included a chance to win free Fatheads, discounts on the purchase of a Fathead, and the grand prize of a trip for two to the Major League Baseball All-Star Game. Topps paid for the additional costs of the burst on packaging and the promotional cards. Fathead absorbed the discounts in selling its products. Both companies split the cost of the grand prize.

The promotion drove immediate sales of Fatheads, and both companies reached a consumer base that they had yet to successfully tap into.

Review a New Product Launch Campaign

One of the first large-scale advertising campaigns that I worked on was for the launch of the golf business at Upper Deck Company. We decided to launch a series of trading cards featuring top golfers and to start a collectible and autograph memorabilia business around Tiger Woods. It was a difficult launch because we had to prepare the campaign and create a new product while we were simultaneously trying to sign Tiger Woods to an exclusive marketing deal. Until we were sure that Tiger's deal would be finished, we couldn't let anyone know that we were entering the business. In essence, if that deal was not completed, there was no golf business. At the same time, our goal was to be to market with golf product as quickly as possible if the deal was signed.

When we determined that the Tiger deal was imminent, we decided to act quickly. My golf team put together a list of golfers who we wanted in the inaugural set of cards. The golfers were put into three categories, which we called Young Guns, Current Stars, and Legends.

The Young Guns consisted of about 20 golfers who we determined through internal research had a chance to become stars. The Current Stars were put in two categories: stars and superstars. This was a list of about 40 golfers, including such players as Phil Mickelson and Vijay Singh in the superstar category. Finally, the Legends included both living and deceased golfers and numbered about 20. For the deceased golfers, we typically dealt with their estate or a marketing company in charge of licensing their image and likeness rights. When finished, the first set included 25 Young Guns, 40 Current Stars, and 20 Legends.

While the deals were being executed, we created an advertising strategy to create a buzz around the new product. First, we executed an endorsement deal with Jesper Parnevik. At the time, he was well known for wearing his hat with the brim flipped up. We felt that this distinctive style was one of the most recognizable things on the PGA Tour that wasn't somehow attached to Tiger Woods. By putting the Upper Deck logo on the brim of his cap, we generated an amazing amount of buzz around the brand. His hat was essentially a walking billboard. At the same time, we executed endorsement deals with five other golfers to wear the Upper Deck logo on their golf shirts.

Fans, media, and card collectors started asking what we were up to. Our strategy was to keep quiet until the Tiger deal was executed. After about a month of buzz, we announced an exclusive trading card, autographed memorabilia, and collectible deal with Tiger. We followed this with a print advertising campaign in the leading collectibles industry magazines and online. The initial campaign was a perfect example of a coordinated effort using PR, athlete endorsement, and traditional print ads.

Case Study

Mike Losito is the brand manager for a sunglasses company that has decided it wants to enter the golf market. Mike is in charge of putting together the advertising program to gain exposure in the market. His line of sunglasses has brand recognition in cycling and skiing but little in golfing. It's his job to devise a plan to maximize exposure to the golf enthusiast. There are three main publications in golf that have similar readership numbers. Each magazine has a defined theme. Although they all cater to golfers, one focuses on product reviews, one on tips and coaching, and the third on the coolest places to play. Mike's budget will not allow him to have placement in every issue of all three magazines. He has enough money to run 10 ads.

   1. Should Mike have limited placement in each magazine?

2. If Mike chooses to have a limited placement in each magazine, would you be worried that he is missing many of the readers and not having enough impact with the campaign?

3. Should Mike choose one magazine that best fits his customer demographic and blanket every issue with an ad?

Critical Thinking Activity

Can you name all of the auto manufacturers and movies that advertised during the most recent Super Bowl? Can you recall any taglines? Who were the sponsors of the pregame, postgame, and halftime shows?

At some point, you may be in a position to decide for a company how and when to advertise. Which variables such as medium, reach, frequency, and consumer demographics will help you make an informed decision?

Choose and analyze a sports advertising campaign that you think successfully considered all of the variables and another that did not. Present the two campaigns and defend your analysis.

CHAPTER QUESTIONS

1. Why would a company not involved in sports want to advertise during a sporting event?
2. Besides Zambezi, find and review an example of an ad agency that promotes itself as a digital agency specializing in sports.
3. Find a Super Bowl ad that features a nonsports company being endorsed by a professional athlete.
4. Find a Super Bowl ad that features a sports company being endorsed by a professional athlete.
5. What is meant by *media buy*? What is the best buy placement for your favorite sports brand?
6. What is meant by *frequency*? What is your estimate of the frequency of your favorite brand?
7. Why would an advertising agency engage a seeding company?
8. Find an example of a cross-promotion in sports advertising.
9. Find an example of a company using a grassroots campaign to launch a product.
10. Why is it important that all departments and the client be a part of creating the advertising brief?

Notes

1. Robert Campbell, *The Golden Years of Broadcasting: A Celebration of the First 50 Years of Radio and TV on NBC* (Scribner, Old Tappan, New Jersey, 1976).

2. Gene Youngblood, "Hardware: The Videosphere," accessed September 19, 2014, http://www.radicalsoftware.org/volume1nr1/pdf/VOLUME1NR1_0003.pdf.

3. Bill Ganzel, "World Events During the 1950s and 1960s," Wessels Living History Farm, 2007, http://www.livinghistoryfarm.org/farminginthe50s/worldevents_01.html.

4. Mike Ozanian, "Biggest Spending Sports TV Advertisers Give Shareholders Little to Cheer About," Forbes Sports Money, May 16, 2013, http://www.forbes.com/sites/mikeozanian/2012/05/16/biggest-spending-sports-tv-advertisers-give-shareholders-little-to-cheer-about/.

5. "Top Ten Companies Sports Ad Spending," accessed September 19, 2014, http://www.rjfishingpro.com/Top%2050%20Companies%20in%20Sports%20Marketing.pdf.

6. "Verizon Replaces AT&T Atop List of Sports' Biggest TV Ad Spenders," *Sports Business Journal*, June 6, 2012, http://www.sportsbusinessdaily.com/Daily/Issues/2012/06/06/Research-and-Ratings/Top-Ad-Spenders.aspx.

7. Austin Schindel, "The 50 Most Iconic Sports Commercials," Bleacher report, August 15, 2011, http://bleacherreport.com/articles/804007-the-50-most-iconic-commercials-sports-history.

8. Zambezi Fantasy Football advertising campaign, http://zambezi-la.com/work/vitaminwater-time-to-collect/.

9. Rupal Parekh, "Small Agency of the Year: Pereira & O'Dell Thanks to Its Collaborative Ethos, Energized Staff and In-Demand Digital Chops, This Rapidly Expanding Shop Is on a Yearlong Tear," *Advertising Age*, Agency Editor, July 26, 2010, http://adage.com/article/special-report-small-agency-2010/advertising-small-agency-year-pereira-o-dell/145088/.

10. "About Active.com," Active, accessed September 19, 2014, http://www.active.com/page/about?force_a2=y.

Chapter 8

Media Training and Public Relations

CHAPTER OBJECTIVES

- Learn about media training and public relations.
- Learn the history of media training and public relations.
- Learn how the five Ps affect media training and public relations.
- Identify key benefits of media training and public relations.
- Learn key components of a media training and public relations plan.
- Review a sports media training and public relations plan.

CHAPTER OVERVIEW

This chapter explores the use of media training and public relations and how they relate to athletes and sports marketing. It looks at the techniques used by a leading trainer to prepare athletes for the rigors of dealing with the media and fans successfully. It explores the pros and cons of using public relations as a way to build a brand.

Voices from the Field: Steve Shenbaum
Biography

A classically trained actor and comedian, Shenbaum has worked with some of the most recognizable athletes, colleges, and professional sports teams in the world. He is considered one of the industry's leading experts in character development, team building, and communication training. Steve has created a unique curriculum to teach communication, utilizing improvisation, role-playing techniques, and game dynamics to help clients improve self-awareness and creativity while embracing the power of honesty, humility, and positive humor.

Shenbaum has worked with nine number 1 overall draft picks and more than 50 first-round draft picks. He has helped numerous college athletics teams and teams in MLB, NBA, and NFL, including the New York Yankees and Pittsburgh Pirates organizations. Steve and the game on curriculum have been featured in *Sports Illustrated*, *Sporting News*, *New York Times*, *The New Yorker*, *LA Times*, *ESPN The Magazine*, and on BBC Network, Big Ten Network, ESPN Outside the Lines, ESPN News, and ABC News.

In his past career as an actor, Shenbaum was featured in *American Pie 2*, *EdTV*, *Space Jam*, *The Third Wheel* (with Matt Damon and Ben Affleck), *Will & Grace*, *Married with Children*, *Beverly Hills 90210*, and more than 100 national commercials. Steve graduated from Northwestern University with a degree in Theatre and Performance Studies and also trained at the British American Drama Academy in Oxford, England.

Q&A

Q: *What is your current position?*

Founder and President of game on Nation, LLC.

Q: *What was your career path?*

I took a very diverse career path into sports media training. I studied Theatre at Northwestern University and started my career as an actor in theater, films, sitcoms, and commercials. This led to a job cohosting a sports show on WGN in Chicago called *Energy Express*. During my 2 years on the show, it became apparent that many athletes could use guidance for navigating the media. I realized that being an expert at a sport didn't necessarily make the athlete an expert at communication. My early roots in media training began by talking to the guests before each show and coaching them on how to relax and have fun on air.

In 1997, I was approached by tennis great Pete Sampras, who asked if I could help him become a little more outgoing and comfortable in front of the media.

I developed a 3-month curriculum for Pete and got to work. His agency, International Management Group (IMG), saw the value in what I developed and eventually asked me to become a part of the IMG Academy in Florida. During my 10 years there, I worked with 700 athletes per year in seven different sports. We developed programs in leadership, character development, and communications. In 2012, we ended our partnership with IMG Academy and expanded our services nationwide.

Q: Tell me about your department. Who works with you? How is it structured?

I have one permanent employee and many trained consultants who help me service clients nationwide. We work with individual athletes, professional sports teams, and corporations to help them develop and communicate their images and brands. I have worked with athletes from every NFL Draft since 2004, when I worked with Eli Manning, and in each NBA Draft since 2002, when I started with Carmelo Anthony.

Q: What has been your greatest accomplishment at IMG and game on Nation?

I think that it would have to be working with the 2012 Women's Olympic Soccer team. I had a 6-month old daughter at the time, and to be able to work with these wonderful female role models was a great experience. To watch them win the gold and handle themselves flawlessly with the world media made me very proud to play a small part in their success.

Q: What has been your favorite moment with an athlete?

I think that it would have to be watching Pete Sampras at center court with his kid in his arm after the final match of his career. He looked so calm and comfortable addressing his fans and the media. I realized then how far he had come and that gave me great joy. I also have tremendous respect for Alex Smith, formerly of the San Francisco 49ers and currently with the Kansas City Chiefs. He faced such scrutiny as a top draft pick and during his time with the 49ers, but he never once lost his cool. To see him now succeeding on the field again brings me great joy.

Q: What is the most exciting thing about the field of sports media training?

The development of social media has changed the game, and its continued growth makes this a very exciting space to be working in. You now have to be aware of all of the developments online and be technically savvy to succeed in this industry. Being on the cutting edge of communications is really exciting.

Q: What advice do you have for students interested in sports media training?

Don't get into this industry to meet celebrities. That is part of the reward of media training and PR. Get into this industry to be a resource to the athlete. If you approach it from that angle, the athlete will appreciate it and you will have a better chance to succeed.

Courtesy of game on Nation © [2009] All Rights Reserved. Used with permission.

Introduction

Media training is the process of enhancing one's communication skills and gaining a comprehensive understanding of the media's objectives in order to effectively interact with the media. Public relations (PR) represents the relationship between the public (i.e., fans) and an athlete, team, or organization. The goal of public relations specialists is to help their client create and maintain a positive public image. Although these two disciplines are distinctly different by definition, they often intertwine in the ultimate goal of equipping athletes with a positive image and the ability to articulate it to the public.

Today, athletes and teams are constantly under the microscope of the media and fans, especially with the emergence of social media, where many athletes have become journalists of sorts. TV news, bloggers, and fans with cell phones seem to follow an athlete's every move. Because of this, many athletes invest in media training and public relations to effectively manage their public image. These trainings strive to help the athlete develop the communication skills to project a positive image. Athletes hope that those skills lead to an increase in their likeability from teams, coaches, fans, and endorsement companies. This of course could help them lengthen their careers and increase their earnings. Organizations know that more than just talent is needed when it comes to building great teams. New emphasis is put on interviewing potential players before they are signed to a contract or drafted. These are essentially part job interview and part audition for the player. The teams think that they can learn a great deal about an athlete's character, attitude, and communication skills by conducting a formal interview. Owners of teams want to know whether an athlete can represent their brand responsibly and effectively. Make no mistake, talent is still king when teams choose to sign a player. But when they have to choose between players of equal talent, the one with the more polished image will get the job.

History of Sports Media Training and Public Relations

One of the first high-profile uses of media training happened in 1960. Although not sports, it certainly was a competition. Richard Nixon squared off against John F. Kennedy in what many consider the most influential presidential debate in the history of politics. (See **FIGURE 8-1.**) This was the first debate shown on television, and 70 million people tuned in. Kennedy's team worked hard to create a cool and confident

FIGURE 8-1 The Nixon-Kennedy debate.
© AGIP/Epic/Mary Evans Picture Library.

image for their candidate. He appeared young and vibrant on camera, exuding confidence. Nixon's team, on the other hand, knew that their candidate had knowledge and experience that far exceeded Kennedy's and focused on those attributes. They disregarded his media image in preparation for the debate. What happened on that night may have changed the course of American history. Nixon refused makeup and looked pale, slightly unshaven, and sweaty during the questioning. All of these attributes made him appear nervous. Kennedy looked like the leading man in a Hollywood movie. Interestingly, those watching on television picked Kennedy as the winner while those listening on radio chose Nixon. By the end, public backing had swung to Kennedy, and he went on to win the election.[1]

Sports media and PR training really took off with the evolution of the NFL Combine in the late 1970s. In the evaluation process, NFL teams started looking at more than a player's past performance and physical skills. Cognitive ability tests and an interview were added to the battery of tests players had to endure. The interview process told the team a lot about a player's communications skills, likeability, and makeup. Players and agents realized that millions of dollars could be riding on a single interview with a team owner or general manager. Because of this, they started investing money in media training and PR campaigns to help bolster the player's image and ability to handle journalists.

As the athlete endorsement business grew in the early eighties, the ability to communicate an image became critical to an athlete's endorsement opportunities. Players who could showcase their personalities became valuable to brands. Stars such as Michael Jordan, Magic Johnson, Tiger Woods, and LeBron James were able to create revenue sources that exceeded their contracts and winnings from their sport.

Most sports companies and teams have developed public relations strategies to help support their marketing and advertising messages. The goal of most PR campaigns is to receive placement of a message in a media outlet that reaches the correct demographic. When done effectively, it can have as much impact as an expensive advertising campaign. Another goal is to regulate the athlete's social media postings, hoping to ensure the posts do not contradict the team's image. This has become one of the most challenging elements of the public relations, media training, and marketing fields because countless athletes are posting messages that fall outside the desired brand.

How the Five Ps Affect Sports Media Training and Public Relations

PRODUCT   PR and media trainers sell their ability to craft an athlete's image and coach the athletes through the process of comprehensively articulating that image.

PRICE   Trainers charge the team or athlete based on the amount of time needed to craft the message and coach the athlete through various interview scenarios. Athletes hope that by building their image and learning to project that image in all of their communications, they will be able to demand a higher compensation from their teams and find improved endorsement and advertising opportunities.

PLACE   Media trainers usually promote themselves as experts in corporate or individual communications. Some, like Steve Shenbaum, work with athletes individually and also work for whole organizations such as the New York Yankees. Others, like media coach Barbara Pinson of Media Versed, author of *Athletes and the Media: Bridging the Gap*, convey lessons from a broadcast journalism perspective. She educates athletes and college programs about journalists' expectations and then conducts mock interviews to prepare players for media encounters.

PROMOTION   Athletes and teams conduct media training and PR efforts in order to promote a positive message to the industry.

PROGRESS   At one time, this training was a one-on-one type of scenario. And though it still benefits the client to have face-to-face media training sessions, the Internet is now filled with self-help segments that anyone can practice on their own. Also, video conferencing capabilities have been a game-changing technology for the industry. Media trainers now have the ability to hold face-to-face sessions from remote locations.

Key Benefits to Sports Media Training and Public Relations

The key benefits listed below are some of the main reasons that athletes and their agents often engage a media trainer.

Draft status: People get jobs through the experience listed on their résumés and their interviewing skills. The combines are a demonstration of athletic skills,

FIGURE 8-2 NFL Draft.
© Chris Trotman/Getty Images

communication skills, and job interview skills. (See **FIGURE 8-2**.) The interviewee (the player) tries to convince the company (professional sports team) to make a job offer. Past athletic performance initially predicts the draft status. A good interview will hold the player's spot, whereas a poor performance in the process may get a player dropped from that spot. Media training prepares players to supply smooth and concise answers to interview questions by walking them through practice interviews.

Spokesperson: Teams that are investing millions of dollars in a player would like that player to have the ability to represent the franchise in public. Although this isn't a deal breaker, if the athlete can play that role, it makes the team decision to choose the player that much easier. Media training helps a player build the skills to be a good spokesperson. Whereas some people have great charisma, most need to work to develop a good on-camera persona that they can deliver consistently, no matter the situation.

Likeability: Most winning teams have good chemistry. A player's ability to fit in with teammates has a lot to do with personality, and most players who are willing to engage in media training recognize the need for chemistry on a team. Media training teaches the communication and interaction skills needed to be a good teammate. Players who have such skills tend to be good in the locker room. There are many examples of players who have had long careers because they are good locker-room guys—they may not be the most talented, but they understand their roles and will help the team in any way needed. While media training can't make people like a particular athlete, it can set the tone as fans gain insight into the athlete's personality. Media training can also help position athletes for long-term success by preparing them for broadcasting opportunities after their careers on the court and field have ended.

I represented a player by the name of George Lynch. He won an NCAA National Championship with the University of North Carolina. He was guarding Chris Webber of Michigan in the NCAA Championship game when Chris called the infamous time-out. George went on to become a first-round pick of the Lakers. He wasn't a superstar, averaging only seven points a game, but he had a long career in the NBA. He worked hard, was likeable, and helped the younger players. Because of these attributes, teams always wanted him around. The *Sporting News* once said about George, "He never zigs when he's supposed to zag." He understood how to play to his strength and turned it into a long and profitable career.

Talent alone isn't always enough to make it in professional sports. Every sport has many stories of players with great talent looking for a job because they are simply more trouble than the team is willing to deal with. Those types of players rarely understand the need for a polished image and often can't understand why they aren't playing in the league. Terrell Owens is second in the NFL in career receptions behind Jerry Rice. Despite his amazing talent, he eventually could not find a team that would put up with his antics. His long history of drama has led to him bouncing from team to team and eventually finding it hard to even get an interview with a team. Ironically, Owens tried to revamp his image in the latter portion of his career, especially since leaving Dallas. Because he had already established a controversial image, media outlets always expected to hear controversial statements and baited him accordingly.

Good influence: Charles Barkley is famous for saying that he is not a role model. Some say that Barkley refused to accept the responsibility that came with his privileged role. The reality, however, is that many fans, particularly kids, idolize athletes. That their players are good influences on and off the field or court is important to the team owners and league. Teams are paying millions of dollars in marketing fees to build a brand. Players are the face of that brand. The ability to be a good influence in the community, in the locker room, and during games makes a player more attractive to a team.

Grasp concepts: Teams discuss a wide variety of subjects during the interview process. At times, these interviews can stray far from the sports world. Teams want to see whether an athlete can think on his or her feet, think outside the box, and grasp new concepts. Some teams even try and ask awkward questions to see how an athlete will respond. They know that at some point in time the media will put the athlete in an uncomfortable position that the athlete will have to handle without the help of a media trainer, agent, or coach.

Exams like the Wonderlic Cognitive Ability Test help a team test an athlete's cognitive ability. There are numerous cases of athletes bombing this test. Although it may or may not translate to success or failure in their job, it usually creates media frenzy around the athlete. Leading up to the draft, almost every conversation with a team general manager, coach, or member of the media begins with questions about the test score. How an athlete handles that constant barrage of questions about the same topic shows a great deal about that athlete's patience and character. Media training helps teach the skills to smoothly handle the situation. In addition, a PR plan can help rebuild the athlete's image.

Key Components of a Media Training and Public Relations Plan

Media training starts with an athlete understanding his or her own communication style. Recorded mock interviews help establish this. The idea is to begin with common interview questions, and then to progress to the out-of-the-box, even controversial, questions that reporters may present at any time. Practicing the ability to answer uncomfortable questions tactfully is a great way to prepare athletes to represent and defend their brand in the midst of a real-life, stressful interview.

Media training extends to the social media world and is the number one request of college athletic programs. Media trainers walk athletes through the benefits of social media in brand development and PR while also outlining the types of posted messages and photos that can damage an athlete's image. This is where media training and PR really coalesce. Developing a PR plan involves establishing the desired image, and then crafting messages, events, and opportunities that support that image. Foundations, partnerships with various organizations, and community service events are tools PR representatives may incorporate in a PR plan. It is quite common to invite the media to these events. When asked about the initiatives, it becomes crucial for athletes to exercise what they have learned during media training—how to deliver a well-said message.

Steve Shenbaum's Seven-Phase Media Training Plan

Over the course of his career, Steve has developed a number of strategies for successful training. The list below outlines the key steps of a media training plan.

Make a positive first impression: Improve your self-awareness and authentically connect with owners, general managers, and coaches by sharing your unique story with confidence and clarity.

Perception is reality: Be aware of the signs and signals you give off to ensure that your energy and behavior make the most positive impact in an interview situation.

Communicate with confidence: Maintain confidence in the face of unexpected obstacles so that you can navigate your communication with resourcefulness and creativity.

Think quickly on your feet: Stay cool under pressure and adapt to the unexpected without ever seeming scripted or rehearsed.

Prove your value: Set yourself apart by sharing stories that prove your work ethic, leadership, talent, and intellect rather than making general statements.

Lead by example: Own your leadership style and take accountability for your professional behavior while presenting yourself with honesty, humility, and appropriate humor.

Protect your professional brand: Establish and maintain your professional reputation by staying consistent and confident in your words, thoughts, and actions when interacting in person and online.

Example Sports Media Training and Public Relations Plan

game on Nation has developed a curriculum based on the seven steps listed previously. Each athlete begins with a 90-minute personality assessment and an exercise that game on Nation calls the Coins Exercise. This exercise is an individual interview that helps to determine what makes the athlete shine off the field or court. Topics such as family and interests are discussed to find the areas where an athlete can build a compelling story.

Once the individual assessment is complete, groups of 8 to 10 athletes work together on the seven phases: Make a positive first impression, Perception is reality, Communicate with confidence, Think quickly on your feet, Prove your value, Lead by example, and Protect your professional brand.

Each session consists of a warm-up, entrée, and warm-down. These seven 1-hour rotations of three exercises mean that each athlete completes 21 different stages of the program. Most focus on self-awareness, body language, and listening.

One of the most popular exercises happens during the Think Quickly on Your Feet session. The group plays a game called "Last Letter First." The moderator begins speaking about a random topic. When the moderator stops, the athlete must continue the story by starting with a word that begins with the last letter of the moderator's final word. Not only does it teach the athletes to think on their feet but they also have to listen closely. As you know, listening is a huge component of good communication.

When the athlete completes the program, game on Nation develops a review for the athlete and the agent. This assessment helps both develop a strategy to market the athlete most effectively. To the most savvy agents and athletes, communication training is just as important as strength and conditioning training are.

Sports Public Relations

Is there another industry in the world that receives as much free advertising as sports? When you see a sports program on television, do you think "sports reporting" or do you think "free advertising"? Is the newspaper sports section "sports journalism" or simply an extended print ad for local and national teams? The most profitable division in the Disney Corporation is ESPN. And ESPN is simply a continual visual advertisement for sports, teams, and athletes. And people actually *seek out* this advertising, making sports shows a staple of prime-time broadcasting.

Professional teams are well aware of this gift from the media. It is commonplace to allow journalists privileged contact with athletes, and athletes are expected to cooperate. Players have actually been fined by their team or league for refusing to cooperate with the media. This is most apparent in the 2 weeks prior to the Super Bowl. Every player is assigned to speak with the media. Smart players are happy for the opportunity because that media exposure can easily lead to endorsements or perhaps even a career after sports.

There are many different definitions and uses of public relations. Different industries and companies use PR for many reasons. Sports public relations can be defined as the crafting of a message that is distributed through the media to gain publicity for a team, athlete, or company. This is often done through press releases, press conferences, social media, blogs, or press kits. The hope is that media outlets will pick up and spread the message in a positive manner. Although PR doesn't take the place of advertising, a well-crafted PR campaign can help a company spread its brand message in an inexpensive fashion. Sports public relations takes many forms, but the main three are player relations, media relations, and community relations:

Player relations: Teams or agents often feature stories about their player's off-court/field activities. The goal is to build the player's brand and connect with the fan base.

Media relations: Teams supply interesting stories to help journalists develop unique and interesting content. This type of strategy builds good will and hopefully leads to a writer using a positive tone to describe the team.

Community relations: PR is employed as a way to get the message out about community activities developed by the team. Foundations and charity events are a large part of the PR messaging used by organizations.

Benefits of Public Relations

There are many reasons that companies and athletes engage in PR. The list below outlines the key benefits to a well-run PR campaign.

Promotion: A well-crafted PR campaign can work as a subtle form of free advertising. When consumers read a story about a player, company, or team, they probably

FOR IMMEDIATE RELEASE
January 1, 2015

SPORTRx.
THE BEST PRESCRIPTION EYEWEAR

RED SOX NEW TRADE ACQUISITION, RHP JOE KELLY, FINDS HIS SOLUTION TO PRESCRIPTION EYEWEAR IN SAN DIEGO

SAN DIEGO, CA – Vision is important to an athlete's performance – even if it means resorting to conspicuous spectacles as they did in the days of Kareem and Eric Dickerson. However, times have changed, and glasses have gone from a functional necessity to a fashionable accessory. Just look at LeBron and Russell Westbrook, for example.

RHP Joe Kelly is the poster child for this functional fashion on the face. During the 3-game road trip against the Padres – virtually hours before being traded to the team he faced in last year's World Series – the former St. Louis Cardinals pitcher visited the San Diego-based online sports prescription eyewear company, SportRx. "I needed a direct source [to get glasses quickly]," Kelly explained, as he described how his glasses might "accidentally" get thrown from time to time when he's having a bad day on the field. (Hey, sometimes the competitive nature of the athlete causes one to lose their temper – and their glasses.)

Joe Kelly looking over lens options at the SportRx

In an interview between Kelly and SportRx VP, Rob Tavakoli, the UC Riverside alum recollects his past reluctance of getting his eyes checked for the possibility of needing to wear a prescription, "I could have had a better college career if I would have had glasses," says the Southern California native. During night games, Kelly required special "night signs" from the catcher because he was unable to make distinctions between fingers with usual hand signals. It wasn't until the tail-end of his college career that Kelly gave in and paid a visit to the optometrist.

Joe Kelly getting fitted for prescription glasses at SportRx

Ironically, after spending two years in the Major League, Joe Kelly went from enduring impaired vision and denying the need for prescription glasses, to becoming known by baseball fans for his cool eyewear. "Everywhere I go, if I'm not wearing my glasses, they [fans] are like 'where are your glasses?'" Glasses have paradoxically become a signature piece of Kelly's wardrobe.

Although the MLB pitcher finds it a necessity to wear his glasses on the mound, oddly, he chooses to bat without them, "It's kind of what I'm used to," says Kelly. However, given his recent trade to the AL, prescription-less plate appearances are ironically no longer a question.

Upon visiting SportRx headquarters, Kelly decided this was the go-to company to handle his prescription eyewear needs moving forward, on and off the field. SportRx is outfitting Kelly with Oakley authentic prescription lenses for gametime in his Oakley Fast Jacket XLs, sprinkling some Smith Quinlan eyeglasses into his everyday eyewear collection, and also adding some Ray-Ban Erikas to his wife Ashley's collection. It's a good thing Kelly has been traded from the Cardinals to the Red Sox – his Oakley Fire Iridium lenses still match his red jersey.

Joe Kelly at the SportRx Headquarters wearing Summit™ by SportRx

About SportRx
SportRx is a SoCal-based company that was built by active opticians who ride their bikes, run their races, push their jogging strollers, and bomb down slopes. For nearly two decades, SportRx has specialized in custom prescription sunglasses for athletes in virtually every sport, and have mastered the art of prescription wrap around lenses. SportRx has eliminated the uncertainty of buying custom sports glasses online by providing exceptional customer support with expert sports opticians, free shipping, and easy returns.

FIGURE 8-3 Press release.
Used with permission from SportRx.

don't realize that the story may have been placed by a media consultant. It appears to be an independent endorsement that the consumer is more likely to believe than an advertisement. (See **FIGURE 8-3**.) The media are complicit in this game, receiving and distributing content without working for it.

Cost-effectiveness: Compared to advertising and many other forms of marketing and promotions, PR is very inexpensive. Because teams and companies are not paying for placement of stories, the message can be distributed with little cost.

Awareness building: PR can reach many places where a company or team is not planning on advertising. A story may get picked up by outlets that are outside the current scope of any planned advertising or marketing campaign. This can only help organizations build their brands and solidify their message.

Retention: Many studies show that consumers retain a message delivered through PR better than through advertising. Companies that have the ability to provide both PR and advertising to their consumers have a good chance of creating both awareness and retention.

Market advantage: Many companies don't have a formal PR strategy. Those that do have a distinct advantage over the competition that doesn't use PR to promote their brand message.

Dangers of Public Relations

For the most part, PR has a positive outcome. But, as seen from the list below, occasionally it can be difficult to control the message.

Message control: Although a company can create the PR message, it can't control who uses it or how it is used. Advertising can use a controlled message in an agreed-on publication. Once placed, PR messages are in the hands of the media outlets that receive the message. If they like and agree with the message, they can choose to report it in a positive manner. At the same time, if they disagree with the message, they are within their rights to say so.

Negative press: It's not uncommon for a planned positive PR campaign to turn negative. This can happen when the message appears to be driven by the wrong motives. Not long after Tiger Woods's indiscretions became public, he called a press conference to clear the air and face the media. What people thought was going to be Tiger finally explaining what happened, turned out very differently. The press was handpicked by Tiger, and they weren't able to ask any questions. Tiger simply read a statement that made them want even more to question him and get to the bottom of the situation. What should have been the beginning of the end of the controversy just stirred up more questions and put more pressure on Tiger.

Public Relations Plan

The Internet and social media have been game changers for public relations. The speed of the game has changed. In the past, a PR department had to formulate its plan before the next newspaper hit the stands or the next newscast was scheduled. Today, with almost instant access to teams, players, and companies the message has to be ready at a moment's notice with answers to questions from the public and the media. Although positive PR is always the goal, it seems like almost every day agents, teams, and companies use PR to deal with controversial situations. In one basketball season, Meta World Peace and Rajon Rondo were suspended from their team's NBA Playoff games. Their agents had to do frantic spin control to assure the fans and endorsers that the athletes were still good guys and deserved their support. The Bulls lost Derek Rose to a knee injury, making it a lot less interesting to follow the Bulls for the next year during his recovery. The New Orleans Saints had multiple problems with the NFL, which led to many of the coaching staff being suspended for a year. The Bulls and Saints are trying to control the damage and focus on the positive image their teams and players have developed over the last few years. Donald Sterling created a firestorm with his racist remarks that sent the NBA and its sponsors reeling. NFL stars Ray Rice and Adrian Peterson were suspended for off-field issues. Almost every day there is a need for PR to deal with both positive and negative situations.

While every PR plan and situation is different, most follow a similar format. The steps of a typical structure follow:

Overview: The current situation should be explained in detail.

Goals: The best-case scenario for a PR campaign should be communicated.

Strategies: The techniques planned for the successful achievement of the stated goals are laid out in this section. Media selection and message type are spelled out here.

Target audiences: Based on the goals, the target demographic should be clearly identified.

Key media targets: The media outlets that reach the stated demographic are the main targets of the campaign. These might include specific newspapers, radio stations, or more specifically sports radio magazines and online options. Every category has subcategories. Magazines might be divided into general sports publications such as *Sports Illustrated* or sport-specific publications such as *SLAM Magazine* for basketball or one that targets children such as *Sports Illustrated for Kids*.

Recommendations: Any specific need for the campaign is communicated here. Specific messages and spokespeople are clearly stated here.

Timeline: The campaign should have a specific start and finish and a structured strategy for execution.

Follow-up: All steps should be monitored so that any needed adjustments can be made.

Example Team Public Relations Plan

The example below gives a good overview of a typical professional sports team PR campaign.

TEAM PUBLIC RELATIONS PLAN

OVERVIEW: The lockout has ended, and we are facing negative public backlash regarding the months of negotiating between players and owners. The negotiations were dubbed "millionaires versus billionaires" while the general public struggles in a difficult economy.

GOAL: Our goal is to regain the fans' trust, enthusiasm, and loyalty that we had before the lockout occurred.

STRATEGIES: The PR department will set up a series of interviews using the owner, organization staff, coaches, and players. All will clearly state the same message and show that they get along and are ready to work for the fans.

MESSAGE: The message is a simple one: We're back! Thanks for waiting for us!

TARGET AUDIENCE: Our current fan base is the target audience. The secondary focus is on potential new fans in the city.

KEY MEDIA TARGETS: Local TV stations, radio (both sport and nonsport), newspapers, and team blogs will be targeted.

APPROVED SPOKESPERSONS: All requests for comment must be scheduled through the PR department. The Chief Marketing Officer will answer all event and promotional questions. The Head Coach will handle all team- and player-related questions, while the General Manager will take anything related to the new agreement between the players and the league.

MATERIALS: The campaign will be launched through a press release sent out at noon on Thursday. The release will be sent to all internal staff at 11:00 a.m. along with a list of potential questions and talking points. It is important that all parties communicate the same message.

RECOMMENDATIONS: We are on an incredibly short timeline. All strategies must be communicated to the stakeholders within 48 hours. Buy-in by all parties is critical. We will be asking for an unusual amount of interaction with the media during a very busy period. The importance of this project must be communicated.

TIMELINE: We have 30 days until the first preseason game and 48 days until the regular-season opening game. This campaign will lead into our first game.

ACTION PLAN: The plan will be distributed to all involved at noon today. Because of the tight timeline, face-to-face contact will be made with each stakeholder by end of day tomorrow. Feedback will be reviewed the following morning. Any adjustments will be made at that time.

FOLLOW-UP: Because we are on a short timeline, we must continually monitor this campaign. A daily review of story placement should be reported, including where the story is placed, any known reaction to the message, and whether the story was reported as delivered or altered by the media outlet. Any negative reaction must be addressed immediately.

Case Study

Media trainer Rob Tavakoli has approached an agent who has six players in the upcoming NFL Draft. One is expected to go in the first round while the other five are expected to get drafted in the later rounds. The agent thinks that only the player that will get drafted in the first round should get media training. Rob is trying to convince the agent to spend the time and money and get all of the draft picks trained and ready for their new careers.

1. Do you agree that it is important for all of the agent's clients to get media training?
2. What strategy should Rob use to convince the agent?
3. If Rob works with all six, should he train them all the same or should the first-round pick get different training since he may receive more exposure in the media?

Critical Thinking Activity

Choose one of the four major leagues (NFL, NBA, NHL, and MLB). Using the steps in the public relations plan, choose a team and create a plan for the current season. Typically, each team is at a different stage in is public relations life cycle, which leads to distinct differences in each plan based on league, popularity, and history.

CHAPTER QUESTIONS

1. Search your favorite team's website and find a press release. What was the message? Was it picked up by any media outlets?
2. How can media training affect a player's draft position?
3. Why would a team engage in PR?
4. Why can the likeability of a player be important to a professional career?
5. Identify a successful PR program in sports.
6. Identify a PR program in sports that turned negative.

7. Find a player whose draft status was negatively affected by his performance at the NFL Combine.
8. Why must companies be cautious when using PR?
9. Why is it important to follow up and continually review a PR campaign?
10. Provide an example of an athlete who, in your opinion, is the best at interacting with the media. Identify why that athlete presents well.

Notes

1. "The Kennedy-Nixon Debates," History Channel, accessed September 19, 2014, http://www.history.com/topics/kennedy-nixon-debates.

Chapter 9

Cause Marketing

CHAPTER OBJECTIVES

* Review an introduction to cause marketing.
* Learn the history of cause marketing.
* Identify the tactical approaches of cause marketing.
* Learn key components of a cause marketing partnership.
* Answer the question "Is cause marketing right for your marketing mix?"
* Learn how to avoid the pitfalls of cause marketing.
* Review a cause marketing campaign.
* Review athlete cause marketing case studies.

CHAPTER OVERVIEW

This chapter explores the use of cause marketing and how it relates to sports marketing. It reviews how teams and athletes are using cause marketing to gain a loyal fan following and analyzes the strategies of different athletes and companies for cause marketing.

Voices from the Field: Carly Samuelson

BIOGRAPHY

Carly Samuelson is a 2000 graduate of the University of Maryland, College Park, with a Bachelor of Science in Kinesiological Sciences. Right after college, Carly started working in the nonprofit industry as a campaign assistant for a chapter fund-raising program for a national organization. During her 12 years as a nonprofit professional, she has managed fund-raising campaigns on the local and national levels, planned and executed revenue-producing special events, worked with corporate giving, managed thousands of volunteers, and built countless profitable relationships for her organizations. She's worked in nonprofits of all sizes and has had experience working in both the local and national arenas of nonprofit fund-raising.

Q&A

Q: What is your current position?

National Manager DetermiNation and Sports Initiatives for the American Cancer Society's DetermiNation program.

Q: What was your career path?

I have worked in the charity endurance training program business for over 12 years. I started on the local level of a successful endurance training program where I held all available positions from assistant to director. I've also worked on a nationwide endurance training program with a different structure for a midsize nonprofit. Most recently, before ACS, I was the regional director for a half-marathon charity training program overseeing a specific state.

Q: How did you become an expert in your field?

My years of experience have helped me become an "expert" in my field. Additionally, I have held many different roles within a charity endurance training program and have learned different skills in every role. I've had a major focus in volunteer management and relationship building as well as strategic planning and budgeting and accounting.

Q: Tell me about your department. Who works with you? How is it structured?

My department consists of staff members on the national level as well as in the field. We are led by a National Director for the program who oversees three National Managers (my position). Each National Manager is responsible for a designated part of the country, and our role is to implement the fund-raising program in those markets.

Q: Running a half-marathon or full marathon is a big commitment. When coupled with running for charity, the task could seem overwhelming with the responsibility to also fund-raise. How do staff members ease any time commitment worries potential runners may have?

Good customer service is the key to easing time and worries associated with fund-raising for an endurance event. First, the staff needs to appear knowledgeable and strong in the area of fund-raising, even if they are just learning the ropes themselves. They need to make the fund-raiser feel that their goals can be achieved, no matter how high they may be. Additionally, I think it's important to be honest, telling the fund-raiser that this *is* going to take work and time on their part, but that the effort can pay off. Finally, motivation. The staff member needs to believe that this person *can* raise the funds, no matter their background, their network, or their history.

Once the fund-raiser gets going and starts bringing in funds, it's all about recognition for achievement to keep the fund-raiser going. There are going to be ups and downs in their journey to their fund-raising minimum, and the staff member needs to be there on a personal level to celebrate the successes and help pick them up from the challenges.

Q: What has been your greatest accomplishment in this industry?

I think it's been having the ability to watch a charity endurance training program grow and succeed, specifically, achieving financial goals. Reaching goals means more money going to the charity and further advancement of the mission you are working toward.

Q: What has been your favorite moment working with charities?

Hands down, my favorite moments have been helping people achieve goals they thought were not possible. With charity endurance training programs there is the obvious accomplishment of completing an endurance event. However, we also have the fund-raising success, and that's exciting to see as well. Watching someone who never thought they would raise a substantial amount of money for a charity accomplish their goal is one of the most satisfying moments of my job. It means that I've done my job well, so we can both celebrate.

Q: What is the most exciting thing about the field of cause marketing?

I think it's the fact that you never know who you will affect. That next person you meet at an expo, talk to on the phone, or drop that piece of mail in their mailbox could be your next top fund-raiser for your program. It puts the effort in perspective and it always reminds me that whether I am selling my program to the first person or the hundredth person of the day, I have to have the same energy and passion for my program.

Q: What advice do you have for students interested in sports marketing with charities?

My advice would be not to be afraid to start at the bottom and work your way up. It may not be fun to come in as a "newbie" but if you pay attention and take in all the knowledge you can, you will learn so much and one day find yourself in a management role. Treat your role in any nonprofit as if you are working for a Fortune 500 company, act professional, strive for results, and grow on your success. The end result will save lives and give you a brilliant career in the nonprofit arena.

Courtesy of Carly Samuelson.

Introduction

Compared to many types of marketing, cause marketing is a fairly new discipline. It has really started to become a part of the marketing mix in the last 20 to 30 years. It also takes many forms, which makes it difficult to define. You may see definitions that include philanthropy, corporate giving and responsibility, social capital, point-of-sale donations, and percentage-of-sales offers. All of these and many more can be a piece of a cause marketing program. Whatever the structure of the program, the goal should be to create an inspiring partnership that motivates the consumer to action. The best programs help solve both business and social issues.

For-profit companies offer a service or product that they sell to the public. **Non-profit** organizations are those that render their profits to use toward meeting their goals. **Cause marketing** is the partnership between a for-profit and a nonprofit company. The partnership created is a win-win situation: The nonprofit raises funds for its cause, and the for-profit raises awareness for its brand and hopefully increases sales and profits.

Both parties are driven to succeed by profit. For the nonprofit organization, the profit comes in the form of money and branding. The money raised can go directly to satisfying the organization's mission. In terms of branding, this pairing can create a visibility that is extremely valuable. For-profits are given the opportunity to increase sales as well as gain favor among consumers for this coupling. This also enables consumers who may not typically purchase a for-profit brand to change their minds in order to support a nonprofit.

This mutual benefit is different from the benefit of corporate giving, which typically involves a specific donation that is eligible to be tax deductible. Cause marketing is more of a marketing relationship than one based on donations.

Cause marketing is growing at a steady rate. (See **Table 9-1**.) Just 30 years ago it was virtually nonexistent. Back in 1990, cause sponsorship spending was $120 million. Now it is a billion dollar plus industry—$1.84 billion is spent on cause marketing, up 3.4% year over year—led by the sports industry.[1] Anyone taking a walk through the grocery store is bombarded by cause opportunities. Everything from salad dressings and cereals to chocolate has causes attached to it—to help save the

Table 9-1 Projected Spending, Growth in Cause Marketing Since 2002

Year	Cause Sponsorship Spending	Growth (%)
2002	$816 million	13.0
2003	$922 million	6.3
2004	$988 million	7.2
2005	$1.17 billion	18.4
2006	$1.34 billion	20.2
2007	$1.44 billion	10.4
2008	$1.52 billion	5.5
2009	$1.51 billion	0.3
2010	$1.62 billion	6.7
2011	$1.68 billion	3.7
2012	$1.70 billion	1.2
2013	$1.78 billion	4.8

Source: Data from Cause Marketing Forum, "The Growth of Cause Marketing," 2014, http://www.causemarketingforum.com/site/c.bkLUKcOTLkK4E/b.6412299/apps/s/content.asp?ct=8965443.

environment, increase educational funds, or raise awareness for a disease. Almost every sports team and company as well as many athletes use cause marketing as part of their marketing strategy. Numerous studies have shown that the majority of consumers are influenced to support brands that are attached to a cause. It gives the consumer an easy way to support a cause by simply purchasing products that they already use or are willing to try. The right partnership between a brand and a charity becomes a winning situation for all involved. The consumer feels good about helping a cause. The brand builds social capital and increases sales by supporting the cause. The cause raises funds to help pay for its mission. These reasons have led to cause marketing becoming a part of the marketing mix of many brands.

Enthusiastic sports fans seem to be the ideal candidates to get behind a cause. They are extremely loyal to their teams, favorite athletes, or sports product. Because of this, sports-related cause marketing has skyrocketed. The sports category is by far the leading revenue-generating category in cause marketing, and it is projected to keep growing at a steady rate.

Every league has its cause programs, and each team within the leagues has its individual programs. The NHL has teamed with the Leukemia and Lymphoma Society to help fight cancer. The NBA and MLB have affiliations with the Boys & Girls Clubs of America to help promote fitness. The NFL has a long-standing affiliation with the United Way through the Hometown Huddle program that helps raise money for local causes. Most also have some sort of a green initiative that addresses environmental concerns. The goal of earning profits while raising funds works well in the sports industry.

History of Cause Marketing

One of the first cause marketing campaigns to emerge was a partnership between the Marriott Corporation and the March of Dimes in 1976. The Marriott Corporation was scheduled to announce the opening of its new 200-acre family entertainment center in Santa Clara, California. It believed partnering with the March of Dimes would help generate cost-effective public relations and media coverage for this new park. The March of Dimes was quickly approaching its fiscal year end and needed a spark to increase its fund-raising efforts. This pairing enabled the March of Dimes to complete the most successful promotion in its West Chapters region. In turn, Marriott Corporation benefited from hundreds of thousands of dollars' worth of free publicity while breaking the admission rate for a Marriott property opening day.

In 1979, Famous Amos and the Literacy Volunteers of America teamed up. Wally Amos, founder of Famous Amos, became the national spokesperson for the cause. Amos was able to spread the word of how serious illiteracy was in America. This partnership helped tell the Famous Amos Cookie story and helped expand and create new literacy programs.

A few years later, in 1982, Nancy Brinker helped to pave the way for a cause marketing campaign that would span decades. Brinker is the founder of the Susan G. Komen for the Cure organization. She has enabled millions to participate in the fight against breast cancer through organizations that share the Komen commitment to ending the disease. Komen and Yoplait's "Save Lids to Save Lives" campaign has raised more than $30 million for breast cancer research and advocacy.[2]

American Express and the San Francisco Arts Festival agreed to work together in 1981. Every time a patron of the festival used an American Express card, a 2-cent donation was made. When a patron opened an American Express account, a larger donation was made. Card usage increased significantly, and the relationship between American Express and its merchants was strengthened.

Product Red was created to support the Global Fund to Fight AIDS, Tuberculosis, and Malaria. In 2006, it launched a campaign involving a number of companies, including Apple, Nike, Beats by Dr. Dre, Starbucks, and Coca-Cola. This partnership is one of the largest cause marketing campaigns to date. Six years later, the combined efforts had generated $180 million for charity.[3]

One of the biggest cause marketing efforts is the Pepsi Refresh program. In 2010, for the first time in 23 years, Pepsi decided to forgo spending $20 million on Super Bowl ads in favor of creating a cause marketing campaign. The program created a monthly contest in which people could submit ideas and receive votes for a chance to win grants. The program has had a huge response, and more than 400 grants between $5,000 and $250,000 have been awarded.

Pepsi tapped into competitors' personal social networks to gain support. This helped the company spread its message quickly and receive 77 million votes. Of those votes, 19% were cast through Facebook, and many participants used the hashtag #PepsiRefresh to spread the word.

"This was not a corporate philanthropy effort," said Shiv Singh, head of digital for PepsiCo Beverages America. "This was using brand dollars with the belief that when you use these brand dollars to have consumers share ideas to change the world, the consumers will win, the brand will win, and the community will win. That was a big bet. No one has done it on this scale before."

As this chapter discusses, defining whether an event or sponsorship is a success or failure can be difficult. In this case, Pepsi's sales fell 6% compared to a 4.3% decline in the carbonated beverage industry. Do those stats spell failure for the project? Pepsi doesn't think so. As you will read in this chapter, success or failure depends on the goals of the project. It is not always linked strictly to sales numbers. Pepsi has considered the project a success because it has built brand awareness and stronger relationships with consumers. The marketing team used a matrix that included brand equity, brand health, and sales to help measure success. After receiving 120,000 ideas, they feel that they have a better understanding of what is important to their customers.

By forgoing traditional advertising, Pepsi acknowledged a consumer shift to social media. To reach this new consumer, Pepsi needed to create an impactful program that would motivate this consumer to participate. Pepsi believes that this program will establish it as an innovative and modern brand.[4]

How the Five Ps Affect Cause Marketing

PRODUCT   The product is an athlete, team, or sports company using a cause to develop social capital for its brand. Many times, the marketing is based on an event such as the Breast Cancer Three-Day Walk. Other times it maybe an ongoing effort by a team, for example, the San Diego Chargers Community Foundation, which promotes education and physical fitness.

PRICE   The price of a cause marketing campaign is often paid for by the consumers who interact with the sponsors. Many programs ask consumers to donate extra money with each sale to help support their team's favorite charity. Or the team or company may donate a portion of each sale as a way to pay for the interaction with the cause.

PLACE   Cause marketing partnerships are similar to cross promotions. In a cross promotion, the partnership is formed because both entities benefit from tapping into the other's demographics to promote their product. That is why place in cause marketing is so interesting for a sports brand. Partnering with the correct cause can help a sports brand access niches of demographics that would otherwise be very difficult to reach.

PROMOTION   The brand wants to be perceived as a good corporate citizen, and the promotion is part of a defined marketing strategy. Building a positive consumer perception through supporting a cause helps the brand create positive social capital. That good image hopefully translates to sales and greater fan loyalty. Comedian Jerry Lewis was a great example. He prolonged his career by decades with his good work for March of Dimes.

PROGRESS   Cause marketing was a revolutionary concept in the advertising field. Progress here meant a new and more subtle way of bringing a brand in front of the public. Finding a targeted demographic to help raise funds for a cause has enabled many more events to succeed. In the past, a great deal of money was spent on mailings and advertising to help raise funds. Now, social media has taken the lead as the most innovative way to spread the message of a cause.

Tactical Approaches to Cause Marketing

There are three main tactical approaches, which equate to benefits. They are point of sale, percentage of sale, and licensing.

POINT OF SALE

Point-of-sale programs are the backbone of cause marketing. Most point-of-sale efforts include a **pin-up**. A pin-up is a paper cutout or icon that can be scanned during the checkout process, whether in person or online. They are typically sold for $1 to $5. When customers reach the checkout point of a restaurant or a department store, the pin-up is sold as a donation and is tacked onto the bill. Most pin-ups allow purchasers to sign their name on the pin-up, which is displayed somewhere in the business.

Most pin-ups are only inches tall and wide. The shape primarily depends on the cause. Most pin-ups are inexpensive because, at the end of campaign, they are thrown away. These pieces shouldn't cost more than 10 cents to produce.

A successful pin-up strategy is to include the nonprofit's logo on the pin-up and a barcode that can be scanned at the register. Depending on the space available, the nonprofit's mission statement could be a good addition.

An alternative to pin-ups is having cashiers ask customers if they would like to add money to their purchase or round up to the nearest dollar for the nonprofit. Many shopping malls partner with St. Jude's Children Hospital to raise money through point-of-sale asks.

PERCENTAGE OF SALE

In this type of cause marketing, when a company sells a qualifying product or service, a dollar amount or percentage of the purchase is dedicated to the cause. Beginning in 1989, New Balance created a partnership with the Susan G. Komen for the Cure. Each year, New Balance contributes 5% of the suggested retail price of sales of the Lace Up the Cure Collection.[5] New Balance guaranteed a minimum donation of $500,000 to the Susan G. Komen for the Cure through 2012.

LICENSING

This approach is dominated by big charities and companies. Notable large charities include the American Heart Association and the Arthritis Foundation. A long-standing licensing agreement has been created between the Arthritis Foundation and Advil.[6] Advil developed an Easy Open Arthritis Cap for bottles of its product. The new cap, and the implied Foundation endorsement, suggests Advil as a good treatment for arthritis.

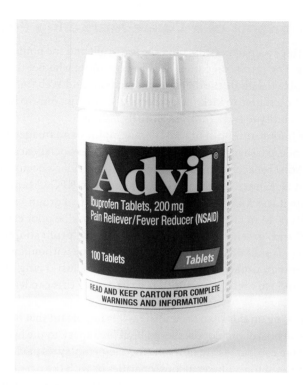

FIGURE 9-1 Long-standing licensee Advil.
© George W. Bailey/Shutterstock, Inc.

FIGURE 9-2 American Cancer Society.
© iStock Editorial/Thinkstock

Key Components of a Cause Marketing Partnership

Before committing to a partnership, both the for-profit and the nonprofit need to do their homework. For-profit companies need to investigate whether their nonprofit partner will be able to handle the increase in donations and Web traffic that will soon occur. It would be a shame to kick-off a successful campaign only to have website crashes or the inability to track funds in a timely fashion.

Proper fit is important. Both brands' demographics and images should align. It would be an odd partnership if the American Cancer Society accepted donations on behalf of a tobacco company. A "clucking" backlash occurred in 2010 when the Susan G. Komen for the Cure partnered with KFC.[7] Many questioned how appropriate it was for a fast-food chain to be tied to a group known for helping save women's lives. Many terms have developed to describe poor cause alignments. "Pinkwashing" and "greenwashing" happen when a for-profit simply attaches itself to a breast cancer (pink) or environmental (green) issue without any real fit or plan. Consumers can usually tell when the for-profit is just trying to take advantage of a trend and isn't really a supporter of the cause. This can lead to negative backlash.

When embarking on this type of campaign, it is important that both organizations' teams be on board. Employees should be able to speak to the benefits of their counterpart. Some companies are now offering their employees paid volunteer time. This time can be used to volunteer at local charities or with the partnered nonprofit. Texas Instruments employees tracked 35,200 volunteer hours along with hours of their own time.[8]

It is important to manage the expectations of each side of the partnership. Successful campaigns are those that are sustainable with mutually beneficial partnerships. Creating researched plans that include milestones, deliverables, and return on investment, the companies can track and monitor their commitment to one another. When synergy is created, consumers, the company, and the cause win.

Not every project can shine. The best thing to do if a partnership falters is to be honest and transparent about what went wrong. In the Komen/KFC example, Komen told its audience there was a mistake, but it stood by the message. About halfway through the start of the campaign, Buckets for a Cure, $1.8 million had been raised. In the future, a better partner for the Komen message might be a product such as sports training or workout apparel.

In addition to a proper fit, it is important for the cause to define return on investment. In a recent survey identifying specific challenges to increasing sponsorship revenue, the number one obstacle was "difficulty demonstrating return on investment (ROI) for corporate partner," selected by nearly 60% of respondents.[9]

Steps to a Successful Cause Marketing Campaign

Every campaign is unique, but there are common steps that most follow. Following is a sequence you can find in many cause marketing plans:

Situation analysis: As with the start of any marketing campaign, an audit should be conducted. A thorough understanding of current market position and the reasons why a cause marketing campaign is being considered should be evaluated.

Reasoning: The reasoning for a cause marketing campaign must be established. Is it a campaign to build awareness for a cause? Is it a campaign based on social action? The reasoning will help determine campaign structure.

Goals: Especially in the sports industry, goals can vary. Whereas a products company may have the singular focus of using cause marketing to increase sales, a team may not. Although teams always want to sell more tickets and licensed product, building long-term social capital may be just as important. Many teams have newly formed green programs, which go as far as getting their stadiums LEED certified.[10] Teams that sell out all of their games may not sell a single additional ticket as a result of their environmental efforts. They are, however, building social capital with their fan base that can help keep fans loyal to the franchise over time.

Demographics: As with any program, understanding the consumer is critical to success. This understanding affects partnership choices, the type of campaign, plan engagement and interaction, and the message. Whereas many sports products companies have very specific demographics, teams tend to have a diverse fan base. A company selling women's running gear probably has a pretty good idea who its consumer is. An NFL team has a demographic mix that spans every niche imaginable. Because of this, cause marketing campaigns for teams must have multiple layers and even multiple partners. For example, the Chicago Bears Holiday Initiative works with seven different charities. The Bears also have military, green, and education initiatives. Each cause addresses a different segment of their fan base.

Type of campaign: Demographics often determine the type of campaign designed. The initiative must reach the demographic where they live. A point-of-sale campaign may not work if the demographic buys predominantly online.

Messaging: The goal is to create a message the will resonate with the consumer of the company or team. The benefit to the cause must be communicated clearly. Consumers should understand the link and what is expected of them to participate.

Engagement: Every touch point with the consumer should be considered. The Bears ask for donations, create events, and have online initiatives to reach their fans. This engagement gives the fan a feeling of camaraderie with the team and a good feeling about being a part of the cause.

Marketing mix interaction: All of a team's or company's marketing programs must interact. A cause initiative should not stand alone. It must be supported by all of the other marketing initiatives: PR, advertising, online, and any other pieces of the marketing mix. The marketing efforts should all have consistent messaging and should support each other.

Review: Constant reviewing and monitoring of the campaign must take place. Are goals being met? If not, why not?

Is Cause Marketing Right for Your Marketing Mix?

The following are some simple questions to ask to determine whether cause marketing will work in a product mix:

Is there a natural connection? A professional sports team partnering with the Boys and Girls Clubs to promote the importance of fitness or a WNBA team starting an awareness campaign about breast cancer seem to be good fits. It doesn't take a whole lot of explaining to see the correlation between the brand and the cause. When a brand tries to attach itself to the hot cause and there isn't a natural fit, the effects of the campaign can become more negative than positive. Consumers will see it as disingenuous, and the campaign can fall apart and actually promote negative chatter rather than build social capital for the brand.

Will your consumer relate to the cause? Successful campaigns happen when the consumer is motivated to act. This is why many professional teams have multiple cause marketing campaigns. The environment and going green or breast cancer awareness may not resonate with a 40-year-old football fanatic. Getting in shape and learning more about fitness might be just the message to motivate that fan. As with any marketing decision, it comes down to understanding the consumer base. This can be done only through constant interaction and research.

What do you have to offer? The days of simply stating, "A portion of the proceeds will be donated to the cause" are over. With the advent of social media, consumers want to interact with their favorite brands. They also want to be rewarded for that interaction. Discounts, recognition, access to special events, and information are all motivators beyond just supporting the cause.

FIGURE 9-3 Bill Duffy is an agent and founder of BDA Sports Management.
Courtesy of BDA Sports Management.

Can you make this easy for the consumer? Multiple research studies have shown that when brands are considered equal, a high percentage of consumers will choose a brand attached to a cause over brands not so associated. While consumers can feel good about themselves by interacting with a cause-related brand, most don't want to do any work beyond purchasing the product. If I want to support the Boys and Girls Clubs, I could research online, find their information, figure out how to donate, and send my donation. If interacting with my favorite team or sports product will handle that for me, I'm sure to take that into consideration on my next purchase.

Will you have internal company support? If management and your employees are not engaged, it is unreasonable to expect your consumer to get behind the campaign. It is important that everyone involved internally is on the same page, understands the campaign, and conveys the same message.

How to Avoid the Pitfalls of Cause Marketing

Sometimes teams, athletes, and companies look at cause marketing as a sure thing and jump right into an opportunity without doing their due diligence. Four categories should be initially evaluated to avoid entering a partnership without a good fit.

Partnerships: Choosing the right partner is critical. It is very similar to an athlete choosing a brand to endorse or two companies agreeing to create a cross promotion. There must be a demographic match for the partnership to make sense and succeed.

Fund-raising: Too often, nonprofits are focused more on raising funds than on creating sales impact. While the nonprofit can survive only by raising funds, it must realize that by creating an impactful program for its partner, long-term success can be achieved. An athlete, team, or company should try to determine whether the cause is simply after access to its fan base or is truly going to act as a partner and build a program.

Programs: Too often companies are focused on using the nonprofit's logo without backing it with any real program that makes sense to the consumer. Consumers will see right through a marketing program that is trying to take advantage of a cause rather than promote it. If there isn't a good fit between the brand and the cause, the consumer won't get behind it. To ensure success, companies must focus on creating an impactful program. If the program resonates with the company's consumer, the goal of the program will usually be met. Similarly, the nonprofit must determine whether the athlete, team, or company's interest is genuine.

Impact: Both the for-profit and the nonprofit should be focused on developing ideas with both social and professional impact. The goal should always be to create impactful opportunities for both stakeholders. For the nonprofit, this is usually raising funds. For the for-profit, it may be building brand awareness, raising social capital, or increasing sales. Both parties must understand each other's business and communicate freely to develop the program. Impactful partnerships lead to successful long-term programs.

Athlete Cause Marketing

Athletes have two choices when deciding on a cause marketing strategy. Many will build a relationship with a cause, whereas others start their own foundations. This section looks at an NBA player who is very active in cause marketing. This is the more typical and manageable way for an athlete to build a cause marketing campaign. There are very few success stories of athletes who have attempted to build their own foundations. It takes a great deal of time and a huge commitment of resources to run a foundation, and most athletes have neither the time nor skill to do it successfully.

Spotlight on Antawn Jamison

NBA veteran Antawn Jamison is a great example of an athlete who believes in cause marketing. He has partnered with the nonprofit organization KaBoom to build playgrounds in a number of communities. KaBoom's goal is to build play spaces to promote leadership and participation in the community. Jamison is an athlete who has gone above and beyond the average professional athlete to become involved in a cause. He has personally funded a number of builds and takes it upon himself to personally promote the cause. He has talked about the partnership with media and in the NBA Cares newsletter and on the website, sent out information to his fan base via e-mail and Twitter, and donated signed memorabilia to events. In addition, he filmed a public service announcement spot that was played at a game that highlighted the partnership, and he dedicated his regional Sportsman of the Year award to KaBoom, giving the cause further promotion. This illustrates how a professional athlete can get behind a cause.

Case Study

Reilly Tierney recently started as the Chief Marketing Officer of an NFL team. The team owners strongly believe that there should be a cause marketing component to their marketing mix. The owners don't have any personal connection to a cause and are looking to Reilly to choose a category and partnership that will resonate with the team's fan base.

1. What criteria should Reilly use to pick a cause?
2. What types of causes would resonate with a football fan base?
3. Would you recommend that Reilly choose a cause that connects mainly with men, or should he pick one that has a broader demographic?

Critical Thinking Activity

Develop a sports cause marketing campaign detailing the rationale behind the pairing, the benefit to each party, and the projected longevity of the movement. Also, include what goals will be used to measure success or failure. You can make the perspective specific to a team or include the company.

CHAPTER QUESTIONS

1. What is cause marketing? Give an example of a professional sports team that uses cause marketing as part of its marketing strategy.
2. How did American Express partner with the San Francisco Art Festival?
3. What are the three tactical approaches to cause marketing?
4. Why is proper alignment important for the partnership?
5. What steps should be taken when a partnership begins to fall apart?
6. What are the main charity partnerships with the NBA, NFL, MLB, and NHL?
7. Review your favorite team's website and describe the team's charity strategy.
8. Does your favorite athlete have a charity partnership established? If so, describe that partnership. If not, find an athlete who does.
9. Find a sports company with a charity partnership. Which of the three tactical approaches is the company using to fund the charity?
10. Describe a sports charity event that you have attended or been involved with.

Notes

1. Cause Marketing Forum, "The Growth of Cause Marketing," 2014, http://www.causemarketingforum.com/site/c.bkLUKcOTLkK4E/b.6412299/apps/s/content.asp?ct=8965443.
2. g-Think, *Yoplait's Got It Right*, 2004, http://www.g-think.com/keepout/articles/35/article_35.pdf.
3. Red, "Buy Red Save Lives," accessed October 1, 2014, http://www.joinred.com/red/#impact.
4. Jennifer Preston, "Pepsi Bets on Local Grants, Not the Super Bowl," *New York Times*, January 30, 2011. http://www.nytimes.com/2011/01/31/business/media/31pepsi.html?_r=3&ref=media.
5. New Balance, "Lace Up for the Cure," accessed October 1, 2014, http://www.newbalance.com/komen/.
6. Arthritis Foundation, "Ease of Use Sponsors," accessed October 1, 2014, http://www.arthritis.org/ease-of-use-new.php?p_id=31.
7. Rosemary Black, "Eat Fried Chicken for the Cure? KFC's Fundraiser with Susan G. Komen Group Raises Some Eyebrows," *Daily News*, April 22, 2010, http://www.nydailynews.com/life-style/health/eat-fried-chicken-cure-kfc-fundraiser-susan-g-komen-group-raises-eyebrows-article-1.166080.
8. Texas Instruments, "TI Volunteer Recognition Results in $15,000 in Donations to Nonprofit Agencies in Communities Around the World," April 16, 2012, http://newscenter.ti.com/index.php?s=32851&item=127847.
9. "Survey: More Nonprofits Earning Majority of Revenue from Sponsorship," IEG Sponsorship Report, November 12, 2011, http://www.sponsorship.com/iegsr/2011/11/21/Survey--More-Nonprofits-Earning-Majority-of-Revenu.aspx.
10. U.S. Green Building Council, "LEED," accessed October 1, 2014, www.usgbc.org/LEED/Cached - Similar.

Chapter 10

Social Media

CHAPTER OBJECTIVES

- Gain an overview of social media.
- Review the history of social media.
- Learn how the five Ps affect social media.
- Answer the question, Is social media really free?
- Learn the five Rs of social media.
- Identify key benefits of social media.
- Learn key components of a social media plan.
- Review a Twitter campaign.
- Review a Pinterest campaign.

CHAPTER OVERVIEW

This chapter addresses the fast-growing use of social media in sports marketing. It explores how teams, companies, and athletes are using social media to expand their fan and customer bases. It also discusses the pitfalls of real-time messaging.

Voices from the Field: Zack Sugarman

BIOGRAPHY

Born and raised in coastal San Diego, Zack started his career as a high school intern at Transworld Media. He realized immediately that Action Sports and youth lifestyle marketing were where he wanted to make his mark. After attending college at Amherst, he moved back to the West Coast to pursue his career at Wasserman Media Group.

Currently the Senior Director of Social Media and Digital, Zack has more than 8 years of new social media experience creating award-winning campaigns and initiatives for corporate brands and youth lifestyle brands. Zack has worked with athletes such as Travis Pastrana, Ryan Sheckler, Ken Block, Jimmie Johnson, Travis Rice, Paul Rodriguez, and Bob Burnquist; brands include Red Bull, Puma, Dodge, JCPenney, DC Shoes, and Boost Mobile. He has handled high-end properties, including DEW Tour, X Games, Global RallyCross Championships, and Mammoth Mountain.

Q&A

Q: What is your current position?

Senior Director of Social Media and Digital.

Q: What was your career path?

My background is sales, specifically, digital sales. I started with Wasserman in Los Angeles in 2005 as a Business Development Associate, brokering producer deals and selling sponsorship for Studio411, Wasserman's Action Sports Film Division. Studio411 evolved into Sportnet, a network of Action Sports–specific websites, including Motocross.com, Skateboard.com, Wetsand.com, and Newschoolers.com. I was in charge of West Coast sales for all Sportnet websites. In 2008, I left Wasserman for appssavvy, a direct sales force for leading application developers such as Zynga, RockYou, and LivingSocial. At appssavvy, I served as West Coast Director of Sales, responsible for all brands and agencies on the West Coast. I sold integrated advertising solutions, including custom in-app placements to brands like Sony, 20th Century Fox, and Universal Pictures. In late 2009, my wife and I moved to San Diego where I returned to Wasserman, this time working out of the Lifestyle and Action Sports office. I launched our Social Media and Digital department in this office and have successfully grown it into a seven-figure revenue stream.

Q: How did you become an expert in your field?

Tons of reading and tons of practice. I subscribe and read every industry article/blog I can get my hands on. I attend several webinars and workshops and am constantly striving to stay at the forefront of the space. Over the years, I have honed my posting strategy and skills through many types of execution. Activating at an event like X Games for 4 days straight, responsible for 33 athletes, will really improve your skills!

Q: Tell me about your department. Who works with you?

My department currently consists of two Senior Account Executives and one intern. We work closely with our Creative Services and Client Relations department to deliver turnkey programs. We also work with our Sales Division to include social media deliverables to help up-sell their current and new clients.

Q: How is it structured?

I run the division and have assigned specific accounts to each Account Executive. I report to our COO, Brad Lusky.

Q: In the past, athletes have handled their own Twitter and Facebook accounts. What guidelines do you recommend for those athletes who wish not to turn their accounts over to their representation?

The most important rule is simple—Don't Drink and Tweet/Post. Otherwise, here are some additional guidelines:

Tips for Effective Facebook Posting

1. Content is king.
2. Leverage your assets.
3. Fans only.
4. Keep it fresh.
5. We have a winner!
6. Comments spur conversation.
7. Let users guide content.
8. Set engagement goal.
9. Start a conversation.

Tips for Effective Tweeting

1. Follow wisely.
2. Take full advantage of Twitter Search.
3. Time your tweets.
4. Aim for Friday.
5. Think retweet.
6. Importance of #hashtags.

Q: What has been your greatest accomplishment at Wasserman Media Group?

Successfully launching and growing my division. Specific accomplishments include being part of Gymkhana, which was named a Top 10 Viral Brand of all time by AdAge.com in 2010. (Gymkhana 4 was also the most shared video in social media in 2011, according to Mashable.)

Q: What has been your favorite moment working in social media?

Running a Twitter Scavenger hunt from Travis Pastrana's account (@TravisPastrana) and watching throngs of people do the worm in front of the Chick Hearn statue at Staples Center.

Q: Your field is constantly evolving. What do you foresee in the future?

The emergence of mobile as the primary consumption and engagement platform; additionally, an increase in voice-to-text functions.

Q: What advice do you have for students interested in working in social media?

Start participating. Social media is still in its infancy stage. Jump in and participate: read, comment, test out ideas on your own social media platforms, and, most importantly, engage with other users!

Courtesy of Zack Sugarman.

Introduction

Individuals form social circles with others who are like-minded to satisfy the need to feel connected to others. Media is an outlet that enables people to feed these connections. Social media was born from the combination of the two. Once thought to be a fad, social media has become a mainstay in the way companies and organizations interact with their sponsors and clients. It allows for real-time responses as well as two-way communication. In the quickly changing world of sports, this outlet has already proved its worth.

The key to making social media a success is in knowing how to utilize each platform. Many companies have Facebook and Twitter accounts. It is important that each account is used to distribute different information. If each site pushes the same information, then individuals and sponsors will not be engaged. Apathetic readers don't increase the number of site visits, likes, and retweets, and site analytics are very important when pitching new sponsorship deals.

Social media outlets allow for consumers and fans to stay on top of their favorite products, teams, and players while enabling them to feel a personal connection. This perceived interaction between a fan and an athlete or team is what makes social media so powerful. In virtually all traditional types of advertising, the target

Team	Facebook Friends	Twitter Followers
Lakers	20M+	3M+
Heat	15M+	2M+
Celtics	15M+	1M+
Yankees	8M+	1M+
Cowboys	7M+	800,000+
Steelers	5M+	700,000+
Knicks	5M+	900,000+
Patriots	5M+	800,000+
Spurs	4M+	700,000+

FIGURE 10-1 Active U.S. professional teams in social media.

audience is passive at best. Often the audience is completely uninvolved. Social media content can be used as a subtle form of advertising. An interactive audience is an advertiser's dream. Twitter mentions have become this new age's autograph. Athletes use Twitter to connect with their followers on a level that has never been dreamed of before.

Sports teams have embraced the use of social media as a way to engage their fan base. As shown in **FIGURE 10-1**, teams are building followings of millions of fans on both Twitter and Facebook. European soccer teams have taken the lead in promoting their messages through Facebook, while American sports seem to be migrating more toward Twitter. It will be interesting to watch how this develops in the coming years. Will they migrate to Facebook? Will readers take to new offerings such as Instagram and Pinterest? What marketing opportunities will emerge as social media matures?

Whereas most athletes have a Facebook page, not all have adopted Twitter. As shown in **FIGURE 10-2**, in American sports, NBA players lead the way in the use of social media. Can you spot any trends in the popularity of players who are active in social media? Are there any trends based on age? It will be interesting to watch the development and use of social media by athletes.

History of Social Media

It is hard to believe social media has been around for the past 30 years. It seems as if only in the past decade has it truly emerged (Facebook was founded in 2004). Today's ease of use and accessibility were not the case when this form of networking began. This new forum challenges old media sources that have existed for decades or centuries.

The first noted form of social networking has been traced back to 1971 when the initial e-mail message was sent. Ironically, the transmitting and receiving computers

Athlete	Facebook Friends	Twitter Followers
LeBron James	20M+	1M+
Larry Fitzgerald	800,000+	7M+
Jeff Gordon	800,000+	500,000+
David Ortiz	1M+	700,000+
Kobe Bryant	19M+	5M+
Tiger Woods	3M+	3M+
Serena Williams	2M+	4M+
Magic Johnson	3M+	2M+
Jimmie Johnson	9M+	6M+
Robert Griffin III	9M+	1M+
Carmelo Anthony	4M+	5M+
Kevin Durant	9M+	7M+
Dwyane Wade	11M+	4M+

FIGURE 10-2 Active U.S. athletes in social media.
Source: Data from Top Athletes on Facebook http://fanpagelist.com/category/athletes/.

were sitting right next to one another. Six years later, in 1978, a type of online bulletin board system called Usenet was designed so that users could post and read messages. This site was also the birthplace of flame wars and trolling.

A lull occurred until 1994 when Beverly Hills Internet was launched. The concept behind this site was for users to create their own websites. There were six different categories or "neighborhoods" in which these sites could be listed: Coliseum, Hollywood, Rodeo Drive, Sunset Strip, Wall Street, and West Hollywood. As Internet usage grew, so did these communities. In 1995, Tokyo, Silicon Valley, Paris, and Capital Hill were added. This site was eventually acquired by Yahoo, and the name was then changed to GeoCities.

The .com bust of 2000 saw the emergence of **Friendster**. This online connection allowed for real-world friends to be united on the Internet. In its first 3 months, Friendster boasted 3 million users. At the time, that equated to 1 in every 126 Internet users.[1] The next big social media site to hit the scene—also considered the first clone of Friendster—was **MySpace**. The first version was coded in a mere 10 days. This site became well liked by users because they were able to personalize the site's background as well as music on their page. Eventually, MySpace became better known as a place for musicians and artists to promote their material and less known for friend-to-friend interaction. Following the launch of MySpace, a number of other social networking sites were launched, including Tribe.net, LinkedIn, Classmates.com, Jaiku, and Netlog.

Facebook was launched in 2004 as a means for connecting U.S. college students. The effort began at Harvard University before spreading to colleges and universities across the country. More than half of the 19,500 students at Harvard University signed up for the site in the first month. Two years later, Facebook was opened to anyone over the age of 13 years who had a valid e-mail address. After overtaking MySpace as the leading networking site in 2008, Facebook has not shown signs of slowing. In May 2011, the site reported a monthly user number of 138.9 million.[2] The April 2012 purchase of Instagram helped boost those numbers.

Twitter was created and launched in 2006. The site allows for mircoblogging and enables users to send and read texts that contain 140 or fewer characters. These texts are also known as tweets. This service has been described as the "SMS of the Internet."[3] This site most notably took off during the South by Southwest Conference in 2007. Twitter's usage increased from 20,000 a day to 60,000 a day.[4] In 2012, Twitter claimed more than 140 million active users, and the site generated 360 million tweets per day.[5]

How the Five Ps Affect Social Media

PRODUCT   Social media as a product can be defined as another means of spreading a company's marketing message. This addition to the traditional marketing mix can help a company become laser focused in delivering its message. Whereas athletes used to rely on PR and fan clubs to interact with their fan base, they can now interact on an almost one-to-one basis. Athletes using social media can give their fans a behind-the-scenes look at their lives off the field or court.

PRICE   Defining price in the world of social media is incredibly difficult. There is a pervasive thought that social media is free, which is simply not true. Although there may not be a direct cost to send a message through social media, there are creative, human resources, and maintenance costs associated with each message and campaign. To run a successful business campaign requires investment in analytics tools to track interaction, engagement, and which tactics are working best.

PLACE   How do you describe the World Wide Web? The Web is fluid and always changing. New vehicles and mediums are available almost daily to spread a message. With so many ways to distribute a message using social media, companies, teams, and athletes must constantly audit their delivery methods. If the methods aren't reviewed and updated, it is easy to fall behind in the new delivery methods offered. Many companies are attempting to identify key promoters and influencers using programs such as Klout to make sure the message is delivered in the right place to the right target market.

Compared with traditional newspaper and television, social media have radically altered the consumer experience of place. For receiving content, *place* used to mean watching the television, listening to a car radio, or reading the newspaper at home. Now *place* means, well, *any*place. Sports fans can read current content and retweet it from an airliner at 37,000 feet. An athlete's self-absorbed comments are available while fans stand in line at Starbuck's. Teams, players, and advertisers can *always* find the sports fan now. To paraphrase boxing great Joe Louis, "The consumer can run, but he can't hide."

PROMOTION   Social media has completely changed the way people and companies define promotion. A few years ago, only the most tech-savvy companies were using social media as a part of their marketing mix. Now it's difficult to find a company that doesn't use social media to promote its product. Many are using social media exclusively to spread their message. Teams especially have taken to social media as a way to interact with their fan base and promote the team's message. In the past, promotions were almost exclusively defined as game day giveaways. Social media has unlocked many opportunities for teams to create fun ways to engage the fan.

PROGRESS   The fifth P was created because of social media. Social media has been a game changer for the sports industry. The days of a controlled message being distributed by the local reporter who covers the team are over. Although local reporters still exist, their role is less important because of the flow of information in the many social media outlets. The best reporters have now themselves embraced social media and use it to enhance their own image and distribute their message where the fans live.

Sounds revolutionary, but don't forget the demographics. The Millennial Generation is by far the most attuned to social media. There are a couple of problems with that. Being young, Millennials have far less disposable income than earlier generations do. And the newest generation is less attracted to traditional team sports. Older fans are much wealthier and are more likely to follow traditional sports through traditional media. Advertising spend is suddenly much more complex. How do we apportion a limited ad budget between old and new media?

Is Social Media Free?

Let's start with a one-word answer to the question of whether social media is free: No! Although the placement of the message online may be free compared to placing a traditional advertisement, the message development costs are equally expensive or even greater. Many companies, teams, and athletes plan to promote their message through social media because it is considered free. The reality is that the development and delivery of the message still take human resources and a great deal of time, which have costs. In traditional advertising, a company may create an ad and place it in a magazine for a fee. That ad then is distributed through the chosen vehicle. The company's work is pretty much done when the ad is placed. Very little direct interaction with the consumer of that ad takes place. In social media, that same message is placed for free but must constantly be reviewed, refined, responded to, reacted to, and refreshed. A large portion of the work is just beginning with the placement of the ad.

Using social media takes work. I once listened to a consultant tell a client that she should be tweeting at least five times per hour. The client responded by asking when she was supposed to be doing her actual work. Although tweeting is free, the development and delivery of the message take time and resources, which must be adequately defined and allotted for a program to be successful.

I recently reviewed a company's social media plan. The company seemed to have all of the parts covered. It had tweets scheduled, a prominent athlete to participate and promote the brand, a new logo, a YouTube channel, a Facebook page, and a number of promotions scheduled across its social media channels. The company was discouraged when it didn't see much of an increase in likes, followers, and, subsequently, sales from these efforts. After I took a deeper look into the situation, a few critical flaws became apparent. First, the company viewed its social media, website, and offline marketing as three different channels. Although this might be true, they must be coordinated with each other. Second, the company's offline messaging did not match its online efforts: Whereas the company had changed its logo and marketing in the social channels to make them edgier, it was still using the old logo and message offline. Third, the website had not been updated. As with many product sites, it looked more like a catalog than an interactive site, and the messaging was old and stale. The social media icons for Facebook, YouTube, and Twitter were not linked to the new pages. Last, the content and promotions that the company scheduled as part of its new *free* social media campaign never materialized because the company had not allocated the resources to produce and place the material.

This is a classic example of a company viewing social media as a free outlet for the promotion of its product. When this is the driving force for the start of a campaign, the results are often less than stellar. It is critical to allocate the appropriate resources, including both time and money, to execute the plan effectively. In addition, the social media efforts must coordinate with all other pieces of the marketing mix.

One point to note in this case is that the company had paid an athlete and even had given him equity in the business to help launch the social media strategy. By not having a coordinated strategy for the launch, the company completely wasted its money on the athlete's endorsement contract. I have seen many cases in which companies sign endorsement contracts and then do not utilize the assets in that contract. An activation plan is essential to success.

How Should a Brand Use Social Media?

The question is how should a company, team, or athlete manage social media to build brand equity? We know that content is king, but managing that content is just as important. Many companies are intimidated by all of the new technology that is available. A number of third-party apps can help companies manage their social media programs. One of the leading apps for Facebook is Wildfire, which helps manage contests and promotions. Booshaka enables companies to track their most active fans; some use this app to identify and reward their most engaged customers. Woobox helps brands create contests, promotions, and coupons. For companies using

Twitter, third-party apps include Tweetdeck, Hootsuite, and Splitweet, which all help manage multiple accounts. Tweet Reach allows companies to determine how much influence their campaigns are wielding. Twylah helps companies build customizable pages for their tweet offerings. For those using Instagram, Statigram helps them manage their accounts. Finally, Pinterest management apps include Pinerly and Pinreach.

New apps are developed daily. Being an expert in social media is almost impossible. The key is to stay up-to-date and to apply the new technology to your campaigns. Even though technology changes, good and disciplined business strategies still apply. Someone needs to be in charge of that advertising content. Having multiple employees with access to social media can be difficult to manage. Many companies allow multiple contributors but appoint one person responsible for filtering and actually placing the social media message. This helps keep the messaging consistent and on point. Even many athletes have someone managing their accounts. This is particularly true with an athlete's Facebook page. Often that responsibility falls to someone in the athlete's agent's office. Unfortunately, Twitter is usually still controlled by the athletes themselves. Amar'e Stoudemire of the New York Knicks famously found trouble with the NBA league office for an offensive tweet. The league took exception to his scurrilous interaction with a fan and fined Stoudemire $50,000.

Five Rs of Social Media

Successful social media campaigns do not happen by accident. Using social media may appear to be fun and simple, but a defined strategy is behind most successful campaigns. Regardless of the sport, company, or athlete, a social media campaign must be a coordinated and strategic part of the marketing mix. Each component of the mix should support the others and present a consistent message. I have developed the five Rs to help brands stay on track and build successful social media campaigns. Once a campaign is launched, these steps can be used as a guide to success.

REVIEW   Every piece of information placed through social media must be continually reviewed and monitored. Social media is being used to give fans and consumers a vehicle to react to the message. That reaction might be positive, negative, or indifferent, but, whichever, it must be reviewed to help steer the message successfully in the future.

REACT   Once the fans or consumers react, the team, company, or athlete must in turn react. The responses to the message must be analyzed and a strategy formed on how to move forward. If a team launches a new ticket package and the initial response to the pricing is predominantly negative, the team must analyze that response and decide what to do. Should it lower the price and relaunch? Should it ride it out? Should it scrap the whole plan? These decisions must be made quickly with the information that is gathered.

RESPOND   Social media is a fluid marketing medium. Interaction is expected and needed to increase the chance of success. Once the reception of the initial message has been analyzed, it is time for the athlete, company, or team to respond. This back-and-forth engagement is what drives social media and keeps fans coming back.

REFINE   Every interaction in social media should be viewed as a chance to refine the message based on all of the feedback gathered. No other marketing medium gives such an interactive opportunity to a brand. In the case of the team ticket package, small tweaks to the offering could be the difference between success and failure.

REFRESH   Once an interaction has run its course, it is time to refresh the message and reinvigorate the process with the fan or consumer. Keeping the message fresh is one way to ensure that the consumer will keep returning and engaging with the brand.

Key Benefits to Social Media

Many companies still struggle to determine the success and benefits of using social media. The list that follows will give a company or athlete the perspective needed to determine return on investment.

Reach: Reach is a key component of advertising. It is also a key benefit of social media. Companies, teams, and athletes can infiltrate social circles and promote their brands. Individuals can act as brand ambassadors through word of mouth and promotion through their social media accounts. Because news can spread much like wildfire on these sites, companies must have teams dedicated to social media in order to tame the irate and reward the pleased.

Quickness: The emergence of these sites has created an expectation that consumers and fans want news as it happens. For example, cell phone companies base their data packages around the amount of data and speed of transmission their consumers can process. As great as it is to know the latest breaking news, it also has a detrimental side: In an age when news can be broadcast at the click of button, time can be the enemy. Athletes have learned this the hard way, making impulsive comments about the commissioner, referees, umpires, or coaches and then having to deal with the consequences. Some players thrive on getting a quick laugh with their witticisms, but it is always smart to think twice before sending thoughts and comments out to the world.

Numbers game: Organizations and companies thrive by engaging well-connected individuals. A connected individual has many social circles and has an audience that spans more groups than a single company can reach alone. A company, team, or athlete can reach a larger audience by courting these strategic nodes in social networks.

Comments: When fans direct comments to teams, leagues, or companies, there is a science behind the organizations' responses. A response to negative comments is warranted regardless of the number of friends, followers, and repins an individual has. A response to all negative comments is necessary because customers notice when companies do not respond to someone regardless of their Klout score or influence.

Marketing and contests: Contests are becoming more prevalent on social media sites. No longer must companies pay for setup costs and printing fees. Much like the theory behind the numbers game, individuals can encourage their friends to take part in a contest simply by forwarding posts or retweeting. The distribution radius goes far beyond the original targeted audience.

Viral: Going viral is the dream of many companies and athletes. YouTube and other sharing programs have enabled viral spread. Marketing teams have been created to convert commercials and advertisements into shorter segments in hopes the bits will go viral. Athletes are able to have highlights and news conference clips span farther than the typical outlets of ESPN and local regional sports networks. Twitter hashtags also enable thoughts to go viral or to trend. Hashtags are the use of the pound sign (#), called a hash mark, to mark keywords or topics in a tweet. Hashtags were created organically by Twitter users as a way to categorize messages.[6] These tags help people search for and find particular information in tweets, which can help them go viral—if my company tweets about our sponsorship of a bike ride (the Trek Century) only my followers will see it. If we tag Trek, now we open the tweet to anyone seeking info on Trek. The correct use of hashtags is critical to any team, athlete, or company using Twitter. It is recommended that in a tweet users tag no more than two words that are relevant to the topic.

Key Components of a Social Media Plan

There are six key parts to a social media plan. Each of the following steps is vital to rolling out a new social media campaign and succeeding.

AUDIT

Before opening an account on every social media site possible, take a moment to inventory which sites the company is already using and to what capacity. How many friends and followers does the company or athlete have? How are the sites being used? How are sites sharing information? Athletes and companies have a tendency to jump on a new trend, but this can lead to a disjointed flow of information.

COMPETITIVE REVIEW

Go to Facebook, Twitter, Pinterest, and YouTube. Search the competition and see what they have already set in motion in their social media campaigns. Are their templates visually appealing? How many followers do they boast? Are they running contests and promotions? When you check out their sites, think about what is most eye-catching and what would draw in a potential fan or client.

GOALS AND OBJECTIVES

The information delivered on each social media site should be distinct from information delivered on other sites. If the information is the same across sites, companies and athletes are limiting themselves in engaging fans and clients. Know how each site is going to be used and explain the vision for each site. At this stage, it is also important to decide how frequently information should be delivered. It is unfortunate to lose people as a result of overcommunicating or, worse, having nothing to say. As with any part of the marketing mix, the key is good, fresh content. Companies with good marketing plans don't put advertising in press releases or player stats in an advertisement. With social media, each segment should have a purpose and a distinct message and voice.

CONTENT, CONTENT, CONTENT

Breaking news is great to report because it allows clients and fans to feel empowered and "in-the-know" before their friends and coworkers. Sadly, breaking news cannot be the only content delivered on a social media site. Developing and implementing content calendars are extremely helpful in planning what content will be posted when. Of course, breaking news can trump planned stories, but adhering to a content calendar ensures that followers are given their daily or weekly dose of information.

CROSS-PROMOTION

Once a site is launched or rebranded, it is important to have wholesalers, sponsors, conferences, leagues, and news outlets cross-promote it. This form of boosting site views allows both parties to have a win-win experience. When each party is successful, it then reflects on each other's bottom line. It is typical to see the NHL retweet players' tweets along with team tweets. Retweeting, for example, helps push the message to other audiences who may not be following a particular individual or team. Another example of cross-promoting is when college athletic directors retweet comments made about their athletic team or department.

ANALYTICS

Setting a plan in motion is great, but seeing and understanding the results are even better! Most sites are equipped with simple analytic programs; however, companies may find it worthwhile to investigate more sophisticated programs that generate detailed analytics such as number of retweets per hour, mentions per day, unique site visitors, click-through rates from cross-promotions, where users come from, and popular device types. Being able to evaluate the site's analytics is important for knowing when to launch campaigns, how to introduce a site, and how to bring in new clients and sponsors. It also is critical to determining ROI. Ultimately, a company is using social media to make money. For companies selling their products online, the nice thing about using analytics is that ROI can be tracked. Analytics allows a company to determine where each of its visitors came from and if they converted to a sale. Let's say a company has a promotion on Facebook. They can determine how much traffic that campaign drove to its site and how much of that traffic converted to a sale. These conversion numbers allow a company to determine if the campaign was a success.

In 2010, the San Francisco Giants became one of the first professional teams to use social listening analytic tools to help build their social media strategy. Before, during, and after their media campaign, they used tools to monitor Facebook and Twitter to determine what kind of buzz their messages were getting. What was particularly impressive and disciplined about this approach is that they took the time to monitor what their fan base was saying before they designed the campaign.[7] Most companies don't take the time to listen first to try to determine needs and establish a benchmark. Analytical programs such as Radion6 have the ability to scan social media and categorize the online engagement as negative, positive, or indifferent. These programs give companies an almost real-time look at whether their offerings are effective. Teams like the Giants can use this feedback to tweak their marketing message at a moment's notice.

Example of a Twitter Campaign

Stephen Curry, a guard for the Golden State Warriors, has taken Twitter by storm. He created and implemented three contests during the 2011–2012 NBA season with the help of Spiracle Media.

Curry kicked off his Twitter campaign by asking his followers to record themselves singing Christmas carols. The winner of this contest won a Skype session with the star. Curry was so moved by a message sent in from one fan about her New Year's resolution that he met with her before a home game.

Sharing his passion with his fans, Curry sent out a call to his fans to play the ultimate game of H-O-R-S-E. He asked his fans to send videos of their best moves so they could play against one another. Curry then took the top 10 moves and posted them on Facebook for his fans to judge. The prize in this contest was Curry recording the outgoing message on the winner's voicemail.

Example of a Pinterest Campaign

Brooks Running Company is well known within the running community. It is the premier sponsor of Competitor Group's Rock 'n' Roll North American Marathon Tour, and its own North America tour stops at prestigious specialty running stores.

In an effort to expand its reach, Brooks launched a Pinterest contest for followers. In order to participate, individuals had to friend Brooks on Facebook. Next, they were instructed to create a "Run Happy" **board** on Pinterest ("Run Happy" is the company motto). These boards were to reflect what running meant to the board creator as well as what motivated and inspired that person. Once the board was completed, followers had to submit the board via Facebook. The best board, chosen by the company, won a $500 gift card for Brooks apparel and shoes.

This contest is quite simplistic yet helps boost Brooks's Facebook fans and spread the word of Brooks through Pinterest. It is important to have a good following on these sites as it is a great statistic to provide when negotiating sponsorship agreements.

Example of a Social Media Campaign

A great example of the use of social media in sports happened when the sports optics company SportRx was awarded the 10th best place to work in America by *Outside* magazine in 2014. The company wanted to take advantage of the award and promote their brand through multiple social networks. They decided to create a campaign using Facebook, Twitter, Instagram, and e-mail marketing. While there was some overlap in messaging, each channel had a unique feel for its followers. On Twitter, the company retweeted the *Outside* magazine award and hashtagged bestplacestowork, which is a very popular search for people looking for great companies to work for. On Facebook, the company created a celebration video announcing the award. Employees were seen popping champagne and celebrating in front of company headquarters. On Instagram, there were a number of pictures of the company's unique headquarters. Finally, SportRx sent out an e-mail to their customer list offering a promotion in honor of the award. The announcements were retweeted, shared, and forwarded, creating a reach far beyond the company's established network.

Case Study

Tom Lepp represents a number of NBA players. He woke up this morning to find that last night one of his clients tweeted a derogatory comment after he'd been drinking at a local club. The player called Tom to say that he was going to claim that his Twitter account had been hacked. ESPN, Fox Sports, and Sports Illustrated have all left messages on Tom's voicemail and want to know how the player will respond to the public's reaction. Tom has to immediately create a social media strategy to address the comment and guide his player through this crisis.

1. Should Tom follow the player's lead and let him claim that his Twitter account was hacked? What are the implications if someone saw him at the club posting the comment?
2. How should Tom handle the media and the social media response?
3. Should Tom contact the player's team?

Critical Thinking Activity

As helpful as social media can be, it can also become a distraction. The tale of two evils can best be seen through the social media frenzy that a number of players and owners created on Twitter. The NFL has mandated rules about tweeting and posting on game day.

Develop a social media plan for the NFL, MLB, NBA, or the NHL. Make sure to explain how players with existing social media accounts will be affected and included in the new plan. Give an example of a current owner or player getting into trouble while using social media.

CHAPTER QUESTIONS

1. I'm sure things have changed since this book was written. What are the latest trends in social media?
2. What is considered the earliest form of social media?
3. How is your favorite athlete using social media?
4. Does your favorite sports company use different messaging for each type of social media category?
5. How did Twitter gain traction? Is your favorite athlete active on Twitter?
6. How is Brooks using Pinterest? What other sports brands are succeeding on Pinterest?
7. Why would a company want to cross-promote its social media sites?
8. How are social circles infiltrated by these sites?
9. How is your favorite team using social media? Describe its social media plan.
10. In your opinion, what company in the sports industry has the most unique social media strategy? Describe that strategy.
11. Has social media ever influenced your choice of a purchase?

Notes

1. "The History and Evolution of Social Media," WDD, October 7, 2009, http://www.webdesignerdepot.com/2009/10/the-history-and-evolution-of-social-media/.
2. Quantcast audience profile for Facebook.com, Quantcast.com, April 29, 2011, http://www.quantcast.com/facebook.com.
3. Leslie D'Monte, "Swine Flu's Tweet Tweet Causes Online Flutter," *Business Standard*, April 29, 2009, http://www.business-standard.com/india/news/swine-flu%5Cs-tweet-tweet-causes-online-flutter/356604/.
4. Nick Douglas, "Twitter Blows Up at SXSW Conference," *Gawker*, March 12, 2007, http://gawker.com/tech/next-big-thing/twitter-blows-up-at-sxsw-conference-243634.php.

5. Twitter Team, "Twitter Turns Six," Twitter blog, March 21, 2012,
    http://blog.twitter.com/2012/03/twitter-turns-six.html.
6. "Using Hashtags on Twitter," Twitter Help Center, accessed October 3, 2014,
    http://support.twitter.com/articles/49309-what-are-hashtags-symbols#.
7. Adam Helweh, "How the Champion San Francisco Giants Scored
    with Social Media," Social Media Explorer, December 16, 2010,
    http://www.socialmediaexplorer.com/social-media-marketing/
    how-the-champion-san-francisco-giants-scored-with-social-media/.

CURSA DE
LA MERCÈ 2012

adidas

Ajuntament de Barcel

Chapter 11

Events and Sponsorship

CHAPTER OBJECTIVES

- Learn about events and sponsorship.
- Learn the history of events and sponsorship.
- Learn how the five Ps affect events and sponsorship.
- Identify key benefits of events and sponsorship.
- Learn key components of events and sponsorship.
- Review an event with sponsorship.

CHAPTER OVERVIEW

This chapter explores the use of events and sponsorship as a way to promote a company's brand message. It reviews how some of the biggest brands in sports marketing use events and sponsorship to gain an advantage over the competition. It also presents the details of a sponsorship proposal.

Voices from the Field: Sean Clottu

BIOGRAPHY

Sean Clottu joined Competitor Group (CGI) as Vice President of Client Development and Activation in February 2009. As VP, Clottu is responsible for directing a team that provides strategic support for the sales staff in developing and outlining creative sales proposals, research, custom sponsorship, and activation programs. He is a resource for national event sponsors and all sales reps to assist and facilitate revenue growth. His primary responsibilities include overseeing all national activation programs for the Rock 'n' Roll Marathon Series, the world's largest series of running events.

Prior to CGI, Clottu served as Sales Development Director of Sportnet, a division of Wasserman Media Group. There, he developed successful programs with major U.S. advertisers, including Toyota, Oakley, Adidas, Nike, Kawasaki, ESPN, and Pacific Sunwear.

Clottu's first position was at Transworld Media, a former division of Time Warner and Time4Media. At Transworld, he built and directed a sales development team through action sport–related advertiser programs and partnerships.

An avid runner and active lifestyle participant, Sean has completed multiple half-marathons across the United States.

Q&A

Q: What is your current position?

VP of Client Development and Activation for the Competitor Group headquartered in San Diego, California.

Q: What was your career path?

My background is in design and marketing. Through working as a Creative Director for a media and interactive ad agency, I decided I was more interested in the business aspects of being on the media and events side and went to work for a media publisher and event entertainment company.

Q: How did you become an expert in your field?

Persistence. Watching and learning from the industry leaders, implementing best practices, and asking a lot of questions along the way. This shows not only that you're curious about the process or project at hand but also that you want to confirm details so the execution is flawless.

Q: Tell me about your department. Who works with you?

I work under the Marketing department, but we work very closely with the national sales team on the revenue-generation side of the business versus the consumer-facing side. I oversee all media and event assets with the most prominent one being the Rock 'n' Roll Marathon Series, the world's largest running platform.

Q: How is it structured?

Our development team assists with the research, creative ideation, and Request for Proposal (RFP) process on the front end, and then once a sponsorship is sold it comes back to us under the activation team for account management and benefit fulfillment.

Q: In the past few years, CGI has seen huge growth in their Rock 'n' Roll Marathon Series in terms of new markets. How do you pitch to existing clients that they should also expand with CGI?

Historically, the running market is, and has been, very fragmented with single-city events, so we view this growth as a unique selling proposition and differentiator. Most of the partners and clients that we're targeting are looking for national scale through one event series or platform reaching the same targeted consumer and demographic. The Rock 'n' Roll Marathon series delivers a year-round opportunity to give them a presence in more than 24 major metros and cities in North America.

Q: What has been your greatest accomplishment at CGI?

Building a client development and activation team that's one of the best in the business. I'm truly surrounded by some of the top talent and creative thinkers, which makes my job exciting and rewarding every day.

Q: What has been your favorite moment working with the Rock 'n' Roll Marathon Series?

Being a part of the Zappos.com Rock 'n' Roll Las Vegas event and watching that event grow into the largest half-marathon in the United States and the third largest in the world. It's also the largest nighttime running event in the world and the only one on the Las Vegas Strip.

Q: What is the most exciting thing about the field of client activation and sales?

I've got my eye on social media. It's going to be exciting to see how this changes the landscape of client activation over the next few years, as sponsors get smarter at leveraging it and using it to engage their consumers and develop a more personal relationship with them. I also think it's going to continue to develop and become a larger asset for event owners and operators to monetize as it attracts new categories and brands.

Q: What advice do you have for students interested in sponsorships?

Learn as much as you can about the industry and trends by reading sponsorship trade publications, pursuing internships, and volunteering at relevant events to become more familiar with how brands are activating.

Courtesy of Sean Clottu.

Introduction

The terms *events* and *sponsorship* encompass many different things. They are usually linked together because many sporting events have some kind of sponsorship. A sponsorship is when a company pays for the right to be associated with an event, which is called a property. The financial range of sponsorships is huge. It could be the local pizza restaurant sponsoring the neighborhood 5K for a few free pizzas and $200 or a major brand being the official sponsor of a multicity marathon series for millions of dollars.

The term *event* has many definitions and meanings in sports. Everything from the Super Bowl to the PGA-sanctioned golf tournament to the Final Four is categorized as an event. While the game itself is an event, most major games host fan fests, concerts, appearances, and parties leading up to the start of the game. Although difficult to define, most events share two things. First, they are created to build awareness for a brand. It could be argued that even the Super Bowl was created to help build the NFL brand. Second, they are usually for profit.

There are many companies in the event and sponsorship business. Some sports event companies handle only the execution of the event itself, while others handle only the sponsorship portion of the event. A few create, execute, and sell the entire event package.

Spending on events continues to grow. According to Reuters, spending on sports, causes, festivals, the arts, entertainment tours, and associations was about $48.7 billion in 2011. More is spent on sports sponsorship than any other category. Spending on sports is expected to rise 6.1% while spending with the big four leagues is expected to rise 7.6%.[1] Companies love to attach their brands to the loyal and passionate sports fan.

Even in difficult economic conditions, sports sponsorship growth continues to outpace other popular sectors such as concert tours, theme parks, and branded entertainment partnerships. In conservative spending times, companies tend to look for stable opportunities that can bundle media exposure and offer activation platforms, including retail, digital, and on-site marketing. Sports sponsorship offers many established options. Companies outside of North America spent $30.8 billion in sponsorships in 2011. London, with the Olympics, and Brazil, with the World Cup and Olympics, have been particularly active. China and India also have emerging sponsorship markets. The growth during difficult economic times shows that sports sponsorship is perceived as a vital part of the marketing mix.[2]

History of Events and Sponsorship

Just as radio and TV helped foster the exploding popularity of sports, sponsorship owes much of its start to the growth of media. Early shows were often sponsored or "brought to you by" a major brand that wanted to link itself to the viewer or listener of a program. Sponsorship grew right alongside the popularity of sports. By the 1970s, sports sponsorship was becoming commonplace. In the 1980s, even historic college bowl games started to give up their names to sponsors. In 2012, there were 35 bowl games, each sponsored by a major brand. Everything from potatoes to insurance companies to the military acted as title sponsors to the games. In addition, almost every stadium is now named after a corporation. Soldier Field in Chicago is one of the few holdouts. Opened in 1924, Soldier Field is named as a memorial to our troops killed in war. The name and the stadium are cherished by Chicagoans. The name will not be easily changed for corporate money. Still, each entrance to the stadium is now sponsored by a corporation. There is simply too much money at stake for teams and events to pass up sponsorship dollars, no matter how strong their traditions are.

Sponsorship strategies really changed in the early 1980s. Peter Ueberroth once recounted how the 1984 Los Angeles Olympic Games were turned into a financial success. He was the President and General Manager of the Los Angeles Olympic Committee. Prior to 1984, it was common for the host city to lose a significant amount of money when hosting the Games. It was also common to have hundreds of sponsors.

Ueberroth was under great stress from the city of Los Angeles because the majority of the population and politicians did not want the Games and the potential tax bill that might follow to fund it. He decided on a very different sponsorship strategy. Instead of having hundreds of sponsors, he capped it at 50. By doing this, he was able to charge a premium for each sponsorship. In return, he was able to offer each sponsor personal service to help it achieve its goals and objectives.

The strategy worked perfectly. A small number of sponsors created a huge revenue source but also received great value in return. The Games produced a $215 million profit and made Ueberroth the toast of the town. Because of the unprecedented success, he was named Time Magazine Man of the Year. While having a small number of key sponsors doesn't work for every program, this Olympics showed that it is a viable strategy.

How the Five Ps Affect Events and Sponsorship

PRODUCT   Although types of events differ, they can usually be defined as a happening in sports created to raise awareness for a brand. The product could be a game (World Cup Final), festival (Major League Baseball Fan Fest), TV show (College Football Skills Competition), or even a race (Ironman Triathlon). The product may be as simple as an award. For example, each year the NBA's outstanding player wins the Kia MVP trophy.

PRICE   Price comes into play when an event creates sponsorship opportunities for companies. Companies must decide how much sponsoring the event is worth and how much additional money must be spent to help promote the sponsorship. Owners of the event must put a value on their offering and create a sponsorship package.

PROMOTION   Games, races, pregame ceremonies, interviews, and halftime shows are held to promote brands and causes. Brands choose events to sponsor based on the demographic of fans watching and attending the event. You can learn a lot about fan demographics by paying attention to the sponsor list. For example, PGA events are often supported by Buick. Who drives Buicks? You would probably say, older, relatively affluent people. And that has been the main golf-viewing demographic for years.

PLACE   Where an event is held is critical to its success. Even the attendance of hugely popular events such as the Olympics can be affected by the location of the games. At the level of national advertising, location may not be so important. No matter where the Super Bowl is played, it is broadcast across the country and around the world. Super Bowl advertisers such as Budweiser sell everywhere. They don't care much where the game is held. But regional events, such as a minor PGA tournament, need to attract regional sponsors. Yes, Budweiser might be there. But the event organizers still need to attract the local auto dealers and restaurant chains to maximize their ad revenue.

PROGRESS   Because of the Internet and social media, the opportunities to promote an event have increased greatly. Smaller events used to depend on local flyers and perhaps a mention on the radio to attract participants. Now even the most grassroots event can promote on a worldwide basis using Facebook, Twitter, and many other social media options.

Key Benefits of Events and Sponsorship

When executed correctly, a company can reap great benefits from a sponsorship. A strategically placed sponsorship can help build a brand faster than most other marketing opportunities.

Brand association: Much like the personality of an athlete endorser sends a message about the brand, the persona of an event can have the same effect. For example, the PGA emphasizes continuity and tradition in its tournaments. The venues are beautiful and rarely change. Star golfers may contend for a decade or longer. This image of safe tradition works well for institutions such as insurance companies and banks.

Brand awareness: A great event with good sponsors can help a company get its message to a very targeted and captive audience. The makeup and size of the audience are quite predictable from season to season. This increases efficiency of the ad dollar spend.

Sponsorship of an event provides instant visibility to a brand. Smaller events expose a brand to attendees, whereas larger events may be broadcast online or on television. The larger the audience, the more expensive the sponsorship will be.

Image building: When a brand decides to sponsor an event, it attaches itself to that event's image. The event says a great deal about the sponsor. A company sponsoring the Olympics puts itself in prestigious company. Everything about an Olympics sponsorship projects a high-end image. A company sponsoring the Masters Golf Tournament is most likely also trying to project a very high-end image. A sponsor of the X Games is probably trying to project a grittier, more hip image, and the demographic would be much younger with different spending levels and habits.

Increase sales: Although brand awareness and image building are important, the most successful sponsorships drive sales. This could be directly at the event through distribution rights, through sales promotions, or through the advertising and exposure gained by being associated with the event.

Hospitality: Hospitality takes many forms. As part of a golf tournament sponsorship, it might be a reserved tent next to one of the greens. As part of an Olympic sponsorship, it might be the rental of an entire hotel to act as headquarters for the client. For the NFL, NBA, NHL, and MLB, it might be a suite where clients can watch a game in a more private setting. The goal of any hospitality is to have the opportunity to interact with a client in a more informal setting than in the office or on a conference call. It's a way to treat a client in a special way and build a great relationship.

Chicago-based event company Intersport has one of the most interesting examples of hospitality in the business. It has created the Double Eagle Club. This high-end club is used only during the Masters Golf Tournament in Augusta, Georgia. Companies pay for the right to attend the Double Eagle Club during the week of the tournament. The club gives companies a base from which to do business that is just outside the main entrance to the golf course. Companies can host clients; use computers, phones, and conference rooms; eat; and even take golf lessons. It's the perfect way to be away from the office but still have the ability to conduct business if necessary. In addition, it's also a great way to impress a client.

Key Components of an Event

Sporting events are wildly different in size, media appeal, and audience makeup. Think of the difference between a local bowling tournament and a major NASCAR race! Some common approaches apply no matter what the sport is.

Concept: Products start with idea generation. Creating an event is no different. Some events are created to help a specific sponsor create brand recognition. Some are created based on an interesting concept in the hopes that it can attract sponsors to spend their events budget on the product.

Later in this chapter, I discuss an actual event being created by Intersport. This company produces events in both fashions previously mentioned. An example of an event it creates specifically for a sponsor is the College Basketball 3-Point Shootout. This event was originally created specifically for Coca-Cola to help Coca-Cola reach the college basketball fan. The College Basketball 3-Point Shootout was formed more than 20 years ago as a marketing vehicle to achieve Coca-Cola's goals and objectives. The event has grown into a staple of Final Four weekend. Intersport is creating the second event from scratch to capitalize on a trend in sports that may attract a sponsor. The College Hockey event is currently being designed to capitalize on the success of the NHL's Winter Classic. The Classic is a number of games each NHL season that are played outdoors. The success of the series has been remarkable. Fan attendance and overall viewership have been great. Intersport decided to create a collegiate version of the game. The event and its offerings will be constructed and then shopped to potential sponsors that might benefit from reaching the hockey audience. By the time you read this book, the first event should have taken place. Was it a success?

Design: Once the concept has been generated, all of the components of the event must be created. There are two steps in the design process. First, the event itself must be created with all details spelled out so they can be correctly executed. Second, the experience of the sponsor must also be clearly defined so a sales team can sell sponsorships.

Sales: Selling an event concept to a sponsor is critical to the success of the event. Finding a sponsor with the right fit can ensure long-term success. Selling a sponsorship package that meets the needs of the company makes it easier to create long-term partnerships. Just like brands trying to keep loyal customers, salespeople know that it is easier to keep a sponsor than it is to find a new one. This makes understanding the needs of the company an important part of building a program. The more input the sales group can contribute in the conceptual and design phase, the better tailored the sponsorship package will be. Communication is the key.

Execution: Execution varies widely depending on the event. Think of the execution phase as making sure every detail of the event contract is handled correctly. Details may include sample distribution, signage placement, ticket distribution, public relations, hospitality, promotions, and much more. Event activation is very difficult. Every event is different based on the sponsor. Each sponsor has its own needs. Being detail oriented helps event companies succeed.

Distribution: Any televised event needs to find a home on the air. Sometimes companies create an event, sell the sponsorship, purchase airtime, and sell the commercial inventory. Other events may be made for a network, and the event company acts merely as a producer. In any case, when and where the event is shown say a lot about the event. Now even small events can be shown online and can generate an audience that is attractive to a sponsor.

Key Components of a Sponsorship Proposal

Many companies use boilerplate sponsorship proposals. These proposals contain the same information regardless of the companies that they are being sent to. If you simply plug a company's name into a proposal, the company will know that it is an impersonal solicitation.

History: A successful history certainly sets the tone for a proposal. Many proposals go into great depth about their history. While some events may warrant this, most should keep this short and focus on the future.

Objective: Clearly identify the needs of the companies and show the company how you will satisfy those needs.

Demographic: The attendees and viewing audience should be clearly categorized so companies can find the right match for their brands.

Key benefits: The benefits of the sponsorship should be clearly stated.

Promotional opportunities: Any options for a company to promote its brand should be mentioned. If there is an opportunity for onsite giveaways or sampling, it should be noted. Having a live audience, in the correct demographic, try a product can be a huge selling point for a potential sponsor. Any potential retail tie-ins are also interesting to companies trying to stimulate sales. Buick was the longtime sponsor of a golf tournament at Torrey Pines in San Diego. Buick cars were driven by all of the players during the week. Buick dealerships ran promotions for attendees to test ride vehicles. All of the promotions gave Buick huge exposure during the tournament.

Components: While every sponsorship package is different, most have similar components:

Term: Whereas the term of an event may be clear-cut, the term of the sponsorship must be determined. Sponsors may want to promote their association with an event for months or even years in advance. They may also want to continue promoting that association after the event has finished. An event such as the Olympic Games or the World Cup may warrant years of association, while a smaller regional event may be promoted only for a few months. The term clearly states when the marketing of the association begins and ends.

Logo and trademark rights: Most rights holders are very protective of their intellectual property. When and how logos and trademarks can be used should be clearly stated in the contract. Companies may want to include the event logos in advertising or online. The frequency, size, and placement of logos should all be detailed.

Distribution rights: Some sponsors can benefit from having their product sold at an event. A beverage company may be granted pouring rights at an event. This is usually done by soda or beer companies. These companies feel that the demographic represented at the event includes current or potential customers. Having the pouring rights ensures sales and an immediate and measurable return on the sponsorship investment.

Exclusive/nonexclusive: Most companies that sponsor an event want some protection from direct competition. The level of protection usually depends on the amount spent on the sponsorship. Any major sponsor expects that no other product in its category will be showcased and promoted at the event.

In nonexclusive cases, competing companies could be side by side. A golf tournament may have numerous golf companies as sponsors. This means that attendees and viewers may see multiple equipment manufacturers present at the event.

Any sponsor, whether exclusive or nonexclusive, needs to be aware of the possibility of ambush marketing. Ambush marketing takes place when a nonsponsoring company tries to associate itself with an event. This could be done by the display of billboards around the event. Other companies try to infiltrate an event through street teams that use grassroots marketing techniques to distribute samples. Most major events go to great lengths to avoid ambush marketing. Some events go as far as purchasing the rights to all billboards near an event to control the message that the attendees will see.

I attended the Olympics in Atlanta, Georgia, in 1996. One of the most famous cases of ambush marketing occurred during those Games. Reebok was the official sponsor of the Games. Nike, however, was everywhere. It seemed that every billboard in the city was sporting the Nike Swoosh. There was a Nike Center right in the middle of all the festivities. Street teams handed out Nike souvenirs at every turn. I'm sure that the average attendee would have said that Nike was the official sponsor of the Games.

Signage: Signage is often a large component of a sponsorship plan. The quantities, placement, and size should all be determined as part of the agreement.

Designation: Most events have multiple tiers or levels based on the price of the sponsorship. The top sponsor is usually called something like Presenting Sponsor or Official Sponsor.

Event tickets: Especially if the event is popular, tickets can become an important component of a sponsorship package. The number of tickets will vary depending on the event. Events such as the Super Bowl, World Cup, and the Olympics can leverage the difficulty in getting a ticket to lure sponsors. The right to buy additional tickets, often at a discount, may also be a part of a package.

Hospitality: Hospitality is often one of the driving components of a sponsorship. Hospitality provides a sponsor the ability to entertain clients and even host its own employees at an event. It gives the sponsor time to interact with its customers in a more casual setting. The details of the hospitality will be spelled out in the proposal.

Creating a Successful Sponsorship

Successful sponsorship companies are the ones that act as marketing teams rather than sales teams. Some companies are in the business of simply selling sponsorships. These types of programs rarely succeed. Most successful sponsorship programs include these components:

Listen to the client: The best sponsorship companies are great at sales. Whereas sales are the primary goal, many of these companies spend the first meeting with a potential client listening rather than selling. They then take the information learned back to their creative teams and design a sponsorship proposal that meets the client's needs. Especially in a tough economy, sponsorships must be tailored to the client's needs.

Build a marketing program: Most successful sponsorship sales groups view their jobs as helping their clients market their businesses. Instead of showing a client what they will get for their sponsorship, they will create a plan that tailors the available assets to meet the client's needs.

Meet financial needs: Working within a client's budget is essential to building a strong partnership. Giving great value within that budget further strengthens the relationship and enhances the chance of a long-term commitment to a sponsorship.

Leveraging: Leveraging refers to the marketing efforts that occur outside of the sponsorship agreement. These efforts are supported by incremental dollar spend above and beyond the actual sponsorship package. While no exact ratio works for every sponsorship, many agree that the incremental spend should at least equal that of the sponsorship spend. Some sponsorship consultants recommend as high as a five-to-one incremental spend ratio. The point is that sponsorships typically can't stand alone. They must be supported. Things like advertising, promotions, public relations, and sales contests can all be done to help build awareness.

The single biggest reason for sponsorship failure is lack of leveraging. When a company thinks that its work is done when it signs the sponsorship agreement, it usually ends up disappointed. The reality is that the work is just beginning. A sponsor must have a great activation plan to succeed.

Review: Determining whether all the deliverables were met is an essential part of a successful sponsorship. This can be done formally where each part of a sponsorship is rated both internally and externally by the client. More often, the review is done informally with a simple discussion with the client regarding the event.

Evaluating Sponsorship Opportunity Costs

Return on investment (ROI): One of the most difficult parts of managing a sponsorship is determining the return on investment. The return on some components of a sponsorship plan can easily be determined. Items such as free tickets or program advertising have a predetermined value associated with the asset. Other components are more difficult to value. It is challenging to assign a financial number to the amount of good will a company will generate by sponsoring an event. A company definitely gets branding value by having thousands of spectators see its name on signage, in programs, and on promotional giveaways. But it is sometimes hard to determine the direct correlation to sales. A local company sponsoring a small event may be able to track results. But a large company such as Nike may have trouble determining the effect of any single event.

Especially in a difficult economy, companies want to feel that their spending will achieve the results that they need. Stating as clearly as possible the value of each component of a proposal will make it easier to sell.

Defined assets: Defined assets are those to which it is easy to assign a value. An example would be the allocation of tickets that come with many sponsorship deals. If tickets are sold at $50 and the company receives 10 tickets per game, then it is easy to value that portion of the proposal at $500 per game.

Invisible assets: Invisible assets are intangible assets that do not physically exist. The prestige of an event, the media coverage, or the association and use of well-known logos or trademarks add a value that is difficult to define.

Pricing: Determining value can be tricky. Although no one way works for all sponsorships, there are a number of ways to determine value:

Identify benefits: All sponsorship proposals include a list of benefits that the sponsor will receive in exchange for the required payment. The first thing a potential sponsor should do is review those benefits and try to establish a cost for each one based on its value to the brand and company objectives. Each potential sponsor will have different values based on their company's needs. One sponsor may put a large value on sampling, while another may want to use the opportunity for hospitality.

Competitive review: Some companies review similar sponsorship opportunities. Say a golf tournament in Chicago is offering a title sponsorship for $2 million. A potential sponsor could perform a competitive review of similar tournaments to determine whether the $2 million asking price is reasonable.

Media review: Another way to compare value is to conduct a media review. A company could look at the cost of sponsoring the event. It could then determine how many impressions it would get using traditional advertising. Although the type of impression may be different, and not quite an apples-to-apples comparison, it does give the company a ballpark figure on the value of the sponsorship package.

Equivalency: Equivalency means tracking exposure. Say that an announcer will mention the sponsor three times for a total of 00:30 seconds. During the broadcast, the sponsor's logo is visible in the background 40 different times for a total of 3:30 minutes. The sponsor now has 4:00 minutes of airtime for its brand. The cost of 4:00 minutes of commercial airtime can easily be determined, giving the sponsor a solid number to compare with the sponsorship cost.

These are by no means foolproof ways to analyze the opportunity, but they can give a sponsor an idea of whether the price tag is at least in the ballpark of the value offered.

Sponsorship Payment

Once the value is established, most sponsorships are paid for in one of the following ways:

Cash: As with any business, cash is king. Most sponsorships are paid for through an agreed upon cash payment.

Product/service: A company that has a product or service that is compatible with an event can often use that for all or part of the sponsorship fee. For example, if Nike becomes the official sponsor of a university football team, it might pay for the sponsorship by providing all of equipment needed for that football program during a season.

Combination: Many sponsorships are paid for with a combination approach. Some cash is usually included and a product or service rounds out the rest of the payment. When both sides are willing to be creative and are open to ideas, the sponsorship has a greater chance of being financially successful. In the example mentioned previously, Buick paid for part of its title sponsorship by providing vehicles for the participants and staff during the gold tournament. Buick could later market and sell those cars at the local dealerships.

Example of an Event with Sponsorship

For 25 years, Intersport has been an award-winning innovator and leader in the creation of sports- and entertainment-based marketing platforms. Intersport has a profound understanding of how to harness the power of sports and entertainment to effectively produce results for clients.

Intersport combines its two award-winning divisions, Sponsorship and Event Marketing and Programming and Production, to provide turnkey solutions for global brands. When housed within one organization, these disciplines merge to offer a powerful, diverse, and integrated marketing solution for the world's biggest brands. This proposal examines a college hockey event that Intersport has created from start to finish. The project can give you a great overview of the industry because Intersport is one of the companies that handle all aspects of an event.

Ice Hockey Challenge Sponsorship Proposal

Featuring four college powerhouses battling on Presidents' Day weekend at Chicago's iconic Soldier Field

A Multiplatform Approach to Reach the Targeted Audience

National Promotion
- Television partner(s) pre-event promotion

Participating School Markets
- Local markets (use of school markets subject to individual school restrictions)

Chicago Market
- Television, radio, newspaper, billboards advertising
- Online messaging—event site, sponsor sites, social media, etc.
- Outreach to local youth, college and alumni organizations, hockey clubs, etc.
- One million Chicago hockey fans

Title Sponsorship
(Other options include Supporting, Corporate, and Local Sponsorships)

Event
- Event logo integration
    - Integration of event logo on outside dasher board wall wrap
    - Integration of event logo on Soldier Field wall wrap
    - 1 primary center-ice event logo
- 2 secondary on-ice company logos
- 8 dasher boards
- 20-minute LED signage (:30-second rotations) (10 minutes per game)
- 2 video board features (1 per game)
- 4 video board commercial spots with PA copy (2 per game)
- 2 intermission promotions (1 per game)
- 2 in-game promotions (1 per game)
- 4 concourse marketing booths
- Event suite
- Full back-page advertisement in event program
- Opportunity for premium item giveaway (*production costs covered by Sponsor*)
- Inclusion in all marketing and PR support materials
- Rights to own an additional day/night during the 17 days (*incremental costs may apply*)

Title Sponsorship (continued)

Media
- 32 total (:30) commercial units (eight :30 commercial units per game broadcast, including 1 encore of each game)
- 8 total billboards (opening and closing billboards per game broadcast, including 1 encore of each game)
- Event logo graphics utilized throughout
- Branded backdrop for play-by-play and color commentators
- 4 on-air verbal mentions by play-by-play and color commentators (2 per game)
- 2 customized, in-game features (1 per game)

Digital
- Event website integration
    - Company logo presence
- Social media exposure
    - Brand presence on all event social media platforms
    - Facebook, Twitter, YouTube, etc.
- Opportunity for digital campaign (*incremental costs may apply*)

Case Study

Rick Leese is in charge of sponsorship for a PGA Tour event held in February in Arizona. For the past 10 years, the presenting sponsor has been a luxury watchmaker. But that company decided to end its sponsorship. Rick has been struggling to find a new presenting sponsor. It is now 6 months before the tournament. Rick has been approached by a legal Internet gambling site that wants to take over as the lead sponsor.

1. Should Rick hold out in hopes of finding a sponsor that better fits the high-end demographic of the attendees of the tournament?
2. Should Rick care who sponsors the tournament as long as the top-name players are participating?
3. How important is it that the presenting sponsor matches the demographics of the people attending and watching an event?

Critical Thinking Activity

Following the steps for a successful sponsorship given in the chapter, create a simple sponsorship proposal for a golf tournament. Spell out all of the key benefits that will be provided to the sponsor (tickets, signage, programs, hospitality, etc.). Be sure to define ROI.

CHAPTER QUESTIONS

1. How can a company determine whether the price of a sponsorship is fair?
2. Go online and find the website for your favorite event. Who was the main sponsor?
3. Choose an event in sports. How many different tiers of sponsorship can you identify?
4. Identify a sponsor of an athletic team at your university. What are its primary objectives?
5. Describe ambush marketing. Provide an example of an ambush campaign in sports.
6. Why is it important to leverage?
7. Choose an event. Describe the leveraging strategies used.
8. What is the difference between a tangible and intangible asset? Give an example of each.
9. What are the five steps to creating a successful sponsorship?
10. How do most companies pay for a sponsorship?

Notes

1. Ben Klayman, "Global Sponsorship Spending to Rise 5.2 Percent in 2011," IEG, January 11, 2011, http://www.sponsorship.com/About-IEG/IEG-In-The-News/Global-Sponsorship-Spending-to-Rise-5-2-Percent-in.aspx.
2. "Economic Uncertainty to Slow Sponsorship Growth in 2012," IEG, January 11, 2012, http://www.sponsorship.com/About-IEG/Press-Room/Economic-Uncertainty-To-Slow-Sponsorship-Growth-In.aspx.

Chapter 12

Product Development

CHAPTER OBJECTIVES

* Learn about product development.
* Learn the history of product development.
* Learn how the five Ps affect product development.
* Identify key benefits to product development.
* Learn key components to a product development plan.
* Review a sports product development plan.

CHAPTER OVERVIEW

This chapter discusses how sports products are developed. It provides an analysis of the structure and strategy behind building a sports product from scratch and reviews an actual product to discover how creative, licensing, approvals, and production affect the time line for bringing ideas to market.

Voices from the Field: Jamie Kiskis

BIOGRAPHY

Jamie Kiskis became an expert at sports product development during his career at the Upper Deck Company. When Jamie worked there, Upper Deck was the world's leading manufacturer and distributer of sports collectibles. Jamie created sports memorabilia and trading card products. Through his experience he gained expertise in product development, marketing, media, and licensing. He left Upper Deck in 2008 to pursue full time the development of his own intellectual property. As the founder and CEO of On the Record Sports, he created an innovative new version of online fantasy sports games dubbed "reality sports." He has also created a consulting business to provide product development, sales, and marketing services to clients that include technology, trading cards, memorabilia, and restaurants.

Q&A

Q: What is your current position?

After closing the doors of my start-up, On the Record Sports, at the end of 2012, I have had the privilege of working with several companies in sports, technology, gaming, and trading cards that include a few start-ups. I love the opportunity to work with other entrepreneurs, who are chasing their dreams and can benefit from my experience and contacts in the industry. I get to wear many hats depending on what each company needs from product development, product ideas, marketing campaigns, social media, business development, etc. I'm currently heading up Sports Partnerships for an exciting start-up called Ribbon. Ribbon is the first full-scale social media platform focused on connecting people in time and place. For consumers, Ribbon will change the way people make future plans. Ribbon offers the most complete and robust feature set for people to engage in social discovery, event discovery, planning, inviting, sharing, conversing, and purchasing tickets to events. People will use Ribbon to plan all of their future activities—everything from dinners, birthday parties, weekend plans, and holiday to concerts, sporting events, business conferences, and other types of public events. Ribbon's B2B platform, Ribbon for Business, can be described as "Google Analytics for Event Brands" (professional sports teams, music artists, business conferences, etc.). Ribbon for Business will deliver social media and marketing teams, at companies of all sizes, valuable fan behavior data about each fan's relationship with each brand; this unique data and intelligence will be delivered real time and on an ongoing basis. Brands will use this information and Ribbon for Business to generate highly targeted marketing initiatives while promoting the use of the Ribbon consumer application to their fans worldwide. The Ribbon platform will drive event awareness, fan engagement, merchandise and ticket sales for event brands. It's the brainchild of a friend/colleague of mine, and it has the potential to be something special. Great ideas require a lot of hard work, timing, and a bit of luck.

Q: What was your career path?

I grew up playing sports; going to see the Lakers, Dodgers, Rams, and Kings play in Los Angeles; collecting trading cards; playing video games; and even making the volleyball team at San Diego State University. I was a Political Science major, and I was interested in the theory and history of the political process. Then, I had an internship in Washington, D.C., during an election year, and I got to see the "peaceful" transfer of power and how politics really worked. It was cold and ugly—both the weather and the politics. I missed San Diego and being involved in sports, so it was fate that placed me on Washington, D.C.'s, streets one Saturday afternoon that coincided with the Hoop-It-Up street basketball tournament. A close friend from college was working for Upper Deck and traveling the country with the Hoop-It-Up tour. Within minutes of finding him in the Upper Deck booth, I was judging a slam dunk contest along with former Washington Bullets great Phil Chenier and a Bullets cheerleader. He asked me if I wanted his job for the next season, as he was getting promoted into the office full time. I couldn't resist the opportunity. The rest was history.

I did three different tours of duty at Upper Deck that totaled 15 years. I took two breaks that I thought were for good, but I came back to better positions each time. After traveling the country with Hoop-It-Up, I worked my way up through marketing, new business, and product development. In 1998, I help form the Product Development Team at Upper Deck. We completely revamped all of our product lines and changed the development culture at UD. After being given the freedom to do what we wanted to products, the results were staggering. Within 2 years, we had captured first place in 10 of 12 *Trade Card Magazine*'s industry awards, and most importantly, we created and maximized trends that are still relevant in the trading card industry today over 10 years later.

At that point, I realized it was time for a new challenge, as there was no place left to go from there. I left my career and went to Australia for the Olympics and then flew to Tonga where I jumped on a friend's boat and sailed throughout the South Pacific. When out at sea and on the other side of the world for several months, I started getting e-mails that Upper Deck was going to get the Manchester United trading card license, and I was asked to build the brand and run all international products. It was an offer that I could not refuse. After building the best soccer card products the industry has ever seen, Manchester United sold David Beckham and our sales went down without him, especially in Asia-Pacific.

So, I made another jump within Upper Deck to the Authenticated division, UDA. There, I was able to lead the team across all sports and athletes in several different categories. Everything from toys and figurines to one-of-a-kind pieces of signed, game-worn equipment. It was a wonderful experience and great exposure, as I also worked directly with each of the major sporting leagues and players associations.

I knew that I had the experience, confidence, tenacity, and creativity to be successful with my own venture, so I made another great leap of faith to start my own version of fantasy sports with On the Record Sports. There is always a conflict within fantasy sports of having to cheer against your favorite players to win at fantasy. I started it as a pool for friends that then went to message boards and eventually needed to be automated as a website. That was the beginning of an expensive hobby that turned into a business. What we have created at OTRS is a game that can allow fans in any sport to predict how their favorite teams and players are going to do each game and get more points for being the closest to the correct answer. We have launched in NFL, NBA, NCAA Football & Basketball, and World Cup soccer. We have created games for the websites of Comcast/NBC Sports channels.

Recently, working with the team at Ribbon has been extremely exciting. It feels like everything that I learned from my own start-up comes up in some way on a daily basis at Ribbon. It drives me to work smarter and apply the wisdom that will help navigate the inevitable challenges of business and creating something new and disruptive in technology.

Overall, I'd say that my career path has been with a passion to innovate, work hard, stay positive, help others advance, be a valued teammate, make contacts, build relationships, drive revenue, and then go "all-in" when it was time create my own way.

Q: What has been your greatest accomplishment in the sports business?

Besides being married to an extraordinary woman and having a beautiful daughter in my life, I would say that starting my own vision in the sports world and developing a business around it has been a true labor of love. There have been so many peaks and valleys, but to create something new that is my own makes everything worth it in the end.

Q: What has been your favorite moment with an athlete?

Having worked in sports my entire career, I have had so many moments with athletes. In my first week of working at Upper Deck, I was sent to the NBA All-Star Game weekend in Salt Lake City. I met Reggie Jackson and Julius Erving at the first event I went to. Reggie even gave me a look, knowing that I had beaten out a friend of his for my position. That was one of my most awkward moments. Of all of the athletes, it was a pleasure to work personally with Kobe Bryant on creating his product line for

UDA and to meet David Beckham when working on Manchester United products. However, the most memorable has to be playing against and then with Michael Jordan during the Jordan Senior Flight School in 2005. That was nothing short of amazing. It is something I will never forget.

Q: What is the most exciting thing about the field of sports product development?

Seeing your product ideas bring happiness to people and revenue to your own company is similar to playing in an actual game. Sure, thousands are not standing there cheering for you while you make the pitch, but closing the deal and having everything come together to launch an award-winning product that does well in the marketplace is pretty cool, especially when it is about that player who actually did win the game on the field.

Q: What advice do you have for students interested in sports product development?

My advice for students, adults, or anyone who will listen to me is simple: follow your bliss. Do for a living what you are passionate about. Whether it is working for a specific sport, team, player, licensed property, marketing group, agency, or whatever within sports, then you have to go for it. If you are passionate about what you do, then you will enjoy the high times, battle through the low points, and ultimately be successful.

Courtesy of Jamie Kiskis.

Introduction

Product development is the process of creating and bringing a product to market. Every company that has a product has done some kind of product development. In some cases, the process is formal with strict guidelines and time lines. In other cases, it happens organically without formal steps. The time line can vary widely across industries. Boeing typically takes several years to assess a market niche and design a new aircraft. Sports products such as basketball shoes may take more than a year to research, design, engineer, and sell. Other products take just a few weeks. Product development may be done for new products or extensions of existing products. In any case, the goal is to create a sellable product that the consumer will buy.

The process can be a proactive or a reactive one. **Proactive product development** companies have a formal and constant new product development process in place. They are usually perceived as the leaders in their industry. **Reactive product development** companies usually wait to see what innovations are taking place with their competition and then make changes to their own product. There is no one right way to develop the process. Proactive companies, while often market leaders, can spend a great deal of money developing new ideas. Reactive companies, while often looked on as followers, can make changes based on what is successful for the market leader and this may lead to smaller research and development costs and higher profit margins. There are many company battles in the sports industry. Nike versus Adidas and Spalding versus Wilson are two that come to mind. Although each company may be the leader in its respective category, it has many competitors that watch what it is doing and react to those product innovations.

History of Sports Product Development

Specifying an exact date as the start of sports product development is difficult. As long as there have been sports, products have been created, enhanced, and continually improved. It is reasonable to say that there was some product development going on in Greece in 776 B.C. when the first Olympics were held. Perhaps when the Aztecs developed the ball game ollamalitzli or the Mayans created the game ulama, product development teams were fast at work. These teams weren't in a conference room using a whiteboard and computers; yet the fundamental strategies of making the best and most reliable products still hold true today. In more recent times, you can follow the development of the wooden baseball bat from its creation in a woodshop owned by the Hillerich family to its advance as the Louisville Slugger line.[1] And, with a little stretch of the imagination, you can call the creation of a basketball rim from a peach basket a product extension by William Naismith, the inventor of the game of basketball. Today, product development is the lifeline of most companies, and it creates billions of dollars of sports-related business.

How the Five Ps Affect Sports Product Development

PRODUCT There are many different products in the sports industry. It is the job of a company's product development team to create new ideas that lead to the development of successful creations. Product could be apparel, shoes, websites, equipment, premiums, memorabilia, collectibles, and many other items that interest the sports fan.

PRICE The final price of a product dictates the amount of time and money spent in development. On the front end, development budgets are based on pricing and projected sales volumes. Success is determined by profitable sales numbers. Finding the correct pricing can be difficult, but it is essential to the success of the product.

PROMOTION Most products have solicitation sell sheets created long before the product is manufactured. Solicitation sell sheets are concise but detailed advertisements for the product that is being developed. This is often the first thing the sales group shows a buyer or distributor about a new product.

PLACE Each product must be developed with distribution in mind. The look, feel, and packaging of a product are influenced by where it will be sold. Marketers need to understand that retailers may place size and weight constraints on the product that the sales group must consider. Fun and cool packaging that won't fit on a retailer's shelf could kill the purchase of the product line.

PROGRESS The role of the creative team is to keep the product line continually fresh. Teams now try to engage new and existing customers through social media. Shoe companies try to create the latest and greatest innovation that will give an edge to an athlete. Apparel designers use the Internet to track worldwide fashion trends, hoping to catch the next hot design. Designers use technology to speed the process and get their concepts to the consumer more quickly. Staying on top of the latest technology can be the key to a successful product launch.

Key Benefits of Product Development

Companies trying to grow and stay ahead of the curve constantly need to be developing fresh ideas. A strategic product development process can help a company's products stay fresh and relevant in the marketplace.

Fresh products: A company that uses a continual product development strategy will always be giving customers new products. Companies such as Nike and Under Armour have the reputation of being innovators in the industry because of their product development strategies. Not all of their products are successful. However, the consumer is usually willing to try new offerings because they perceive these companies are leaders in their industry. Continual creation of good products is a win-win for the whole business food chain: The company keeps growing profitably, salespeople and distributors have fresh and exciting lines to pitch, retailers have a fresh supply of new inventory, and consumers have new products to try. All of this is created by a strategic product development process.

Product extensions: Not every new product is made from scratch. The running shoe companies have become experts at offering new versions of long-standing brands each year. Much like the auto industry, the shoe industry offers a new model of your favorite shoe each season. Slightly tweaking the design entices many runners to purchase the latest version. Nike has done this masterfully for decades with the Air Jordan line.

Product extensions help a company build off of the brand equity of an existing product. Evolution is cheaper than revolution. Modifying an earlier product and marketing campaign can save the company time and money.

Although new products and product extensions don't guarantee an increase in sales, they do guarantee that the line won't become stale. Product development teams, working closely with sales departments to spot new trends, can usually create popular products and new revenue streams for their companies. Market innovators such as Nike can usually charge more for their products, which leads to higher revenue compared to their competitors'.

Key Components of a Product Development Plan

Every company has its own strategy for product development. Some companies have a solid revenue-producing product, sometimes called a cash cow, and they do very little to ever change it. Most companies, however, need to use a product development process to keep their product lines fresh. There is no one right strategy that works for every company, industry, or product. Most strategies do include the following fundamental steps:

Idea generation: Many times idea generation starts with a group of creative people sitting in front of a whiteboard and brainstorming ideas. These ideas can come from the company's desire for new products, as suggestions from the sales force regarding the needs of customers, or as reactions to competition. An incredible new product can result from a group of people throwing out ideas. Most successful companies have a formal strategy to build concepts that lead to successful products.

Product design: Once the idea is generated, a design team gives life to the look and feel of the idea. This process can take days, weeks, months, or years depending on the product or industry. Companies trying to create product as a reaction to an unforeseen event, such as a sports record being broken or an upset in a championship game, need to have their product to market immediately. These hot market opportunities usually last only a few weeks, and then the sporting world moves on to the next latest and greatest thing. For example, Jeremy Lin became an overnight sensation with the New York Knicks. Jersey sales went through the roof, and his trading card became the hottest item on the market. A few weeks later, after the Knicks lost five or six in a row, Linsanity—as it was called—died down. The companies that were able to quickly design product capitalized on the event. Other times, the product design phase can take months or even years. Performance equipment companies may take years to design and test a product before the consumer ever sees it.

Concept development: Concept development is a critical stage of the new product development process. During this stage, the idea is researched and tested to determine whether the company should pursue it as a new product line. Everything from validity, materials, engineering, sourcing, and packaging to consumer desire is analyzed. This is the stage just before the company commits the funds to developing the product, so it is critical the company makes the right decisions. Both primary research (research conducted for the project) and secondary research (research already conducted) can be used to help decide the fate of the project.

Sales forecasting: Because the sales team members are the ones who have direct contact with the buyers, it is critical that they are involved in each step of the new product development process. At this point in the process, many companies develop something online or use sell sheets, typically a one-page formal and detailed description of a new product. The online page or sell sheet includes product details and may contain conceptual renderings. The sales team uses these marketing materials to introduce the new product to the customer base and to discuss potential sales volumes. Although these are not binding commitments to sales, they give the company a feel for the type of revenue that the new product can drive. Sales forecasting is a crucial part of the process. Correct forecasting gives the product development team the information it needs to determine volumes and potential dollars to spend on the process. Communication with the sales team is a crucial step in the product development process that is often overlooked by the creative team.

Financial review: Armed with the product information developed and the potential revenue the product can create, the finance department will develop a profit and loss statement (P&L). (See **FIGURE 12-1**.) A P&L reviews all of the costs involved with creating the product and helps determine whether the suggested sales price will result in a profit or a loss for the company. A marketer must understand the P&L process of the company. Creating great products that aren't profitable is the way many companies get into trouble. A marketer must realize that raw materials, labor, general and administrative costs, shipping, perhaps licensing royalties, and many other factors combine to create the cost of a product. Although the marketer doesn't need to be an expert in finance, understanding a financial statement and all the moving parts that go into a product is needed. When a marketer has a good financial feel for the product, profitable concepts and merchandise are more likely to follow.

2015 Football Product P&L

1/15/2015

Quarterback - $80 Signature Rate

Description	Avg. Wholesale	Total Units	Proj Gs Rev	SRP	Hobby Stores	Direct Sales	TV	Internet	Internatl.	Total
Jersey -unframed	$353.51	155	$54,794	$649.99	111	28	0	16	0	155
Milestone Jersey -unframed	$457.03	32	$14,625	$749.99	3	25	0	4	0	32
Football	$238.10	127	$30,239	$449.99	105	12	0	10	0	127
Breaking Through	$546.15	26	$14,200	$999.99	14	12	0	0	0	26
Jersey Numbers Piece	$332.35	51	$16,950	$599.99	34	10	0	7	0	51
Sweet Spot Piece	$234.70	34	$7,980	$399.99	15	12	0	7	0	34
16x20 Photo Framed	$242.43	40	$9,697	$449.99	29	8	0	3	0	40
Helmet	$382.61	44	$16,835	$699.99	28	13	0	3	0	44
SUBTOTAL		509	$165,320		339	120	0	50	0	509

(Total Unit Forecast by Channel)

Matl Cost	Overhead 18.36%	Total Matl/Labor	5.5% Roy	Athlete signing fee	Total Unit Cost	Ext Mat/Lbr Cost	Ext 0 Cost	Ext Athlete Cost	Total Extended Cost	Contrib. Margin	Contrib. Profit
117.04	64.90	181.94	19.44	80.00	281.38	28,201	3,014	12,400	43,614	20.4%	$11,180
129.04	83.91	212.95	25.14	80.00	318.08	6,814	804	2,560	10,179	30.4%	$4,446
56.65	43.72	100.37	13.10	80.00	193.46	12,746	1,663	10,160	24,570	18.7%	$5,670
172.18	100.27	272.45	30.04	80.00	382.49	7,084	781	2,080	9,945	30.0%	$4,255
72.90	61.02	133.92	18.28	80.00	232.20	6,830	932	4,080	11,842	30.1%	$5,108
15.86	43.09	58.95	12.91	80.00	151.86	2,004	439	2,720	5,163	35.3%	$2,817
48.35	44.51	92.86	13.33	80.00	186.19	3,714	533	3,200	7,448	23.2%	$2,250
60.67	70.25	130.92	21.04	80.00	231.96	5,760	926	3,520	10,206	39.4%	$6,629
				$80.00		$73,154	$9,093	$40,720	$122,967	25.6%	$42,353

FIGURE 12-1 2015 football P&L example.

Product launch: The product launch typically involves sales, marketing, advertising, PR, and operations. It is up to the creative team to set the tone so the other departments can prepare their strategies and budgets to support the launch. Although the product development team has less responsibility and control of the process once the concept is approved and created, it is important that they stay in the loop and monitor the process. Good teams continually monitor and guide the process from start to finish.

Jamie Kiskis's View on Product Development

Jamie has created hundreds of sports products. Jamie and his team created many of the products in the portfolios of such famous athletes as Michael Jordan, Tiger Woods, LeBron James, and Kobe Bryant. His views reflect years of sports experience.

Product development has perhaps the most challenging job of the sports marketing and product business. As a result, product development has the most overlap with all other phases of sports marketing because it interacts with licensing, legal, marketing, finance, sales, and operations. If you can create a product that sports fans want to buy, then the other departments have a better chance to be successful in their endeavors, as well. Product content is king. If you don't create a great product, then all of the creative marketing in the world may not be able to make it sellable. A sports product is much like the product the team or athlete puts on the field. If the team wins on the field, then the other factors, such as ticket sales, sponsorships, and licensed products, all have a chance to succeed. The same can be said for a successful product launch.

To take the sports team metaphor one step further, there are five key points to consider when creating a winning product game plan.

1. CREATE AN ALL-STAR PRODUCT AND TEAM

First, ask yourself, why is this product more innovative than what is currently on the market? Perhaps you have a new product category that you have created. Perhaps you have an innovative take or new design on a product in an existing category. Or maybe you could be extending a current product line to now include sports licenses.

You should have a basic product profit and loss statement (P&L) spelled out that contains how much the product will cost to create, build, and sell. You won't necessarily know your product volumes yet, but you will have an idea of price breaks that you can get from your suppliers or developers. These price breaks may give you volume targets that can be factored into the development. This obviously depends on the category.

To make a great product, you also need to have the great creative team that can make it a reality. When building a team there are a number of factors that the team leader should consider. Just like a professional sports team, talent doesn't always lead to greatness. Often, the team with the best chemistry is the one collecting the championship trophy at the end of the season. In business, it is no different. While creativity is important, team work is just as critical to the development of ideas, concepts, and products.

One of the most important decisions that you will make when building your game plan is whether you want, need, or can afford licensing from the sporting leagues and/or players associations. As a product developer, you must take the initiative in this process.

Licensed Versus Unlicensed Products

There are two main classifications of sport products on the market: licensed and unlicensed. Licensed products contain team or league marks that may also need additional rights to be acquired if players are being featured. The ultimate sports products require licenses for both leagues and players because the fans have a connection to their favorite teams and its players.

Unlicensed products do not necessarily need team or league marks, but they may use players as spokespeople to help market the product. This is why you see commercials and ads with a well-known player such as Michael Jordan wearing a generic basketball jersey instead of a Bulls jersey in a hot dog ad, Brett Favre wearing a yellow #4 T-shirt instead of a Packers jersey while in a jeans commercial, or Blake Griffin selling foot-long sandwiches in a red sweat suit.

Determine whether your product will need a league (or team) license and players association license. Having both is more expensive since you are paying minimum guarantees and royalties to two parties instead of one. It is also more effort since you will be getting approvals for your products from both entities. Some product categories such as apparel (hats, T-shirts, sweat shirts, etc.) do not need players to be successful. Fans are more than happy to purchase those items with their favorite team's logo emblazoned on the product. If you determine that the product you are developing could benefit from licensing, the first step is to see if the league has an exclusive partner in that category. If they don't, then the licensing process can begin. If they do, then you must decide whether the new product idea can stand alone without the help of a license.

Are you interested in adding sports licensing to your existing product? First, review current P&Ls for the product without licensing. If the numbers work without licensing, then you can add royalties, which will affect your profit margin considerably. You will need to make decisions on taking price increases for products once licensed based on how much more the market will pay for the enhanced product with licensing on it. Consumers may pay $10 for a simple white T-shirt. They may be willing to pay $20 to $30 for that same shirt with the logo of their favorite team prominently displayed on the front.

2. COMPILE A SCOUTING REPORT

Just as it is important to know who you are going to play against in the sporting world, it is vital to know who the players are in your industry. Your market research will include who is in the marketplace, how much they charge for their products, how well their products are doing, market share, awards won, customer feedback, and ratings. If possible, licensing information should be obtained. The more you know about what licensing categories competitors own, how much they pay, and the status of their licenses, the better decisions you can make at the beginning of the new product development process.

After this, you will know roughly what your product is or should be to win in the marketplace. You will also have completed research on the competition. Now it is time to get real and determine what your chances for success are going to be. It is imperative to create a SWOT analysis with key team members.

Companies use many planning tools, but SWOT seems to be one of the most popular. SWOT stands for strengths, weaknesses, opportunities, and threats. You need a whiteboard and conference room area to let all members of the team weigh in on your projected product offering(s). Write *Strengths* at the top of the whiteboard and ask for input about the new idea from the team. Once you have explored and written down your key product strengths in the market, then you move on to weaknesses, then opportunities, and threats. In the end, you will have an excellent overview of your current situation.

3. SETTING UP YOUR LINE

At this point in the process, you know enough about your basic product offering and the competition to build your plan. That plan begins with your ideal product, as well as pricing and distribution strategies. This is also a great time to look at your planned products versus hot market products. Planned products are products that you can reasonably forecast for throughout the entire year. Hot market products are items created to take advantage of championships, record-breaking events, or unforeseen events that often happen in sports.

Planned Versus Hot Market Products

One of the joys of being a sports fan is the unpredictability of what will happen on and off the field/court/track each game or season. The excitement of seeing an unexpected rookie break through early and take over a starting position, having a team secure a superstar in a midseason trade, and the emerging squad that surpasses all expectations to take a ride into the postseason are all great scenarios for fans, but these are extremely challenging for sports product developers. Even the most experienced product developers can't predict everything that will happen in a season and they will learn something new every year. Although this is a difficult part of the job, it also keeps things exciting.

Product and marketing plans are generally developed well in advance, sales orders against those plans are placed, and product has been produced with specific teams and players called out. When the inevitable dramatic changes occur, companies are looking at potential dead inventory and a loss of profit. Depending on how the player leaves a team, like LeBron James taking his talents from Cleveland to South Beach, the inventory is not only unsellable, but it is toxic for the market being left. Of course, the product for the new team may be extremely hot. It's like a game of sports product "Russian Roulette," so you have to be quick, flexible, and creative.

For stable product categories, a large portion of your sports product business should be around planned products. But a planned mechanism should also be in place to take advantage of hot market scenarios, which can bring in significant upside dollars. For example, in the trading card business, Upper Deck would plan to produce a box set of trading cards for the winning team of the Super Bowl, World Series, Stanley Cup, NBA Championship, and so forth. The problem is that, because of production time lines, they have to create products for eight teams knowing that only one in each sport will ultimately win. The difference in popularity and market demand for each of those eight teams can be dramatic. You will have already sunk the costs of creating new designs, packaging options, player photos, and so forth, as well as getting them preapproved should any of the teams win, so that you can go to market.

Let's say that the Yankees are playing the Devil Rays in the World Series. It's safe to say that Yankee product will outsell Devil Rays product by a mile. You may find yourself rooting for teams that you never thought you would be cheering for because they give you the best opportunity to turn a profit.

4. CREATING YOUR GAME PLAN

Once you have your products lined up, you will need to create your product launch strategy. This includes the timing of production and delivery, marketing/advertising/PR efforts, and a sales plan. Include the ability to capture potential upside should a popular team win. Also formulate an exit plan should something change the success of the product (player team change, major slump, off the field issues, etc.). This is what makes a job in sports unique. Whereas individuals designing automobiles, clothing, or shoes can have a stable 5-year plan, sports marketers may need to change their plan many times over that period based on player and team decisions.

Many companies create a document called a strategic brief. (See **FIGURE 12-2**.) The name is ironic, because it is anything but brief. The document included a detailed overview of the products, the promotion, the distribution, and so forth. It was generally more than 30 pages long. Like an advertising brief, it is a document that helps all departments stay on track.

XYZ Sporting Product Company
Product Game Plan Document
NFL Super Bowl Champions Product

Contents
1. Product Summary
2. Product Positioning/Key Notes
3. Past Product Performance
4. Market Feedback
5. Competitive Position
6. Product Details
7. Player List
8. Packaging and Design Direction
9. Marketing and PR Notes
10. Financials and P&L
11. Initial Schedule

Product Summary

Previous Line/SKU Release: $2 million
Current Year Company Revenue/Margin Plan: $2.25 million/25% margin
This Plan Revenue/Margin: $2.5 million/28% margin
Difference vs. Plan: + $250,000 /+3% margin
Product Game Plan Due Date: 10/01/13
Final Sales Volumes Due: 12/31/13
Product Go-Live Date: 02/03/14@game conclusion
Delivery Date: 02/14/14
Primary SKU SRP per Unit: $40.00

Product Positioning/Key Notes

Provide a top-line description of the product or products, why it is important, how much customers want it, and so forth. Tell everyone why this product is important to the company.

SAMPLE LANGUAGE   This is one of our most popular sports-related products every year, and, depending on the team that wins, we have seen up to a 25% increase in sales of this product.

Product Positioning

Who do you want to buy this product and how should you go about building and marketing it?

SAMPLE LANGUAGE   Provide sports fans with a value priced item that commemorates the season of the Super Bowl championship team.

Product Description

Provide a description of the contents of the product or products, stock keeping units (SKUs), and any special bonus items/features.

SAMPLE LANGUAGE   This product will commemorate the winning team from Super Bowl XLI. Each item will have the names and pictures of all of the key players on the team and include any significant details for the product.

FIGURE 12-2 Product brief.

Key Product Drivers/Differentiation
- Our launch date is very aggressive, and we should be the first to market.
- New, innovative card designs incorporate the Super Bowl logo.

Target Consumers
- Football fans
- Team-specific football fans
- Sports fans
- Gift buyers

Target Distribution Channels
- Retail accounts
- Specialty retail accounts
- Distributors
- Direct to consumers (via e-mail, catalogs, postcard mailers)
- Online store
- Retail online accounts
- Television shopping networks

Past Product Performance

It is important to review the performance of past products. The knowledge gained from that experience should be applied to the current strategy.

SAMPLE LANGUAGE   The following data are from last year's NFL Super Bowl product as of last week's sales reports.

Quantity of product produced last time: 100,000 units

Overall sell-through: 85% (85,000 units)

Remaining inventory:

Item/SKU No.	Description	Units	Unit/Wholesale Cost	Extended Cost
00756	Individual units	5,000	$20.00	$100,000
00757	200 boxes of 50 units	10,000	$20.00	$200,000
	Total Inventory	15,000		$300,000

Market Feedback

This is where you include initial feedback from end customers, dealers, retailers, product reviewers, focus group testing, and so forth, as applicable.

You should also include feedback on past performance of the product or products if this is not the first release.

FIGURE 12-2 Product brief. (*continued*)

Competitive Position

In this section, you highlight the competition within your category, as well as potential competitive products from outside of your category that might attract your customers away.

For example: If you are launching a video game and a mobile game app around the same time or a similar property is planned for roughly the same time frame, then it is important to note. Identifying potential competitive issues and providing key differentiation points are vital to your plan's success.

Depending on your category and the company you will work for, this section can be several pages or it can be a top-line overview. Following is an example:

Competitor 1: Company A

Brand(s): Hot Market Product

Price Point: $35.00

Customers: Sports fans, football fans, gift buyers

Provide a description of what this competitor has done in the past with its product(s) and what you know about its current product(s).

Also, point out the key differences and product attributes that make your product(s) more attractive to potential customers.

Competitor 2: Company B

Brand(s): Hot Market Product

Price Point: $39.99

Customer: Sports fans, football fans, gift buyers

Provide a description of what this competitor has done in the past with its product(s) and what you know about its current product(s).

Also, point out the key differences and product attributes that make your product(s) more attractive to potential customers.

Recommendations and Key Points Regarding Competition

Provide a bullet point list that everyone can quickly read to summarize your competition, what to watch for, and recommendations for how to react.

Product Details

This is the portion of the plan that spells out what goes into the product and how it should be built. This section will vary greatly depending on the category, but it should call out the sales details of the product such as price points, discounts, margins, channels of distribution, and so forth.

For example: Gaming releases (from video games to online and mobile games) will contain a specification document that clearly states what will be developed, what a user should be able to do while utilizing the end product, and how it will work.

Player List

Provide a list of all teams and players that will be featured in the products.

This is important for making sure the developers, designers, and producers make the product(s) correctly. It informs Legal and Finance so that they can distribute the licensor and athlete royalties. Also, it guides marketing as to whom to feature on packaging, sales materials, and advertising.

FIGURE 12-2 Product brief. (*continued*)

Packaging and Design Direction

This is where you give clear direction of what you envision the finished product and product packaging look like.

You call out which logos and players should be featured on packaging and any legal rules and requirements for the design and packaging—these could be from your own company, the licensors, the athletes being featured, or even governmental regulations (depending on category).

If possible, you should also include legal lines, copy, and anything else that is important for designers to consider when developing the product.

You may also want to utilize this section to communicate the vision for the line look and other marketing materials such as ads and product sales sheets.

Marketing and PR Notes

This is where you call out marketing and PR suggestions so that Marketing, Advertising, and PR can create their plans and budgets to support the launch.

Tactical Marketing Vehicle	Tactics Used	Notes	Timing
Direct Mail			
Catalogs	X	Feature in the Spring catalog	02/14
Mailers			
Postcards			
Direct Response			
E-mail Campaign	X	Start week before Super Bowl	01/14
Online Store Feature	X	Buy 2, Get 1 free promotion for 1 hour following game	02/14
Banner Ads	X	Place with key sites week before Super Bowl	01/14
SEO Campaign	X	Key words will be expensive to buy, so going light	02/14
Social Media Campaign	X	Use all social networks to post videos	02/14
Company Fan Club	X	Offer 15% discount to club members	02/14
B2B			
Outbound Call Center	X	Provide selling notes for calls to key customers	01/14
Customer Solicitation	X	Send solicitation to customers 2 weeks prior to game	01/14
Television	X	Provide samples of final product for potential shows; final four teams Samples must be received by the customer by 01/25/13	02/14

FIGURE 12-2 Product brief. (*continued*)

Tactical Marketing Vehicle	Tactics Used	Notes	Timing
TV/Radio			
TV Spot 1	X	Utilize overall brand TV spot with product-specific callout at the end Run for 1 week prior to the game and 1 week after the game Marketing to create specific placement schedule and budget	01/14–02/14
Radio Spot 1			
Leagues/Athletes			
League/Team Websites	X	Run banner ads on league site and winning team site	01/14–02/14
Athlete Websites			
Non-TV/Radio Advertising/PR			
Trade Print Ads			
Trade Websites			
Advertising			
Press Releases	X	Prerelease during week to generate hype	01/14
Industry/Company Events			
Trade Shows	X	Booth staff to wear gear promoting product	01/14
Company Events			

Financials and P&L

This is where you highlight key financial aspects of the product, including budgets for marketing, advertising, PR, and so forth.

Also, attach a product P&L that shows the product meets the financial objectives and rules of the company.

Initial Schedule

This is where you call out the key milestones and dates for production, launch, and marketing.

FIGURE 12-2 Product brief. (*continued*)

5. POSTGAME ANALYSIS

Just as announcers break down performances after the game, it is important to review a product launch to determine what happened, why it happened, what can be done better. Try to refrain from just running off to the next product without properly reviewing and getting feedback on the current launch. This is part of the sales follow-up process that enables you to make better decisions about your products in the future. You can conduct this through customer surveys and looking at key market indicators (product sell-in and sell-through figures, product downloads, profitability and margin thresholds, etc.).

It is important to write up the postgame analysis so that you have this for future releases, sales reports, and key learning for expansion into other channels of distribution or categories.

To create a solid postgame analysis report, you can also have several key cross-functional members of the team score the team's performance over a set number of key variables, such as On-Time Product Delivery, Sales Number Achieved, Profitability, Teamwork Between Departments, Product Design, Usability, Packaging, and so forth. Whatever key success factors are important to your organization can be included for rating. Each team member scores the category on a scale of 1 to 5, with 5 being the highest score possible. This will give your product an overall internal numeric score to go along with sales figures and helps paint an overall picture of product success or failure. It also gives the cross-functional team members a feeling of ownership in the process.

The Five Fs of Sales

Much of the strategic brief is centered on how and where to sell the product. In this text, you have read about the five Ps. Jamie Kiskis uses the five Fs of sales. The major disconnect in the product development process often happens between the creative team, who are stuck in the office, and the sales team, who are out interacting with customers. Designs often happen without complete buy-in from the sales team. This can result in a product that the sales team can't or doesn't want to sell. Either way, it hinders the success of that product. To be a complete marketer you must involve every department in the process and manage your idea through the entire process. For that reason, the five Fs of sales were developed.

The five Fs of sales can help bridge the gap between sales and marketing/product development. They are as follows:

Focus: Sales teams that can focus on the needs of the customer, the marketplace, and where their product fits can be invaluable to a creative team. Companies that listen to customers, have good communication between departments, and satisfy their customers' needs are often the most successful. Part of the job of the product development team is to foster that communication. Engaging the sales team and giving them a feeling of ownership in the process encourages them to focus on the needs of the marketplace and not just the immediate sale.

Feedback: Because the sales team are on the front line, and are the company's direct link to the buyer, they are a critical step in the development process. Getting feedback from end users, customers, distributors, dealers, and others helps give direction to the creative team. It is imperative not to take everything that the customer says as gospel. You need to have confidence in your research and development.

Forecast: Understanding potential sales volumes is essential to product success. A great sales team should have the ability to predict sales volumes. This helps the product development team determine market viability, potential revenues, strength of the P&L, and how much money is available to spend on marketing and advertising efforts.

Finalize: As you get closer to the launch of the product, all details need to be finalized. The sales team should make sure that commitments to volumes that their customers have provided are still accurate.

Follow-up: Sales teams that continually follow-up with customers have the ability to stay in the loop on product performance. Also, they can determine whether the customer can use additional product, whether there are new ideas for the future, and whether any hot market product opportunities exist for the new product. During follow-up, some retailers request or require help in moving through a product. This may include markdowns, discounts, and returns. If you want to do business with the party in the future, then it is a good idea to negotiate and help that customer be successful at selling through the product. Your last option should be to take the product back via returns, as returns can disrupt cash flow and kill P&Ls.

Example Product Development Plan

Deuce Brand is a sport watch and lifestyle company based in San Diego, California. The Deuce Brand has created an interesting product extension using professional athletes. Deuce took a product that had been on the market for many years and rebranded it as a sports watch. (See **FIGURE 12-3**.) Prior to the rebranding, this rubber-coated watch had the look and feel of a very simple timepiece without many bells and whistles. Deuce recognized that the rubber coating made it ideal for wearing while engaging in sports. Much like they wear cause-related rubber bands, athletes could now wear something similar that also functioned as a watch.

The initial product launches were well received. The next product development done at Deuce was completed using a product extension strategy. Deuce recognized

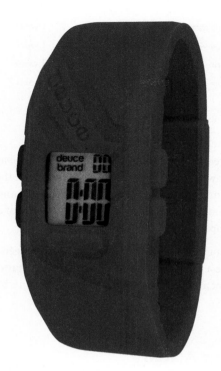

FIGURE 12-3 Deuce watch.
Courtesy of Deuce Brand.

that by using licensing and adding team logos to the watches, they could reach new demographics and distribution. They completed a licensing deal with the NBA, NBADL, WNBA, and a number of universities. The third product in the development process was the Signature Series, which featured professional athletes. Each watch was designed using logos that represented items that were important to the athlete. This customization gave customers a behind-the-scenes look at what the athlete cared about most. Each watch carried a story about the design.

The Deuce Signature Series had a very succinct time line. The company can produce a new line in only 17 weeks.[2] Here is how the time line is organized:

Contract time of completion	2 weeks
Design concept with story	1 week
Design concept to digital rendering	1 week
Digital rendering delivered for approval	1 week
Factory creates preliminary run product	5 weeks
High-resolution photography shoot	1 week

Digital strategy organized	1 week
YouTube video shot and edited	1 week
Initial pre-sell program	3 weeks
Program launch	week 17

Case Study

Mike Szala has been hired as the new brand manager for a licensed sports product company. The company wants to create a product line to reach the teen demographic. The company holds licensing rights for apparel, memorabilia, and collectibles with the NBA, NHL, NFL, and MLB. Mike has been given the task of creating this new product line for the company.

1. What new product should Mike create to attract the teen demographic?
2. Should he create a product extension or create a new product?
3. What price point and distribution method would work best for the teen demographic?

Critical Thinking Activity

Using the 11 steps in the project development brief, develop a product for a sport. Include a brief description for each of the 11 steps.

CHAPTER QUESTIONS

1. Why is it difficult for many sports-related companies to have long-term marketing plans?
2. Give an example of two companies that use a reactive product development strategy.
3. What is the importance of a solicitation sell sheet?
4. What role does sales forecasting play in product development?
5. Why is it important for a company to review each product that it launches?
6. Give an example of a successful product extension in the sports industry.
7. Why would a sales team be involved in the packaging design phase of the product development cycle?
8. Review your favorite team's website. What new products are available in the team's online store?

9. Provide an example of a hot market product. What was the event? How was it sold?

10. How was your favorite sports product created?

Notes

1. "The Slugger Story," Louisville Slugger, accessed October 6, 2014, http://www.slugger.com/story/index.html.

2. Deuce website, accessed October 6, 2014, http://www.deucebrand.com.

Chapter 13

College Athletics

CHAPTER OBJECTIVES

- Learn about college athletics.
- Review the history of college athletics.
- Identify key benefits of college athletics marketing.
- Review college athletic realignment.
- Review the SEC television deal.

CHAPTER OVERVIEW

This chapter reviews what it is like to work in the upper management of college athletics. It takes a behind-the-scenes look at the skill and strategies needed to build a successful college athletic program and analyzes how the NCAA, conference TV deals, and realignment affect universities' athletic departments.

Voices from the Field: Donna Woodruff

BIOGRAPHY

Donna (Mulhern) Woodruff serves as the Chief of Staff for the Stony Brook Department of Athletics. She manages the daily operation of the Department of Athletics and oversees several administrative units. Her purview includes Student-Athlete Development, Compliance, and Facility and Events Operations while she also supervises men's and women's basketball, men's soccer, and women's lacrosse. Recently, Donna was named a recipient of the 2011 National Association of Collegiate Women Athletic Administrators (NACWAA) Administrator of the Year for her tireless efforts with the Seawolves.

Donna arrived at Stony Brook after serving for 7 years as an athletic administrator at both Villanova University and the University of Pennsylvania. As a member of the compliance office staff, she was connected to all day-to-day operations and in charge of specific programs such as the NCAA Special Assistance Fund, the Student-Athlete Opportunity Fund, and drug testing.

Donna spent 4 years as an athletic administrator at the University of Pennsylvania. She served as the contest scheduler for all 34 intercollegiate sports while creating and monitoring contest contracts for each sport.

She earned a Bachelor of Arts in English in 1990 from the University of Pennsylvania where she earned All-America status as a field hockey player. She helped lead her team to the Final Four of the 1988 NCAA Championship and remains the only player in school history to be named to the NCAA All-Tournament team. She also was an All-Ivy and Regional All-America pick in lacrosse. She later went on to receive her Master of Science in education in 2000, also from the University of Pennsylvania.

Q&A

Q: What is your current position?

I am the Executive Associate Director of Athletics and Senior Woman Administrator for Stony Brook University's Department of Athletics.

Q: What was your career path?

My experience as a collegiate student athlete was so rewarding that I found myself gravitating to opportunities that allowed me to stay in the field of intercollegiate athletics. After graduation, I progressed into coaching when an assistant position opened up, which allowed me to work with my alma mater's field hockey and lacrosse teams. While coaching at the University of Pennsylvania, I also found myself intrigued by the organizational dynamics and infrastructure of an athletics department. I was fortunate to be given the opportunity to assume additional responsibilities within the department, and, after earning my master's degree in Higher Education Administration, I accepted a position to become the Director of Administrative Services for Athletics at Villanova University.

Q: How did you become an expert in your field?

I attribute any personal success I may have had in this field to one fact. I have been extremely fortunate to work with, and for, great people during my career. By paying attention and learning from their actions, mostly all good, but sometimes not so good, I have been able to use that knowledge to influence my own work. In addition, I have sought out opportunities where the individuals I would work with had the potential to make waves in this industry so I can learn from their outstanding successes and individual styles.

Q: Tell me about your department. Who works with you? How is it structured?

Like at many institutions, the Stony Brook Department of Athletics can be viewed in two distinct and separate ways with regard to my responsibilities: internal and external. Internally, I work very closely with our Director of Athletics and our Senior Associate Director of Athletics as we consider ourselves the senior staff. I also have direct individual oversight responsibilities for the Office of Student Athletic Development, Compliance, Facilities and Events, and four sport programs: men's basketball, women's basketball, men's soccer, and women's lacrosse. Externally, I work closely with many departments across campus such as the Sr. Vice President's office, Financial Aid, Admissions, Provost, Office of the General Counsel, and the Dean of Students. So many areas on a college campus are connected to what happens in an athletics department, and our close relationships with those offices are key to much of our success.

Q: What would you classify as the most important skill set to have to work at the senior management level?

There are three different skills that I feel are most important to have for success at the senior management level. The first skill is vision. Senior managers need to be able to see where their program or department can be years in the future, as opposed to planning just for today and tomorrow. True leadership is based on the ability to set a course for your staff members even when they cannot imagine the future. The second skill necessary for success is the ability to build strong relationships. It is essential not only to know the right people who can help you to achieve your goals but also that you devote energy to building relationships with those people so that when you do call on them, they are on your side. For example, if there is an issue with finances, it is extremely beneficial to be able to turn to a decision maker like a Vice President of

Finance for assistance; however, that is only possible if you have made a commitment to building the appropriate relationship. Lastly, the ability to appreciate the need for earning respect is also an incredibly valuable skill. It is a quality that must be earned through demonstrated integrity in all that you do and how you conduct your business. Once you can earn respect, it is also much easier to build those solid relationships that are essential to achieving the goals you have set as part of the vision for your department!

Q: What has been your greatest accomplishment in this industry?

In the world of intercollegiate athletics, I was both a coach and an administrator, so I have a few different accomplishments that come to mind. In terms of coaching, I am proud that I was able to positively influence young people both on and off the field. Knowing that some of the lessons I taught, some of the relationships I built, and some of the knowledge I was able to share helped to prepare a former player for life after college is very satisfying. I am extremely humbled by any of my former student athletes who in even a small way feel that something I did or said positively influenced a part of their life. In terms of being an administrator, my greatest accomplishments revolve around the work we have done at Stony Brook. I am honored and proud to have been a part of a team that has rebuilt and shaped this athletic department.

Q: What has been your favorite moment working with student athletes?

There is never just one favorite moment in athletics when you work with hundreds of athletes and staff members every year. That said, most of my favorite moments revolve around watching our student athletes progress during their time in our program. Being able to see their hard work put into the classroom and on the field or court pay off is a great feeling. It is all about seeing a student athlete put in the time in the weight room and at practice, then come off the bench and score a game-winning goal or even their first goal ever or to see an athlete who might have struggled in the classroom, but then see them walk across the stage at graduation to receive their diploma. When all of their efforts finally "click," that is a moment that is truly special.

Q: What is the most exciting thing about the field of college sports?

Competition! This industry thrives on competition. It could be the competition of beating a conference rival or the everyday competition such as fighting for space in the newspaper and meeting annual fund goals. It could be competing to hire the best coach possible for one of our programs or helping a coach to land an important recruit. The excitement of competition is what I find the most exciting part of being involved in college athletics every day.

Q: What advice do you have for students interested in collegiate athletics?

My advice is to get involved as early and as often as possible in any capacity. You cannot be hesitant to volunteer for an athletic event or hand out marketing materials or file reports. You must get involved and be willing to roll up your sleeves and get the job done, no matter what that job is. You never know who will take notice and who will have the ability to help influence the next steps in your career. But if you aren't willing to get involved early and often, you will have much less of a chance in this field because so many people think the world of intercollegiate athletics is "fun." While that is true that athletics can be fun, appreciating that success in this field requires dedication and hard work is a much better recipe for success. Also, make sure to ask questions and do your homework to find out everything you can about the areas in which you work. Finally, make connections and get noticed. Like all careers, who you know is very important and could help open the right door for you as you move forward.

Courtesy of Donna Woodruff

Introduction

College athletics are viewed as the front porch to most institutions. Colleges and universities can advertise their brand and mission based on their amount of airtime, conference wins, and national championships. The Department of Education reported that in 2010, Penn State athletics generated $73 million from ticket sales, merchandise, and sponsorships. In addition, non–student athletes take college sports seriously. Of the 600 students who participate in Duke University's study abroad program, only 100 sign up for the spring semester, citing Duke basketball as a reason for not wanting to travel.[1] Former University of Michigan President James J. Duderstadt put it best when he stated, "Nine of 10 people don't understand what you are saying when you talk about research universities. But you say 'Michigan' and they understand those striped helmets running under the banner."

The National Collegiate Athletic Association (NCAA) acts as the governing body for 89 sports in three divisions. It is made up of three membership classifications known as Divisions I, II, and III. Division I schools offer numerous teams and athletic scholarships. Division II schools have fewer of both, and Division III schools do not offer athletic scholarships. This hierarchy helps keep competitive balance among schools. Each division has its own rules in terms of "governing personnel, amateurism, recruiting, eligibility, benefits, financial aid, and playing and practice seasons—consistent with the overall governing principles of the Association." Although Division I sports receive more television deals, sponsorships, and even their own networks, the other two divisions still have some of their championships shown on channels such as ESPN2 and streamed on ESPN3. Other governing bodies include the

National Junior College Athletic Association (NJCAA). This association is responsible for governing 2-year college and community college athletics. NJCAA events are rarely televised unless on a locally or regionally operated network.

History of College Athletics

Before 1850, intercollegiate sports were insignificant. Groups of young collegians played an early form of football, and these games became quite vicious, with physical hazing of incoming freshmen by the sophomore class. In an effort to curb these violent traditions, college officials created intramural sports. Early on, professors feared that intramurals would cause serious scholarly distraction.

The world of college athletics began to take shape in 1852 when the first intercollegiate crew regatta between Harvard and Yale took place. This opened the door to many other firsts, such as the first intercollegiate baseball game (1859), football game (1872), track-and-field meet (1875), tennis match (1883), ice hockey game (1895), and gymnastics competition (1899).

In 1904, colleges and universities realized how promising athletics could be for their institutions. Harvard constructed one of the first known athletic venues for football. Yale followed suit in 1914, constructing a stadium to seat more than 70,000 people. Schools in the Midwest wanted to replicate what was occurring on the eastern seaboard. In the mid-nineteenth century, universities in the Midwest formed the Western Conference. (This conference is known as the Big Twelve Conference today.)

By the 1920s, college athletics had turned to chaos. There was no regulation in terms of recruiting and compensating student athletes. The Carnegie Foundation for the Advancement of Teaching released a report in 1929 stating, "Meaningful reform in American collegiate sports could take place only if campus presidents replaced the 'downtown crowd,' comprising a city's businessmen, alumni boosters, and commercial interests, as the source of leadership and responsibility."[2]

Despite its creation in 1906, it was not until World War II that the NCAA took control of the ever-growing chaos. The NCAA instituted the "sanity code," which established guidelines for recruiting and financial aid. Even with the rules in place, colleges and universities paid little attention to them. In 1951, the NCAA named Walter Byers the organization's Executive Director and established Kansas City, Missouri, as the national headquarters in 1952. Byers quickly took control of which games were to be televised and passed legislation governing postseason football bowl games.

As the college athletic scene continued to grow, the NCAA recognized the need to create different divisions to even the playing fields. In 1973, the association divided its membership into three legislative and competitive divisions (I, II, and III). In 1978, Division I football programs were further divided into subdivisions known as I-A and I-AA, better known now as the Football Bowl Subdivision (FBS) and Football Championship Subdivision (FCS).

The 1980s were plagued with many serious and high-profile rule violation cases. Academic standards began to be questioned. In 1984, the NCAA lost its regular-season football television rights when the U.S. Supreme Court found the group guilty of antitrust issues. The 1980s did, however, introduce women's athletics to all three of the governing levels. Nineteen events for women were added, many of them Division I and National Collegiate Championships. Despite the ups and downs, the NCAA has steadily asserted dominance and control over college and university sports. Schools and coaches have sometimes chafed under its control. But the NCAA rules on amateurism and reimbursement have been a huge boon to university general funds.

Recently, a legal challenge to decades-old policies on athlete reimbursement has arisen. The NCAA rules can be summarized as follows: "College athletes are amateurs, and ineligible for any form of compensation." More specifically, the following rules are taken from the NCAA website:

> An individual loses amateur status and thus shall not be eligible for competition in a particular sport if the individual:

Uses his or her athletic skill (directly or indirectly) for pay in any form in that sport (unless expressly permitted under NCAA or Ivy League rules).

Accepts a promise of pay even if such pay is to be received following completion of intercollegiate athletics participation.

Signs a contract or commitment of any kind to play professional athletics, regardless of its legal enforceability or any consideration received.

Receives, directly or indirectly, a salary, reimbursement of expenses, or any other form of financial assistance from a professional sports organization.

Competes on any professional athletics team even if no pay or remuneration for expenses was received.

Subsequent to initial full-time college enrollment, enters into a professional draft.

Enters into an agreement with an agent.

These rules may sound familiar because they echo policies long held by the International Olympic Committee. The IOC spent decades gradually losing the battle against professionalism in sports. In the face of flagrant cheating and defiance, the IOC finally allowed professional athletes to compete after the 1988 Olympics.

The NCAA may be forced to follow the example of the IOC. In 2009, former UCLA basketball player Ed O'Bannon filed suit against the NCAA for using his likeness without compensation. Other players joined, and *O'Bannon v. NCAA* may now attain class action status. The risk to the NCAA and member institutions is substantial. O'Bannon and many others could be entitled to compensation from past advertising in broadcast, print ads, and video games. Potentially, athletes might negotiate their own endorsement deals, just like the pros do. The entire landscape of college sports marketing could be revolutionized with one legal decision.

The subject of amateur athletics has also been brought to the forefront by Northwestern University's football team. The team is discussing the possibility of unionizing so that players can be recognized as employees rather than as student athletes. With the amount of time they put into the football program outside of games, it's understandable how the players could make such a request. The amount of money generated by the program also makes it attractive for players to create a union. How this will play out remains to be seen. If they are successful, it may lead to other programs unionizing and changing the entire landscape of the NCAA.

How the Five Ps Affect College Athletics

PRODUCT The product is everything involved with being a student athlete, including grades, test scores, and academic standards that must be met. Also, the product is dealing with the big business of running a college athletics program, including sponsorship, NCAA regulation, and promotion of the school's brand.

PRICE Price takes many forms in college athletics. On one level there is the price of tickets to various events. On a different level there are TV network deals and sponsorships.

PROMOTION Just like professional sports teams, the schools are trying to promote their brand. A strong brand could lead to increased attendance, higher ticket prices, additional sponsorships revenue, and an increase in the sale of licensed goods.

PLACE For most universities, the place decision is pretty clear. The campus holds most marketing opportunities. For the most popular universities, the place decisions may be national and even worldwide. The brands of the most popular schools are often as strong and far-reaching as a major professional brand is.

PROGRESS The collegiate landscape is an extremely volatile business atmosphere. Progress is being made with the distribution of wealth at the college level. Changes are being discussed in regard to paying athletes, the rights and revenue distribution of licensed goods, and television networks being formed around conferences and even teams.

Key Components of College Athletics Marketing

College athletics marketing is very similar to any sports company trying to market its products. Schools are trying to build brands and create fan loyalty to maximize revenues.

Branding: When it comes to developing a brand, collegiate athletic departments aren't much different from how companies such as Nike and Oakley are. All are trying to build a loyal following for their product. Universities can do this in many ways. It might be as simple as having a cool uniform that fans would like to wear. The University of Oregon leads the way in this category. It has picked up many fans who love the groundbreaking designs by Nike that the university's sports teams wear. These are fans who might otherwise never follow the Ducks. Another way to build a loyal following might be deciding to hire a coach who runs a high-scoring offensive scheme. Creating a brand around the excitement that offensive stats generate can attract fans from all over the nation and lead to increased ticket and licensed goods sales. Branding on the collegiate level goes far beyond creating a cool logo, and, if successful, it reaches far beyond the school's alumni base.

Target demographic: In 2011, more than 4.4 million people watched Southeastern Conference (SEC) football, according to Nielsen ratings. And 16.7 million people watched the SEC, Big Ten Conference, Atlantic Coast Conference (ACC), Big 12 Conference, Pacific-12 Conference, and Big East Conference football. Among adult college football fans, 61% are males and 39% are females. In terms of age breakdown, college football reaches 12% of 18- to 24-year-olds, 18% of 25- to 34-year-olds, 19% of 35- to 44-year-olds, 20% of 45- to 54-year-olds, 16% of 55- to 64-year-olds, and 16% of people 65 years and older.[3] Nielsen also reported that 61% have an annual household income of $50,000 or more, while 42% claim income of $75,000 or more, and 25% make $100,000 plus. Of viewers, 32% are college graduates and 61% are married. These target demographics are extremely valuable when colleges are aligning sponsorship deals and television rights.

COMMUNITY OUTREACH

Many colleges and universities have community outreach programs. These programs allow athletes to work with their community's youth and people who are injured, disabled, sick, or elderly. The NCAA created the Student-Athlete Advisory Committee (SAAC), a committee of student athletes who represent each sport at their institution. They serve as liaisons linking student-athlete concerns with their school's administration. Along with major community service projects, the student members are called upon to provide input to improve the welfare of student athletes on campus.

MARKETING

One of the key components of college athletics is marketing. Programs can market directly and indirectly. Indirect marketing is easier for bigger Division I schools than it is at the Division II or III level.

Direct marketing for schools involves ticket sales, promotions, advertising, and alumni support. Fliers, banners, and flags placed in local businesses and throughout the community are forms of traditional marketing. Social media and athletics websites are forms of nontraditional marketing. Stony Brook unveiled a nontraditional marketing strategy to promote its senior running back for the Walter Payton award, which is given to the outstanding player in the Football Championship Subdivision. Stony Brook created a unique website so that viewers could see highlights of the running back as well as statistics and quotes. The university also introduced a Twitter handle for the player that the university managed (@Maysonet4Payton), and it utilized a Twitter hashtag to help the player trend (#Maysonet4Payton).

Indirect marketing for university programs includes, but is not limited to, local and national media coverage. ESPN's Top 10 segment allows for prime coverage, which is played every hour for that given day on one of the ESPN or ESPN2 channels. Also, Cinderella stories produce indirect marketing opportunities for universities. Virginia Commonwealth University, Butler University, and George Mason University received a lot of coverage during deep runs into the NCAA Division I basketball tournaments. These unexpected successes put the universities front and center in almost all sports media coverage.

To reap the marketing benefits of their athletic ability, athletes are given the choice to declare themselves as professionals, or they can remain as amateurs to maintain their collegiate eligibility. The 2012 Olympics made this decision quite difficult for 17-year-old USA swimmer Missy Franklin. Franklin secured her spot in the Olympics record books with her performance in London. Afterward, she faced the decision of remaining amateur or turning professional with lucrative endorsements.

President of Navigate Research, AJ Maestas, believes Franklin is not the typical Olympic swimmer who medals. The average medalists can earn between $300,000 and $400,000 in endorsements per year.[4] Maestas expects Franklin to be able to generate "$1 million to $2 million dollars per year over the next five years through endorsements. Because she is so young, she will be very relevant at the Rio Olympics in 2016." On October 20, 2012, the five-time Olympic medalist made her decision. In August of 2013, Missy Franklin declared to uphold her amateur status and enrolled at the University of California, Berkeley.[5] Cal Berkeley will be able to market its program as home to a five-time Olympic swimmer, and Franklin will be unable to receive any benefits in order to keep her NCAA eligibility.

TOURNAMENT SEASON

Much like professional sports, colleges and universities can earn more money when their teams advance in the NCAA tournaments. Institutions do not reap all the funding as the money is shared among the member universities of the institution's conference. This plays out nicely for schools in major conferences such as the Southeastern Conference. The 2012 BCS Championship game was played between two SEC schools, University of Alabama and Louisiana State University. It is reported that LSU was able to generate $22.3 million, while Alabama secured $6.1 million.[6]

Also bringing in huge revenue is the March Madness Men's Basketball Tournament. Second only to the Super Bowl in terms of ad sales, the NCAA men's basketball tournament is big business.[7] Research firm Kantar Media reports that "a thirty-second commercial during one of the last two rounds of the tournament costs around $1.2 million, far more than a $440,000 spot during the World Series, and more than three times the cost of an ad during the NBA championship." In addition, this ad revenue equates to a new long-term deal for the NCAA March Madness Men's Basketball Tournament and CBS/Turner Broadcasting System. This 14-year deal inked for $10.8 billion, which is roughly $771 million a year.[8]

JOBS

There are many job opportunities in college athletics. The bigger the program a university or college has, the more positions will be available. Smaller schools enable individuals to take part in many aspects of the program rather than being more focused on one specific task. At a Division II or III school, an individual working in the development office may be asked to focus on the annual fund as well as major gifts and special events. In a larger Division I school, such as one in the ACC or SEC, that one position would be broken up into three positions, allowing one person to focus on the annual fund, one to direct attention to major gift prospects, and another to plan all the special events for the department. Besides coaching, sports jobs include marketing/promotions, communications, compliance, administration, sponsorships, ticket sales, academic support, event management, facility management, guest services, video services, sports information, and development and external relations. One of the best places to find jobs available in NCAA-compliant schools is the NCAA market website.

FINANCES

Sports fans assume that athletics must be a financial windfall for universities. Just look at those stadiums full of fans! What are the data? How much money do schools really make from sports programs? To answer these questions, direct income, costs, and indirect benefits must be considered.

USA Today published a study covering the years 2006 to 2011 that detailed the budgets of all public Division I schools. The study examined the costs of sports programs. A breakdown of the numbers showed the different revenue categories of ticket sales, student fees, school funds, contributions, rights/licensing, and other revenue, including game guarantees, media rights, concessions, and more. Expenses included scholarships, coaching staff, building/grounds, medical expenses, travel, equipment, spirit groups, and more.

The University of Texas is the highest-grossing school, taking in a little more than $150 million in 2010–2011, the most recent year for which public schools' filings with the NCAA are available. The outlay for football and 19 other varsity sports was $133.7 million. Texas's program is one in Division I that operates in the black—it generated enough revenue to cover athletics expenses.[9] The bottom three included Coppin State University ($3.4 million), Mississippi Valley State ($4.1 million), and University of North Carolina, Asheville ($4.6 million).[10]

In Division I, 22 out of 346 schools run profitable sports programs. Not very impressive. But what about indirect benefits to the schools? Many believe that football wins translate into increased alumni pride and donations. The evidence is mostly anecdotal, but a recent paper by University of California Professor Michael Anderson applied statistical analysis to this problem. His conclusion was that every unexpected football win yielded $134,000 in added alumni donations.[11] More wins also correlate with higher numbers of freshman applications and even slightly improved SAT scores of applicants!

One might ask, "How much did the Sociology department bring in?" Maybe athletics should not be expected to be profitable. Perhaps the value of sports is simply as part of the overall college experience. Here's an interesting footnote. *USA Today* published an article on the finances of college sports. "Spelman College—a historically black women's college in Atlanta with a far-from-big-time NCAA athletics program—announced how it plans to return to the old model. The school said it would use the nearly $1 million that had been dedicated to its intercollegiate sports program, serving just 4 percent of students, for a campus-wide health and fitness program benefiting all 2,100."

The unique financial nature of college sports makes sports marketing in this area a little different. Professional teams market to a population whose only connection to the team is geographical—most fans connect with their local professional franchises. Marketing income is from ticket sales, parking and food, and merchandise sales. College sports are different. A major marketing target is alumni. Graduates may live anywhere but still follow their school's sports fortunes. Alumni are targeted not only for ticket and merchandise sales but especially for big, tax-deductible donations. The most affluent alumni are generally older, so traditional media are more important than social media. The mix of advertisers may also change. Financial planners and vacation cruise companies may appeal to the older alumni demographic.

College Conference Realignment

The name of the Big East Conference would lead one to believe that the teams aligned with that conference are from the East. Many conference realignments were supposed to begin in 2013. The Big East was to feature football teams from the University of Houston, St. Mary's University (SMU), University of Central Florida (UCF), University of Memphis, Boise State University, and San Diego State University (SDSU). Houston and SMU are located in the South, as is UCF. Boise State is located in the Northwest, and SDSU is as far west as you can get. The conference's former interim commissioner explained that having a conference that extends four time zones in major markets warrants a name change.[12] Why would teams from the West want to become a partner in a conference predominately in the East? The costs of transportation for 75 or more athletes, coaches, and training staff members to bounce from coast to coast can strain an athletic program's annual fund. Most of the realignments didn't happen.

At the time of talks, the commissioner of the Big East Conference Mike Aresco believed a new media deal was in order. He disclosed that the conference was negotiating with ESPN, but other networks had also expressed a lot of interest.[13] If the Big East signs with ESPN, one would be able to better piece together why institutions across four major time zones would want to align. In April 2011, the former Big East commissioner John Marinatto recommended the conference sign a media deal with ESPN worth $1.17 billion. This deal would average out to $130 million annually, allowing full members of the Big East to earn $13.8 million a year and allowing non-football schools such as Boise State and San Diego State to earn $2.43 million a year.[14] The Big East plan was to create a conference with handpicked schools that would rival other current Bowl Championship schools such as those included in the Pacific-12 Conference, Big Ten Conference, Southeastern Conference (SEC), and Atlantic Coast Conference (ACC). These four conferences have "media rights deals worth between $18 million and $21 million annually per school." With money like that on the table, the Big East will continue to shop around for media rights deals.

SEC Television Deal

In 2008, the Southeastern Conference announced a historic television package with CBS and ESPN to run from 2009 to 2024. The deal with ESPN was reportedly worth more than $2 billion.[15] This package was to provide unprecedented exposure for the conference to ensure that SEC fans across the nation would have access to their teams. Some of the package highlights included the coverage of the CBS national game of the week for SEC football, including the SEC Championship Game, televised coverage of every SEC home football game (with 20 games on ESPN or ESPN2 and 13 on ESPNU), every SEC basketball game, SEC men's basketball tournament semifinals and finals, 16 SEC women's basketball games, and SEC championship games in baseball, softball, and gymnastics, and ESPNU was to cover 25 additional SEC regular-season events.[16]

The original 15-year deal between ESPN and the SEC granted ESPN all the rights that CBS didn't take as a way to prevent the SEC from starting its own network. During the early part of the 2012 summer, the SEC began reconstructing its media deal with its original partners. The SEC wanted to increase its rights fee as well as create its own conference channel, which could be ready for production in time for the 2014 football season. The conference began looking into a network deal as the conference expansion welcomed Texas A&M and Missouri. As a result of the expansion, the SEC triggered the clause in its contract that enables it to reconstruct a deal with CBS and ESPN. Precedent had been set on this matter as the Atlantic Coast Conference (ACC) renegotiated its media contract with ESPN after it expanded with the addition of Pittsburgh and Syracuse. If the SEC is able to renegotiate its deal with ESPN, it could be worth a reported $150 million per year over the course of 15 years.[17]

SEC was the pioneer in establishing television rights. Since its initial groundbreaking deal, other conferences have taken notice and have been able to exert more leverage with their television networks. The Big Ten established a deal with Fox Network in which the conference is 49% owner of the Big Ten Network and can have a share of the revenue. The Pac-12 conference set up a deal in which it owns all of its regional networks. The University of Texas, on the other hand, broke ties with its conference and created its own network and then sold the rights to ESPN, and ESPN now owns the Longhorn network.

Case Study

Adam Greene, the NCAA compliance officer at a university, noticed something while doing his annual review. The need-based scholarships offered to members of the school's football team exceeded the limits set by the football conference. The scholarships were instead in compliance with the limits set for the general student body of the university. The team just finished the season with an undefeated record and received an offer to participate in a bowl game. The violation of NCAA rules would result in sanctions against the university. Self-reporting the infraction and declining the bowl bid may lead to no other sanctions by the NCAA. But being caught by the NCAA without reporting the problem could result in the loss of scholarships and a potential future bowl ban.

1. If you were Adam, what would you do?
2. Is it fair to the current team to be penalized when they did nothing wrong?
3. Would you take the chance of not reporting the infraction because it was an honest mistake and not a deliberate violation?
4. Would you take a risk and report after the bowl game?

Critical Thinking Activity

As colleges and universities begin to capitalize on their athletes' talent through television deals and conference realignment, many argue that college athletes should be paid for their abilities. Develop a plan to pay collegiate athletes.

Discussion points should include equity between schools and equity between sports. It's easy to say athletes should be paid but difficult to determine how.

CHAPTER QUESTIONS

1. What is the difference between the divisions in the NCAA?
2. What is NJCAA? Do any of those schools currently have successful sports marketing campaigns?
3. Explain why the NCAA was created.
4. Given the demographics of the college athletic viewing audience, which companies do you think should advertise in this market?
5. Should collegiate athletes be able to unionize?
6. Are college athletes being exploited? Use examples from the chapter to support your decision.
7. Should institutions switch conferences because of potential media rights deals they could benefit from? Provide evidence to back your opinion.
8. How does your school market its sports teams?
9. Go online to your favorite collegiate team's website and determine whether there is a new yearly theme for the marketing effort or whether the school uses the same theme each year.
10. How are your school's teams raising funds for the athletic department?

Notes

1. Laura Pappano, "How Big-Time Sports Ate College Life," *New York Times* January 20, 2012, http://www.nytimes.com/2012/01/22/education/edlife/how-big-time-sports-ate-college-life.html?pagewanted=all&_r=0.
2. Howard Savage, Harold Bentley, John McGovern, and Dean Smiley, *American College Sports* (New York: Carnegie Foundation for the Advancement of Teaching, 1929).
3. "College Football Facts and Figures: Attendance, Viewership Keep Going Up." *Hootens*, March 23, 2011, http://www.hootens.com/college-football-facts-figures-attendance-viewership-keep-going-up_335_a.aspx.
4. Alicia Jessop, "College or Pro: Missy Franklin May Miss Out on Big Endorsement Dollars by Competing at the Collegiate Level," *Forbes*, August 3, 2012,

http://www.forbes.com/sites/aliciajessop/2012/08/03/college-or-pro-missy-franklin-may-miss-out-on-big-endorsement-dollars-by-competing-at-the-collegiate-level/.

5. Cheryl Preheim, "Missy Franklin Will Swim at Cal for Olympic Coach," *USA Today*, October 21, 2012, http://archive.wbir.com/news/article/239033/16/Missy-Franklin-will-swim-at-Cal-for-Olympic-coach.

6. Chris Greenberg and Chris Spurlock, "Bowl Game Payouts Map: Money Earned in 2011–2012 BCS and Other Football Bowls," *Huffington Post*, December 29, 2012, http://www.huffingtonpost.com/2011/12/29/bowl-game-payouts-map-2011-2012-bcs_n_1174808.html?.

7. Sarah Morgan, "10 Things NCAA Basketball Won't Tell You," *Smart Money*, March 25, 2013, http://www.marketwatch.com/story/10-things-ncaa-basketball-wont-tell-you-2013-03-22.

8. Brad Wolverton, "NCAA Agrees to $10.8-Billion Deal to Broadcast Its Men's Basketball Tournament," *Chronicle of Higher Education*, April 22, 2010, http://chronicle.com/article/NCAA-Signs-108-Billion-De/65219/.

9. Steve Wieberg, Jodi Upton, and Steve Berkowitz, "Texas Athletics Overwhelm Rivals in Revenue and Spending," *USA Today*, May 15, 2012, http://usatoday30.usatoday.com/sports/college/story/2012-05-15/texas-athletics-spending-revenue/54960210/1.

10. Brent Jones, ed., "USA TODAY Sports' College Athletics Finances," *USA Today Sports*, accessed October 6, 2014, http://usatoday30.usatoday.com/sports/college/story/2012-05-14/ncaa-college-athletics-finances-database/54955804/1.

11. Linda Gorman, "The Benefits of College Athletic Success," The National Bureau of Economic Research, accessed November 25, 2014, http://www.nber.org/digest/nov12/w18196.html.

12. Curtis Eichelberger, "Big East Conference Considers Name Change After Adding Schools," *BusinessWeek*, September 6, 2012, http://www.businessweek.com/news/2012-09-06/big-east-conference-considers-name-change-after-adding-schools.

13. Brian Hamilton, "Big East Commish Aresco Talks TV Deal, Bowls, Future," *Chicago Tribune*, October 5, 2012, http://articles.chicagotribune.com/2012-10-05/sports/chi-big-east-commish-aresco-talks-tv-deal-bowls-future-20121005_1_aresco-big-east-basketball-schools.

14. Brett McMurphy, "Big East Shopping for New TV Deal," *ESPN*, October 26, 2012, http://espn.go.com/college-football/story/_/id/8554125/big-east-negotiate-networks-other-espn-new-tv-deal-according-sources.

15. Associated Press, "ESPN Signs 15-Year Deal with SEC," *ESPN*, August 25, 2008, http://sports.espn.go.com/ncaa/news/story?id=3553033.

16. "New Television Agreements for the SEC and UF to Begin in 2009–10," Florida Athletics, September 8, 2008, http://www.gatorzone.com/story.php?id=14419.

17. John Ourand and Michael Smith, "SEC Media Talks Revolve Around Possible Cable Channel—Again," *Sports Business Journal*, May 21, 2012, http://m.sportsbusinessdaily.com/Journal/Issues/2012/05/21/Media/SEC.aspx.

Chapter 14

Controversial Issues in Sports Marketing

CHAPTER OBJECTIVES

- Review the most controversial issues in sports.
- Examine which issues the experts face in their careers.
- Learn how the experts deal with controversial issues.
- Understand marketing responses to controversy.

CHAPTER OVERVIEW

In this chapter, experts give their opinions on the most controversial issues in sports. Because each expert works in a different niche of the industry, you will read about a variety of issues that affect the business of sports marketing on a daily basis. Even though the executives featured in this text are some of the most accomplished people in their field, they still have to deal with difficult situations and navigate turbulent waters. The field of sports marketing is one of the fastest changing of any industry in the world. It is filled with passionate fans and incredibly skilled employees, often with huge egos. This combination makes the development of controversy almost inevitable.

Advertising

I have been paying particular attention to the 2009 Federal Trade Commission "Guides Concerning Use of Endorsements and Testimonials in Advertising." The guidelines influence what my athletes can and cannot say regarding products and companies that they endorse. Whenever they are discussing a product that they endorse, they must make it clear that they are getting paid by that company. If they don't, they leave themselves open for fines from the FTC. This may seem easy, but in today's world of interviews and social media, even a quick mention of a product could get them in hot water. Think about the possibilities. Could hitting the like button on Facebook for a product that they endorse put an athlete at risk from the FTC? The examples are endless, which is why choosing the right partners and athlete education is so important.

Courtesy of Bill Sanders.

As an athlete marketer, Bill Sanders has many responsibilities. When it comes to creating endorsement opportunities, his clients depend on him to develop a portfolio with which they can maximize profits and truly get behind a company's brand. They also depend on him to understand issues such as FTC rulings. The ruling Bill mentions stipulates a set of guidelines intended to ensure the disclosure of the endorsement relationship between an athlete and a company.

Say, for example, that one of Bill's NBA clients appears on ESPN, and the announcer comments on how much muscle the athlete has gained since last season. If the player mentions that he's done it with the help of a specific protein supplement, but he fails to mention that he is a paid endorser of that product, the FTC could hold him liable. If that same player then Tweets that he was just on ESPN talking about how great that particular product is and again fails to mention that he is getting paid by that company, he could be in violation of the ruling.

Former Major League Baseball player Steve Garvey was part of a case that pitted him against the FTC for a weight loss product that he endorsed. The FTC received many complaints about the ineffectiveness of the product and decided to bring charges against the company and Garvey. The 1980 FTC guidelines stated that "an endorsement may not contain any representations that would be deceptive, or could not be substantiated if made directly by an advertiser." The FTC argued that because Garvey was an endorser of the product, he was liable for the material misrepresentations. Garvey was able to escape prosecution because he did actually lose weight by using the product. The court ruled that because it was his belief that the product worked and he substantiated those beliefs by actually using the product he was not liable.

The 2009 version of the FTC guidelines takes the rules even further. It is now not enough for athletes just to say that a product works for them. It is their duty to do the due diligence to determine whether the advertising claims are deceptive and whether the product will work for the general public as well. Closing this loophole puts direct responsibility on an advertising agency and an athlete to make sure that product claims are not false or misleading.

In the FTC rules, the responsibility starts with the advertising agency. It must inform the athlete that he or she must make it clear that there is an endorsement in place whenever the product is discussed. Once that fact is established, then it is the responsibility of the celebrity to comply with the rule.[1]

Another interesting point in the 2009 guidelines is that they also apply to bloggers. Online writers touting products in which they have a material connection must make that connection clear. It would seem almost impossible to monitor all of the blogs online, but the regulations are in place. Athlete marketers don't expect the FTC to suddenly start cracking down every time an athlete mentions a product and forgets to state the endorsement connection. But which marketer wants to be the one who failed to educate a client when the FTC does begin to strictly enforce the guidelines?

Rule 40 Olympics

Rule 40 of the Olympic Charter limits athletes competing in the Olympic Games from appearing in advertising for non-Olympic sponsors around the Olympic Games. This helps prevent ambush marketing that might otherwise utilize athletes to create an association with the Games.[2]

> Given the growth of social media, Rule 40 has increased the divide between the haves and the have-nots when it comes to athletes. It creates an enormous competitive advantage for those athletes who have personal sponsorship deals with the official Olympic sponsors by preventing athletes who have non-Olympic sponsors from promoting those relationships before, during, and after the Olympics. It is a regressive rule that fiscally punishes second- and third-tier athletes, or athletes of lesser known sports, by eliminating their ability to market themselves and their sponsors. Athletes voiced their displeasure in London and I expect the resentment to escalate heading into Sochi and Brazil. It is a parallel to the growing divide between the 1% and the other 99% in our economy.
>
> Courtesy of Zack Sugarman.

The rationale for Rule 40 goes back to the amateur roots of the Olympic movement. The rule ensured that athletes maintained their amateur status. International Olympic Committee (IOC) policy has changed, and in the majority of sports professional athletes now compete. However, to protect against ambush marketing, to prevent unauthorized commercialization of the Games, and to protect the integrity of athletes' performance at the Games, the IOC places certain limits on how participants' images can be exploited during the Games period. Ambush marketers have, in the past, used their association with athletes and National Governing Bodies (NGBs) to suggest or imply that they have an association with the Olympic Games. This undermines the exclusivity that Organizing Committees and/or National Olympic Committees (NOCs) can offer official Games and team sponsors, without whose investment the Games could not happen. An implied association with the Games through use of athletes is particularly powerful during and immediately before the Games. Rule 40 protects the sponsors and the IOC but at the expense of some athletes. Is Rule 40 fair to Olympic athletes? There are strong debates on both sides of this subject.

Off-Field Issues

You may have noticed that off-field issues have surfaced numerous times throughout this text. Whereas the brands of many professional leagues are strong and hugely popular, the real appeal lies with the players who make up the teams. Those players are human beings who sometimes make mistakes. Because of their high-profile jobs even the smallest mistakes are magnified in the media.

At Upper Deck, we used the phrase "You don't own your own equity" to describe this situation. Although the company spent hundreds of millions of dollars building a brand and creating world-class products, both were dependent on athletes. Upper Deck borrowed the athletes' images and likenesses to help its products succeed. Of course, Upper Deck paid the athletes, but it had no control over how the athletes lived their lives.

My most difficult situation happened when a recently signed high-profile NFL client was arrested in a hotel room in what the media likes to describe as a compromising position. The good news was that Upper Deck had a morals clause in the contract that allowed the company to cancel its contract with that athlete. The bad news was that the company had just finished a major autograph signing with the athlete. We had a substantial investment in inventory of jerseys, photos, balls, and helmets signed by an athlete who just lost his fan base by receiving significant negative publicity. The company had to cut its losses and move the inventory at any price to recover some of the costs. Thus the importance of including a morals clause in every contract. It works like an insurance policy. The morals clause won't prevent problems, but it will limit losses for the sponsor when a PR disaster occurs.

> In your sports marketing career, you will likely have to handle client mistakes. Imagine that you have committed extensive time and money to create a sophisticated campaign. Then the athlete destroys their own credibility in just five minutes. Now you find out what you are made of as a sports product developer, marketer, manager, agent, etc. The historic list of athlete mistakes is long. It includes saying something stupid "on the record," getting caught driving while intoxicated, murder, running a dog fighting ring, or molesting children. While not an athlete mistake, a career-ending injury will also be devastating to your campaign.

Know that things can and will go wrong with your athlete clients, their families, and teams. Plan for the occasional disaster by protecting yourself and your company. Until you have experience with contracts, get sound legal advice in writing them. Paying lawyers is pretty annoying. But when the chips are down, those legal fees could be the best investment you ever made.

In my experience, included in the starting line-up for your game plan has to be a well-written contract. You need one that gives you the ability to easily (meaning without any penalties to your business) and immediately (meaning like NOW!) terminate the endorser for serious brushes with the law. Remember, it's not baseball with "3 strikes and you're out." One bad strike can take down your business plans and possibly lead to your job being lost. Having a good contract lets you take the next steps, knowing that if things continue to get worse for your endorser, you can always make the decision to make it stop.

Crisis plans are like a 2-minute drill with your backs to the goal in football. You don't have much time to make decisions, and you will need exceptional teamwork to get out of trouble.

Here are 10 steps that will help lead the way:

1. Get as much information as you can on the situation, including the name of the source and their representation. This will probably include contacting the athlete's agent or representative to try and get the real story.
2. Monitor public opinion and stay close to PR throughout the process of creating your plan. Your company's official comment may be necessary before you want it to be.
3. Consult legal to discuss contractual options and possible outcomes for the individual's situation. You want to protect the client. But first you must consider your own liability.
4. Project the worst-case scenarios for the situation now and in the future as more details emerge. The public has a short memory for most things. Rather than terminate a client, maybe just go dark for a few weeks or months.
5. Determine how the situation will resonate with the core values and messages of your company.
6. Find out where your current plans and products are in the development process.
7. What are costs, deadlines, and alternatives available to make adjustments to those plans?
8. Get feedback from your customers and gauge interest in possible alternatives.
9. Finalize options, present them internally, make recommendations, and get approvals.

10. Notify the individual of your plans and then make public statements as necessary through PR.

Courtesy of Jamie Kiskis

Performance-Enhancing Drugs

Performance-enhancing drugs (PEDs) seem to have been around as long as sports themselves. Before the era of skilled testing, most doping issues lived in the form of rumors with little proof to back up the accusations. Many Olympic Games have been shrouded in accusations that German swimmers or Russian weightlifters were "on the juice." As testing started to catch up with illegal drug manufacturing, it became a little easier to catch athletes cheating at their sport. Sports such as baseball, American football, and cycling have had numerous controversies regarding PEDs.

The issue goes beyond simply improving testing methods. Athletes and their unions must agree with their leagues to allow testing. The leagues themselves must want to "clean up" their sport. Although this seems like an obvious thing for both groups to agree on, it never is. Some leagues have turned a blind eye toward PEDs because, frankly, stronger athletes make for more exciting games. Nobody in baseball in the late 1990s seemed too concerned when Sammy Sosa and Mark McGuire were hitting home runs at a pace beyond any ever seen in the history of the game. The league was coming off of a strike that negatively affected attendance numbers. It was more than happy to watch two of its biggest stars battle it out trying to break the long-standing home run record of Roger Maris. Attendance was up, and the game was back in the national spotlight. The fans didn't seem to care, so why should the league?

So, how do PEDs affect sports marketing? The athletes who use PEDs are putting current and future endorsement opportunities at risk. The athletes could be suspended or even face jail time. Lance Armstrong had all seven of his Tour de France titles and Olympic medals stripped as a result of PED accusations. Marion Jones lost her Olympic medals and spent time in jail over her use of PEDs. Numerous baseball players have been suspended for 50 or more games. Brands do not want to do business with athletes who are associated with using PEDs. In the case of Armstrong, some sponsors are even trying to recoup bonuses given to him.

From a marketing perspective, having an endorser athlete test positive can be a fiasco. The sponsor may overnight find its good name linked to a drug abuser. Lance Armstrong's sponsors could hardly get away from him fast enough the day after he admitted to doping. "I don't like thinking about it," he said. "But that was, I don't know, a $75 million day." Similar to a morals clause, PEDs should be specifically addressed in a contract.

Paying College Athletes

Should college athletes be paid? Are some already being paid, under the table? The debate has been ongoing for years. Each individual is presumed to be both a student and an amateur athlete. That model works well at small institutions and with club sports. Big-time Division I sports are entirely different. National media, sponsors, and fans create tremendous hype around the college-aged athlete. It's easy for everyone to forget the purpose for which the student is in school.

At top Division I schools, it is argued that the amount of exposure sponsors and the universities receive—not to mention revenue based on television deals and bowl/tournament appearances—easily exceeds the amount of a full scholarship. A full scholarship consists of tuition, room, board, fees, and books costs. The average cost for a full scholarship for an in-state student athlete is $15,000, whereas it is $25,000 for an out-of-state student athlete and $35,000 per year for a student athlete attending a private institution.[3] But are the values received by institution and athlete equitable? Allowing athlete compensation would radically alter the marketing of college sports.

Title IX

Title IX is a federal law designed to give women equal access to college sports and athletic scholarships. Most agree that Title IX has given a great boost to women's athletics. But the law also created controversy. In its fortieth year of existence, Title IX has been the topic of much debate. More women have been given the opportunity to compete on the collegiate level thanks to Title IX, but for institutions to be in compliance with the ruling, they have to make arrangements to include female sports in their programs, which sometimes have included and are not limited to cutting men's sports. In Division I Football Bowl Subdivision (FBS), football and men's basketball make up 80% of the men's athletic budget. In order to balance the women's side of the budget, some men's sports were cut.[4]

© Aspen Photo/Shutterstock

In 2011, the University of Delaware announced that it would demote men's track and cross-country teams to club status and no longer financially support them at the varsity level. Program cuts like these are occurring all over the country. Title IX is meant to promote the underrepresented sex. Because more women enroll in universities and college than men do, it will be interesting to watch how Title IX will affect men's teams in the future.

Collegiate Licensing

One of the biggest issues in sports right now is whether the NCAA has the rights to market athletes once their playing eligibility is over. Although athletes do sign a waiver that gives the NCAA marketing rights, should this allow the NCAA to continue to make money from marketing athletes' images and likenesses forever? Some former players take exception to seeing their image used in products without gaining any compensation. Lawsuits between former players and the NCAA have been filed over this issue. Ed O'Bannon was a star basketball player for UCLA in the 1990s. In the 1994–1995 season, he led the Bruins to the National Championship. O'Bannon filed a lawsuit against the NCAA for himself, former, and current players. The suit states that the NCAA is using the image rights of players without their consent and without providing compensation. Former football players have also filed a number of other similar suits. O'Bannon's is particularly interesting because a federal court denied the NCAA's request for dismissal. The denial will give the class-action plaintiffs, led by O'Bannon, access to the NCAA's licensing contract information. These contracts are estimated to be worth more than $4 billion. On August 8, 2014, District Judge Claudia Wilken found for O'Bannon, holding that the NCAA's rules and bylaws operate as an unreasonable restraint of trade, in violation of antitrust law.

There are a number of interesting parts to this discussion. The NCAA requires all student athletes to sign a release that permits their images to be used in promotional materials. Does this go on forever? The right of publicity protects against the use of a person's image without the person's consent. Does the release signed by a teenager deem consent? Do student athletes have the option not to sign? Is it clear what they are giving up? NFL Hall of Famer Jim Brown sued and recovered $26 million for former players whose images were being used in video games without consent or compensation. It seems that O'Bannon is hoping for a similar outcome for his suit. The outcome of the suit may have serious ramifications in the sports licensing business.[5]

Agent Payoffs

As long as there are agents, there will be payoffs. College athletes are not allowed to sign with agents, in most cases, until they finish using their eligibility. But some agents attempt to secure potential clients with secret payments ahead of the signing period. Sometimes it backfires. Since there is no contract, athletes have occasionally kept the bribes and signed with a different agent. "There is no honor among thieves!" The possible financial rewards to an agent for signing an elite athlete will always tempt some to try and cheat the system. Many agents attempt to find loopholes in the NCAA regulations. However, in the end the universities and colleges suffer the NCAA penalties. A number of prominent football programs have been sanctioned and banned from the lucrative bowl circuit because athletes have been accused of reaping extra benefits from boosters and agents. The issue has become so out of hand that University of Southern California (USC) hosted a summit in 2011 to help explain the need for agent awareness and to educate those in attendance about how their actions could hurt the university.[6] For a professional agent or sports marketer, this illegal activity could spell the end of a career.

Bowl Championship Series BCS

Maybe by the time you read this all of the parties involved will agree on a new system for college football playoffs. As it stands right now, a four-team playoff will start in the 2014–2015 season. Determining a national champion in college football has been a major controversy for decades. Too often the final game seemed to be based on confusing and sometimes arbitrary methods. On a number of occasions, these methods left deserving teams out of the final game that would determine a champion. They also gave teams from the smaller conferences little chance to enter the mix for the title. A four-team playoff is a start. Will college football ever see a true tournament like the NCAA basketball tournament? And how will this new arrangement affect sponsors and traditional bowls? Will the playoff games thrive at the expense of lesser games?

Licensing Fees

Consumers sometimes see things that make them scratch their heads. The perfect example happened in the trading card industry. The entire industry is based on collectability, scarcity, and the ability to chase favorite cards. The thought of missing out on their favorite player's card drives consumers to buy more packs until they find the card that they were looking for. The scarcity of cards gives a feel of collectability and value even though the physical card holds little actual value. In the 1990s, the industry thrived. The leagues saw the popularity of the industry and started to raise their licensing fees to their licensees. To pay for these increased fees, the licensees were forced to produce more cards and to create additional brands. This is the exact opposite strategy that an industry based on scarcity needs to take. Consumers shopping for cards faced a barrage of new brands, higher edition sizes, and more launches, so many consumers left the industry, putting it into a steep decline. It was generally assumed that the trading card companies became greedy and overproduced product to take advantage of an excited consumer base. Although this had something to do with the industry's decline, much of the decrease was caused by difficult-to-attain minimum guarantees by the leagues.

Social Media

Universities, colleges, and even professional sports leagues regulate social media. Some athletic departments ban their players from using social media, while others hold their athletes accountable for postings and Tweets.

In 2009, the NFL developed a social media policy that states that players, coaches, and football operations personnel are not allowed to use social media up to 90 minutes before kickoff. Postgame social media usage is not allowed until after traditional media interviews are concluded. NFL officials and the officiating department personnel are banned from using social media, period. In 2010, in typical Chad "Ochocinco" Johnson fashion, the player was fined $25,000 for Tweeting 77 minutes before a preseason game.

The media limit on players is a good example of the NFL taking care of itself first. Above all else, the league is interested in sponsor revenue. The traditional media are the channels to paid advertisers. TV and radio outlets depend on postgame interviews to extend viewership after the game. More airtime equals more ad dollars for the media and the NFL. If players are allowed to Tweet right away, fans don't need to watch the networks and the league is competing with the players for money.

Other professional sports leagues have social media policies as well. The MLB has a policy in place for MLB personnel, but the policy does not apply to players. Players and other clubhouse personnel follow the guidelines set up by their respective teams. Major League Soccer does not have a league policy, but some teams have enacted rules. The NBA has a policy regulating the use of cell phones, but players can use social media during pregame media access. Players are not, however, allowed to use social media during games. A game's duration is defined as starting 45 minutes before tip-off and lasting until after media obligations have been met. The NHL was the last of the Big Four to adopt social media policies. The league's stance is similar to that of the NBA: Players are not to use social media 120 minutes before faceoff, during the game, and until media interviews are completed.[7]

Many athletes have found themselves in controversial situations as a result of social media. During his senior year at Notre Dame, Manti Te'o was embroiled in a national hoax and scandal. He found that the girlfriend he met through social media and who supposedly passed away during the football season actually never existed. This also led to the discovery that a number of NBA and NFL players had online friends that were really people other than who they portrayed themselves as on Facebook and Twitter. Even though these athletes may have been innocent victims, from a sports marketing standpoint, brands don't want to be involved in controversy.

Digital Ambush Marketing

With the dawn of the digital age, ambush marketing has taken on a new meaning. Whereas in the past it was mainly done with street teams and billboards, the Web has made it easy to ambush a brand. In addition, the use of smartphones has allowed digital ambush marketing to reach new heights. Almost anyone can create a website, write a blog, or shoot a video. These capabilities give tech-savvy individuals a stage on which to compete with or sometimes even outcompete the official sponsor of an event. Yahoo's 2012 Olympic site far outdrew NBC's official Olympic site. Yahoo did not pay the enormous sponsorship fees, yet it figured out a way to establish its site as the go-to authority for all things Olympic. The digital age will continue to reshape how we create sponsorships.

NCAA Sanctions

The NCAA is like a bill collector. The only time you seem to hear from it is when the news is bad. As the police of college sports, it seems to surface only when there is a controversy at a university. The NCAA played a major role in the Penn State football scandal in 2012. The NCAA stripped Penn State of the past 14 football seasons' victories and levied a fine of $60 million against the school. Although Penn State University agreed to the fines and sanctions, Pennsylvania governor Tom Corbett filed an antitrust lawsuit against the NCAA, claiming that the Sandusky matter was a criminal offense and did not violate any of the rules stated by the NCAA. This interesting case tests the limits of NCAA authority.[8] Individual athletes are helpless against NCAA decisions. Universities also must be compliant, fearing NCAA retribution for a public disagreement. But state government cannot be intimidated by NCAA lawyers. The court can now evaluate NCAA decisions on the merits.

Proliferation of Technology

Some owners think that allowing wireless service in stadiums and venues will detract from watching the engagement on the field. Others think that by not providing access it's a negative experience that frustrates spectators by not allowing them the ability to further engage with the event and other fans on their mobile device.

Courtesy of Sean Clottu.

There was a time when the ownership of the Chicago Blackhawks would not broadcast Hawks' games on television. They feared that if fans could watch games on television, they would not buy tickets to games. What really happened was that generations of fans never saw the Blackhawks play at all and never became hockey fans. Some teams have been slow to react to technology, but now all know that it must be a part of their marketing efforts moving forward. Fan engagement is one of the most important components in building brand loyalty. The teams that are on the cutting edge of the technology game build their fan base. Whereas athletes are restricted from using social media during games, there is no restriction on the teams. A savvy team marketer might engage fans while they are at the event. The captive audience can get immediate team news coupled with suggestions for merchandise, tickets, seat upgrades, and so forth.

Unique Branding

A lot of the major sporting leagues are discussing if they should allow sponsorships and branding on what's traditionally been forbidden places—jerseys
and bibs, locker rooms and score tables. It will be interesting to see how each
league handles this situation.

Courtesy of Sean Clottu.

The practice of advertising on jerseys has long been linked to European soccer. The
Big Four American sports leagues have avoided this practice despite the potential
lucrative nature of such advertising. The MLS and WNBA were the first to dabble in
this type of advertising. The NBA announced that it would start adding an advertiser's patch to players' uniforms in the 2013–2014 season. Later, it said that it needed
more time to analyze the ramifications. It is estimated that this type of advertising
could bring the league more than $150 million per season.[9] Although the money is
great, considering the practice brings up a few interesting points. First, the uniform
has always been sacred in the Big Four leagues. No one really wants to be the first to
take that step and perhaps damage their image with fans. Second, advertising on team
uniforms could create difficult situations for players with individual endorsement
contracts. Imagine back in the day if the Bulls were sponsored by Reebok and Michael
Jordan had to sport a Reebok logo 82 games each year. Such practices could put individual athletes in awkward situations. But the money is too great for the leagues to
avoid this situation. It looks like the NBA may be the first to take the leap. Once it happens, the other leagues will probably follow.

Collegiate Sports

I am closely watching the major issues on college campuses—Ohio State football, UNC academics, USC penalties, etc., and how they are casting a negative light on college athletics. It will be interesting to see how this plays out
for the university presidents, athletic directors, and donors.

Courtesy of Donna Woodruff.

Some of the most storied programs in sports have been hit by controversies over
the last few years. Well-respected schools such as USC, UNC, Ohio State, and Penn
State have landed in the middle of major scandals. Whether the issues were related
to recruiting, grades, illegal payments, or oversight of the program, these universities have found themselves with public relations nightmares on their hands. Whereas
most watching from the outside focus on how these situations will affect the team or
individual players, those on the inside have a different perspective. These issues also
affect presidents, athletic directors, administrators, coaches, and many others. In this
way, collegiate sports are in a very similar predicament as are many companies in the

sports industry that depend on athletes to promote their products and brands. Both are building their brands based on the work of 18- to 24-year-olds. Unfortunately, these young adults do not always make the best decisions, especially when there is major money involved, and these decisions can affect the careers of university staff and companies in the industry.

Even if the university athletic department and the compliance officers have all the right training, education, and systems in place, things can still go wrong. Mixing teenagers, agents, and boosters has the potential to be a bad combination. When that combination goes bad, the phrase "lack of institutional control" often is used. The usual result is that someone in the athletic department loses his or her job. The media usually focuses on how many scholarships a famous football program will lose or if it is banned from competing in a bowl game. Rarely is there a discussion about the often good and hardworking university employees who lose their jobs as a result of the scandal.

Concussions

Post-traumatic concussions have become a major issue. They are especially common in football and boxing. Even soccer has been implicated because of the use of headers. The controversy exists because a medical link between repeated concussions and chronic brain damage is now widely accepted. Hundreds of lawsuits involving former players, deceased players' estates, equipment manufacturers, and professional sports leagues have been filed regarding traumatic brain injuries. Besides the future well-being of athletes, the images of leagues and companies are also on the line. At first, some professional sports leagues seemed reluctant to comment on any link between concussions and the deteriorating health of many former players.

This situation is a potential nightmare for the NFL. Payouts to neurologically damaged players are currently set at $765 million but could go much higher. Might NFL sports marketing be at risk? NFL marketing has been colossally successful, given the seemingly unlimited American appetite for football. But what if the public begins to empathize seriously with the injured players? Could the NFL fade from prominence, as professional boxing did? Football's sports marketers need to think carefully about brain injury and its multiple consequences.

Case Study

Dave Canin is the digital marketing manager for a major cell phone company. The company has decided to sponsor the NCAA Men's Basketball Tournament. Dave is currently in negotiation with the NCAA about the terms of the agreement. Because Dave is personally in charge of this expensive deal, he is ultimately responsible for its success or failure. One of his major concerns is digital ambush marketing by his main competitors.

1. What should Dave negotiate into the contract to protect his brand from being ambushed?
2. Do you think that digital ambush marketing can be stopped?

3. If you were a competitor in the cell phone market, what would you do to disrupt Dave's agreement?
4. Are there any ethical issues with ambushing Dave's deal?

Critical Thinking Activity

Choose a major professional league—NFL, MLB, NBA, NHL—and create a plan for including advertising on jerseys. What type of revenue would it drive? What would it look like? How would the deals be structured? What kind of feedback would you expect from players and fans?

CHAPTER QUESTIONS

1. What is Olympic Rule 40? Give an example of an athlete affected by Rule 40 in the most recent Olympics.
2. Do you think Rule 40 is fair or unfair? Debate both sides of this issue.
3. Should the NCAA become involved in criminal cases against universities?
4. Do you agree that an athlete should be liable for statements made in an advertisement? Is the 2009 Federal Trade Commission "Guides Concerning Use of Endorsements and Testimonials in Advertising" fair?
5. Describe a controversial issue in sports created through the use of social media. If you were a PR person in charge of strategy, how would you have handled the controversy?
6. Should college athletes be paid? What marketing opportunities should college athletes have?
7. Should companies that make products such as video games and trading cards be able to license images of collegiate athletes from the NCAA after that athlete has finished his or her eligibility?
8. What is the most unique use of technology that you have seen while attending a sporting event?
9. Should the Big Four American sports allow advertising on jerseys?
10. Is the NFL responsible for the traumatic brain injuries of former players, or are the players responsible because they chose a dangerous career?

Notes

1. Jason Goldstein, "How New FTC Guidelines on Endorsement and Testimonials Will Affect Traditional and New Media," *FTC Endorsement Guidelines 28* (2011): 609–629. http://www.cardozoaelj.com/wp-content/uploads/2011/03/goldstein.pdf.
2. "Social Media, Blogging, and Internet Guidelines," Olympic.com, accessed October 6, 2014, http://www.olympic.org/social-media-and-internet-guidelines.

3. "How Do Athletic Scholarships Work?" *Behind the Blue Disk*, NCAA.org, September 24, 2008, http://www.ncaa.org/wps/wcm/connect/public/NCAA/ Resources/Behind+the+Blue+Disk/How+Do+Athletic+Scholarships+Work.

4. Valerie Strauss, "Has Title IX, Now 40 Years Old, Harmed Male Athletics?" *Washington Post*, http://www.washingtonpost.com/blogs/answer-sheet/post/ has-title-ix-now-40-years-old-harmed-male-athletics/2012/06/14/gJQArSC-qdV_blog.html.

5. "Former College Athletes Sue NCAA over Licensing," Lawyers.com, accessed October 6, 2014, http://intellectual-property.lawyers.com/intellectual-prop-erty-licensing/Former-College-Athletes-Sue-NCAA-over-Licensing.html.

6. Gary Klein, "USC to Stage 'Summit' Dealing with Agent-Related Issues," *Los Angeles Times*, February 8, 2011, http://articles.latimes.com/2011/feb/08/ sports/la-sp-usc-agents-20110208.

7. Maria Burns Ortiz, "Guide to Leagues' Social Media Policies," ESPN Page 2, September 27, 2011, http://espn.go.com/espn/page2/story/_/id/7026246/ examining-sports-leagues-social-media-policies-offenders.

8. Michael Martinez and Stephanie Gallman, "Pennsylvania Gov. Announces Plans to Sue NCAA over Penn State Sanctions," CNN, January 10, 2013, http://www.cnn.com/2013/01/02/justice/pennsylvania-penn-state-lawsuit-ncaa/index.html?iref=allsearch.

9. Darren Rovell, "NBA Tables Jersey Ad Talk," ESPN, October 25, 2012, http:// espn.go.com/nba/story/_/id/8551120/nba-puts-decision-placing-ads-jerseys.

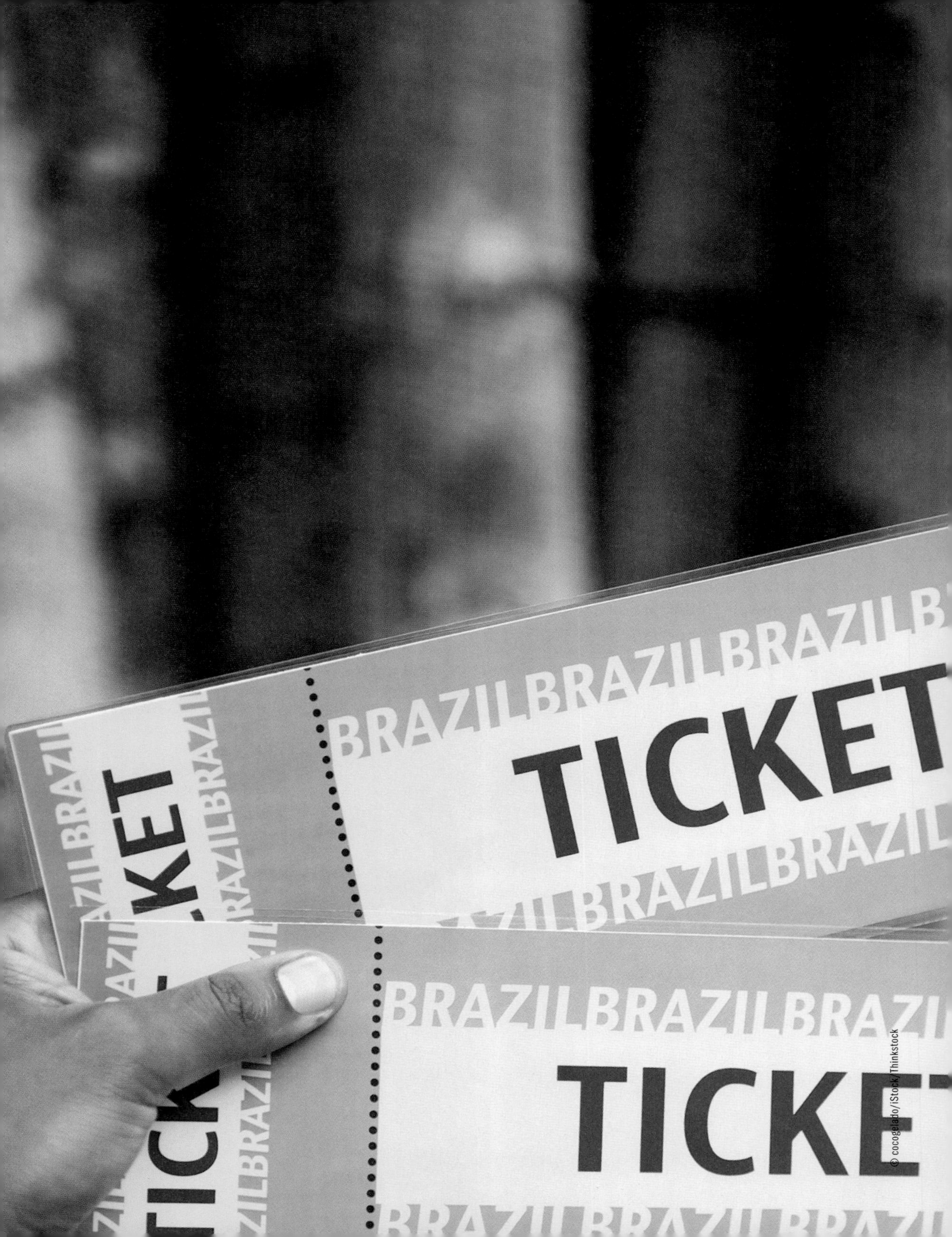
BRAZILBRAZILBRAZIL
TICKET
BRAZILBRAZILBRAZI
TICKET

Chapter 15

Emerging Markets in Sports Marketing

CHAPTER OBJECTIVES

* Review the emerging markets in the sports industry.
* Learn what markets the experts foresee as the most intriguing in sports.
* Learn how the experts are adapting their brands to meet the needs of new markets.

CHAPTER OVERVIEW

This chapter presents the trends and emerging markets that industry experts see in their particular niche of the industry. Marketers must always have their finger on the pulse of the industry in order to stay ahead of the competition. Positioning their companies or athletes to take advantage of new market trends helps them stay relevant in the ever-changing sports industry. It's very easy for marketers to get caught up in their day-to-day jobs and to miss opportunities. The best in the game have the ability to see trends as they develop and to adapt their offerings to take advantage of opportunities. This can be accomplished only by constant research and engagement with the customer base. Marketers who aren't engaged often are left behind.

Mobile

Everything is going mobile and brand marketers need to accept that it is a new marketing medium that cannot be effectively measured via traditional marketing metrics. Expect more sports facilities to become mobile friendly as it pertains to content consumption, in-venue purchases, fan-to-fan and fan-to-athlete interaction, customer service, etc. The days of fans simply coming to a venue to watch a game are over. If there isn't a text-to-win contest or some other mobile fan interaction, the experience won't live up to expectations for most fans.

Courtesy of Zach Sugarman.

Sports fans are truly a marketer's dream. Their need for information about their favorite team, player, or brand seems to be insatiable. The ability to have information at one's fingertips through mobile marketing applications is a perfect fit for sports enthusiasts. A recent survey on the use of mobile devices by sports fans uncovered some interesting data:

79% of fans have watched or followed sports on their device.

55% have tracked the score of their favorite team.

87% have checked scores at an inappropriate time, including during church, movies, and dates.[1]

Teams and stadiums have taken the lead when it comes to mobile marketing. They have seen the power in making their message interactive for their fans. The result is the development of contests, games, fan polling, and many other activities that bring fans closer to teams and brands. Many applications use text messaging. Text-to-win contests and polls are a great way to engage fans and build a marketing database for future promotions. Text messaging is also being used in stadiums for such activities as placing food orders, thus creating a more convenient fan experience. Texting is also changing the face of recruiting. Coaches know that most students have their mobile devices with them wherever they go. Because of this, it has become the most reliable way to communicate with a recruit.

Search Engine Optimization and Marketing

Internet search engines have changed the way consumers obtain information. Whether you work for a sports product company, team, league, or sports service provider, you must understand how consumers obtain information to find you and make purchasing decisions. **Search engine optimization (SEO)** is the process of positioning a website in the optimal way, using keywords, links, and site content to make sure that the site is ranked high by search engine results pages.

Whereas just about everyone is doing free keyword search positioning, SEO and search engine marketing (SEM) take more time, strategy, and dollars. Many companies have yet to take advantage of all of the selling tools now available online. Most teams are becoming savvy in these arenas and are seeing the value of connecting with and selling to fans online.

Search engine marketing (SEM) is the process of paying for advertisements, inclusion, click-through (pay per click), and retargeting online to help promote a website. Pay-per-click (PPC) Internet marketing takes place when a company places an advertisement on a website and agrees to pay a fee each time a consumer clicks on that advertisement. Retargeting is the process of advertising online to consumers who visit a site but who do not make a purchase. Say, for instance, that you go to the Chicago Bears website and search for available tickets but don't actually purchase any. Through retargeting, the Bears may place an ad on a page that you visit sometime in the future. The hope is that the placed ad may remind you that you still want to buy Bears tickets. Teams and sports product companies must position themselves to take advantage of all the new opportunities available online to ensure maximum return on their marketing spend.

Soccer

This is an exciting time in sports marketing as the world is more accessible in the digital age, through advances in social media, mobile devices, and online broadcasting of live sporting events. Direct and instant interactions with athletes, teams, leagues, products, and other sports-related entities are now possible, and this trend should continue for generations to come.

Some of the biggest beneficiaries of these advances are the top clubs in professional soccer. Jerseys of well-known clubs such as Barcelona, Real Madrid, Chelsea, Arsenal, Bayern Munich, Inter Milan, and AC Milan, among others, are worn far away from Europe. You can spot Manchester United shirts with Wayne Rooney's name and number on the backs of fans from California to Cambodia and from Mexico City to Moscow. As a result, according to *Forbes*, soccer clubs are some of the most valuable sports franchises in the world. Four of the top 10 are soccer teams. Manchester United is the most valuable franchise in sports at $2.23 billion.

More than half of the English Premier League teams are owned by foreigners, including some of the most prestigious clubs in the history of England: Manchester United, Arsenal, Liverpool, and Aston Villa—owned by Americans.

Television ratings of top European leagues, competitions, and the World Cup, on both the men's and women's sides, are increasing, and options for watching live matches span from specialized soccer channels such as the Fox Soccer Channel to cable and network channels such as ESPN/ABC, NBC, and Fox. ESPN SportsCenter Plays of the Day even include soccer-related plays, when a few years ago the sports anchors might not have known the proper pronunciation of what have become household names for sports fans throughout the United States.

Soccer in the United States has also benefited. The quality of Major League Soccer (MLS) has improved, and the league has become a competitive outlet for some of the most popular names in Europe. MLS has also done an excellent job of feeding off of the traditional soccer rivalries in the Pacific Northwest by expanding to Seattle, Portland, and Vancouver, allowing teams to adopt names from previous leagues, and providing another professional sports option for cities that have passionately embraced the new teams. Sellouts, traditions, and exciting match day atmospheres make it hard to believe that these teams have not been playing there regularly for the past 25 years. In Los Angeles, where a full generation without an NFL team has passed, two MLS teams have filled the gap in the multicultural and cosmopolitan metro region. Attendance at MLS matches now rivals and even surpasses that of some traditional American sports.

There are lots of potential for growth in soccer sports marketing as both attendance and soccer revenues increase. In 2012, MLS passed both baseball and hockey in attendance per game: Bleacher Report (August 8, 2012) cited per game soccer attendance as 18,733 people, whereas NHL games averaged 17,455 attendees, and NBA games drew an average of 17,273 people. Most MLS franchises are worth $100 million, with yearly revenues averaging $26 million. Compared with football, these are small numbers. But they have grown from virtually nothing in the last decade. In the United States, most soccer revenue is from ticket sales, concessions, and parking. There is certainly potential for all forms of broadcast royalties, sponsorships, and licensing and merchandise sales.

League Sponsorship

Sometimes, a league or event sponsorship collides with an individual athlete's sponsorship. When this happens, it often plays out in the media, and no one seems to benefit.

Nike took over the on-field apparel license for the NFL. In 2012, then-rookie Robert Griffin III had an endorsement deal with Under Armour. In week 1, he covered up the Nike swoosh during warm-ups by writing the word *Heart* on his shirt. He was promptly reprimanded by the league office. The next week, he simply wore a gray T-shirt over his warm-up gear. During week 15 of the 2012 NFL season, Griffin was fined $10,000 by the league office for wearing Adidas gear to an NFL press conference.[2]

Some of the members of the 1992 Olympic basketball Dream Team faced a similar situation. The official Olympic sponsor was Reebok. A number of prominent players, including Michael Jordan, were all highly paid Nike endorsers. Although they had no choice but to wear the official Olympic uniforms, some players covered up the Reebok logo by draping an American flag over their shoulders when they received their gold medals.

Most leagues and events now have specific rules stating that sponsor logos cannot be covered in any way. As the stakes in the marketing endorsement game continue to grow, new rules will emerge in the various professional sports leagues to protect the value of the lucrative endorsement contracts that fund the leagues.

Mixed Martial Arts

Dana White, president of the Ultimate Fighting Championship (UFC), and Lorenzo Fertitta, CEO of the UFC, have brought the world of Mixed Martial Arts (MMA) into the homes of millions. Created in 1993, the UFC did not really gain traction until the

2000s. Fertitta developed a reality television show, *The Fighter*, which featured up-and-coming UFC athletes fighting their way each week into the hearts of the viewers while trying to capture the ultimate six-figure UFC fighting contract. The show has now taped 15 seasons and will be expanding into India.

White was able to negotiate a 7-year contract with Fox and its subsidiaries. The deal includes four events on the main Fox network, 32 live Friday night fights per year on Fox's cable network FX, 24 events following *The Ultimate Fighter*, and 6 separate Fight Night events. This contract is estimated to be worth $100 million per year.[3] The other events are still shown on Pay Per View. The first televised fight on Fox took place on November 12, 2011, and attracted 5.7 million viewers.[4]

Although the Fox contract looks great on paper, it remains to be seen whether the UFC can produce enough talent to have competitive and exciting fights to fill the schedule demand of a network TV deal.

Shoe Brands

Nike and Adidas still dominate the shoe landscape, but a number of competitors are emerging with interesting strategies. Li-Ning has been a major player in the Chinese shoe and apparel market, but it has not had a significant reach elsewhere. Recently, the company started to expand into American retail and signed Dwayne Wade as spokesman for the shoe line. Can this brand gain traction in the United States competing against marketing juggernauts such as Nike and Adidas? How can a company break the near monopoly held by Nike and Adidas? A marketer might envision a new brand with several NBA stars holding equity in the company.

App Licensing

> I'm very interested in following the development in the licensing of apps for the computer market. This is truly the new frontier in sports licensing and could reshape the entire industry moving forward.
>
> Courtesy of Linda Castillon.

Licensing has taken a new turn in recent years with the development of apps for computers, tablets, and mobile devices. Some of the apps have become incredibly popular by themselves and have generated enough of a following to actually create licensing programs. EA Sports even went so far as to open its own retail store that included apparel. Entertainment products have seen even bigger successes with the logos from games such as Angry Birds showing up on many different products. Further blurring the lines between sports, entertainment, and licensing, Rapper Jay-Z was the executive producer of NBA 2K13. With the proliferation of gaming and app development, licensing will continue to grow in this category, which didn't even exist just a few years ago.

Equity Endorsement Deals

For the most part, the days of big upfront payments for endorsement deals are gone. More and more, companies are offering backend royalties and equity deals in exchange for an athlete endorsement.

Courtesy of Bill Sanders.

Bill Sanders has seen it all as the top athlete marketer in the business. He knows all too well that the state of the economy can change the structure of endorsement deals. Most companies are no longer willing to give an athlete guaranteed contracts with upfront payments. More and more, the endorsement deals are equity or royalty based to limit a company's exposure. This also gives the athlete an incentive to be actively engaged in the brand to maximize backend revenues. Part of this results from the economy, while some is driven by the problems of former can't-miss endorsers such as Tiger Woods and Lance Armstrong. Companies have become more cautious with their marketing dollars.

Category Designation

Brands have been less strict on owning an entire category. For example, instead of being the official beverage for an event, companies have become more comfortable owning a smaller piece of the category such as the official fruit blended smoothie. This allows opportunities for their competitors to come into the same events and races, but it reduces their sponsorship fee, allows them to focus on their core products, and places more resources into customized activation. The event rights holder then has the opportunity to sell sponsorships in additional niche categories and to potentially make more money in sponsorship.

© Fakhri-sa/iStock/Thinkstock

Social Media

Everyone agrees that social media is powerful and not to be ignored, but the value of and strategy with which brands should be engaging with consumers is just now becoming clear. The brands that embrace the immediate feedback and leverage the ability to have a conversation with consumers will continue to quickly gain market share. Social media is also the most effective platform for word-of-mouth marketing, which still ranks as one of the top factors for driving consumer behavior.

Research

It is important to be able to deliver custom research back to a brand postevent so the company can justify its expenditure and measure return on engagement. It has always been important to provide key demographic and psychographic information to demonstrate a match with the target consumer. Now brands demand more in-depth research as return on investment becomes more critical in a recovering economy. Before deciding on committing to a sponsorship, brands want to see research and case studies on how other companies have activated the sponsorship. Once committed and completed, it is important to give a brand a complete review of the sponsorship. This review should include information on how well promotions were activated and whether they led directly to sales if that was the primary objective. Research plays a key role in developing long-term commitment to a sponsorship.

Delivering a Unique Experience

The experience for a spectator or a participant starts when they purchase a ticket for an event or commit to register for a race. This is also when the opportunity for a brand to market to these target consumers starts. Effective sponsorship is much more than putting up a 10 × 10 pop-up tent at the finish line or parking lot and handing out promo items. The most successful brands think about how they can effectively engage with these consumers through their journey leading up to race day or the big game. The guiding principles for successful experiential marketing are to provide value, educate, be unique, and design it in a way that will enhance the overall experience. It could be in the form of helping the customer to book a flight or hotel, train for a race, gain special access to areas, connect with other participants, form a support group, and share experiences. And it needs to be across multiple platforms and touch points. Brooks is a brand that activates effectively within the Rock 'n' Roll Marathon Series and provides a unique experience for runners. As part of their "Potty Like a Rock Star" program, they allow participants to gain access to VIP porta-potties at the start line of every race if they purchase Brooks merchandise at the Health and Fitness Expo prior to race day. It doesn't sound like much, but it makes a huge difference to providing a positive race day experience for a first-time runner who is at the start line with 30,000 to 40,000 other people.

As a brand it's also important to think about how to collect consumer information and build a database to communicate and celebrate with these participants postevent. A lot of brands do not devise a strong strategy for follow-up to move these consumers down the experience funnel from sampling and building awareness, to product purchase and ultimately brand loyalty.

Courtesy of Sean Clottu.

As advertising sources proliferate, it becomes even more important to provide a unique and valuable experience to the consumer. Although people are passionate about watching and participating in sports, the dollars they spend are disposable income and a great amount of competition vies for that money. Games, concerts, races, and training all compete for the consumer's entertainment dollar. The Internet provides consumers the opportunity to quickly review the value of the experience and decide where to spend the money. Every facet of an event is important to making that a unique experience.

Season Ticket Holder Mode

The model of interacting with our fans for 6 months out of the year is a thing of the past. Our season ticket members want to be engaged with the team all year long.

Courtesy of Jarrod Dillon.

In the past, the sales job of a professional sports team ended with the purchase of a season ticket. For the teams with the best marketing strategies, this is now just the beginning of the engagement process. There is no doubt that the season ticket holder's marketing model is changing. Teams have unprecedented amounts of information regarding the wants and needs of their customers. At the same time, customers have unprecedented access to express their ideas to the team through social media. The one thing that has become clear is that the season ticket holder wants to be engaged with the team on a year-round basis. Because of this, the Padres have created a membership option for their customers. There are four types of events that may appeal to different members: Family, Social, Fanatic, and Business. The Family events includes perks such as the ability to take family holiday pictures at home plate or to have a movie night sleepover at the park. All fun things that a family can do long after the season is over. The Social events includes gatherings at wineries and brew pubs to help fans get together in a fun social setting. The Fanatic events includes private autograph sessions with players and organized road trips to watch the team play when they are not at home. The Business events allow members to use the meeting spaces at Petco Park and even take batting practice with clients. This commitment to fan engagement helps the Padres stay active with their customer base all year long. It is apparent that this marketing model will continue to develop as fans demand more access and engagement.

For the Padres, part of the marketing message urges fans to "buy early and save." They are trying to incentivize their customers to commit to buying tickets in advance. In 2012, 75% of their single game ticket inventory was initially set at or below the previous season's pricing.

A flexible marketing system has evolved, with pricing based on market trends and supply and demand. The airline industry has been using this model for years. Typically, the longer you wait to book your trip, the more expensive the airfare becomes.

In the past, teams might sit down before the season and determine the games that have the most appeal. Perhaps one popular game would be against a division rival or the Yankees when they come to town. These games typically would carry a premium price to help teams maximize profits. Problems often arose when unexpected changes took place during the season. The big game that looked so promising back in January might turn into a dud because the rival team was hit with injuries and is in last place instead of vying for the lead with your club. Or perhaps a team like the Washington Nationals suddenly burst onto the scene, and that game becomes the hot ticket. There is no way to predict these trends in the preseason. A flexible pricing single-game sales system enables teams to capture potential upside when unexpected trends happen and conditions customers to buy early. A fan with a ticket in hand is more likely to attend a game than is one considering how to spend disposable income on many entertainment options. The Padres are one of the leading teams in sports when it comes to the flexible pricing trend. Their fans are conditioned not to wait to make a purchase because they understand the value in pricing—and options—when they commit earlier.

Digital Ticketing

Marketers have witnessed the birth of a practice that will become commonplace in the near future. Digital ticketing has yet to take hold, but it is becoming more popular with each season. Companies such as Flash Seat allow fans to buy, sell, and transfer tickets online. They now have deals with the Cleveland Cavaliers, Houston Rockets, and a number of other NBA teams. Managing the ticket process online reduces delivery and printing costs and enables the team to collect additional data on their consumers. In the past, if one person bought a group of tickets or gave tickets away, the team had information about only the person who purchased the tickets. With digital ticketing, and each fan managing his or her ticket online, the team can at a minimum capture the e-mail information of each attendee. This past season, the Padres gave their season ticket holders a card that they could swipe at the gate to get access to games. The decrease in costs and the ease of use will help this trend continue to build.

Case Study

Mike Miklos is the director of marketing for a Major League Baseball team. He leads a group to determine the team's dynamic ticket pricing strategy. The members of the sales team think Mike should raise pricing as the games near. They believe that taking a long-term strategy will eventually train fans to purchase tickets early to get the best deals. They argue that this will lead to more consistent sales in the future because fans with tickets in hand are more likely to attend a game than are fans making last-minute decisions. Members of the marketing team think that tickets should be discounted as the games near. They worry about the fan experience and think that fans attending a game in a half-full stadium won't feel the same excitement as do fans attending a sold-out game. They think that empty seats are simply wasted opportunities.

1. Which strategy should Mike use?
2. Do you agree with the sales team that there is a long-term benefit to training fans to purchase early?
3. Do you believe that discounting tickets will train the fans to just wait to buy tickets?
4. Is it more important to fill the seats or to take a long-term ticket strategy?

Critical Thinking Activity

If you were in charge of the consumer experience at the San Diego Marathon, what unique experiential marketing ideas would you create? How would you make the race a unique experience for the runners? How would you measure return on investment for your sponsors?

CHAPTER QUESTIONS

1. Explain SEO. Provide an example of a sports company using SEO successfully.
2. What keywords should a professional baseball team use?
3. Explain SEM. Provide an example of a sports company using SEM successfully.
4. On which sites would you recommend that the Pittsburgh Steelers advertise? Why?
5. Explain retargeting. On which sites and by which brands have you been retargeted?
6. Have you been retargeted while visiting a sports site? What was the advertisement?
7. Have you participated in a mobile-based contest for a sports team? If so, what were the circumstances? If not, find one online and explain the strategy.
8. Look online at your favorite team's website. What type of mobile strategy does it have?
9. What type of ticketing structure does your favorite team have?
10. What type of season ticket holder promotions does your favorite team have?

Notes

1. "Sports and Mobile Now Inextricably Linked Says Motricity Survey,"
    Twittweb, March 20, 2012, http://twittweb.com/sports+mobile+inextr
    ica-18567522.
2. Ian Hanford, "Robert Griffin III Fined by NFL for Wearing Adidas Gear in
    Press Conference," Bleacher Report, December 19, 2012, http://bleacherre-
    port.com/articles/1451358-robert-griffin-iii-fined-by-nfl-for-wearing-adidas-
    gear-in-press-conference.
3. Josh Gross, "UFC, Fox Agree to Seven-Year Deal," ESPN,
    August 18, 2011, http://espn.go.com/mma/story/_/id/6874530/
    ufc-reaches-seven-year-broadcast-deal-fox-networks.
4. Richard Sandomir, "Fox's U.F.C. Broadcast a Hit with Viewers," *New York
    Times*, November 13, 2011, http://www.nytimes.com/2011/11/14/sports/foxs-
    ufc-broadcast-a-hit-with-viewers.html?_r=0.

Chapter 16

Review of Sports Marketing Through the 2012 Olympic Games

CHAPTER OBJECTIVES

* Review the 2012 Olympics.
* Review how the topics discussed in this text affect Olympic marketing.

CHAPTER OVERVIEW

This chapter reviews how the various components of sports marketing operate during the Olympic Games. USA Olympian Holley Mangold provides her insight on what it is like to be an Olympian and the struggles that many face in sports marketing.

Voices from the Field: Holley Mangold

BIOGRAPHY

Holley Mangold is the 2012 United States Olympic heavyweight weight lifter. She grew up in an athletic family and excelled at many sports, becoming a champion roller skater and playing lineman in her Ohio high school football state championship. Her brother, Nick, is the All-Pro offensive lineman for the New York Jets. After high school, she attended Ursuline College on a track scholarship but left school to concentrate on lifting. She started lifting in 2008. Holley quickly progressed to a combined lift of 565.2 pounds, which was good enough to land her a spot on the 2012 Olympic team. Her next goal is to medal in Rio de Janeiro in 2016.

   I asked Holley Mangold to contribute to this text because she represents what the vast majority of Olympians face when it comes to following their dream of winning an Olympic medal. We often see the smiling face of swimmer Michael Phelps or sprinter Usain Bolt on various companies' advertisements, but the majority of Olympians struggle to survive financially and receive little or no support from endorsement. Although many assume that these athletes have companies clamoring for their endorsements, this is not the case. Marketing Olympians who are not the most elite athletes at the Games can be a very difficult task. This chapter looks at Holley's story and how the other topics of this text applied to the 2012 Olympics.

Q&A

Q: In what Olympic sport do you participate?

Weightlifting.

Q: What was your career path to becoming an Olympian?

My path started when I played football in high school. I began powerlifting to get stronger for football and quickly found that I was pretty good at it. I set multiple national records in powerlifting and wanted to see what else could I do. I discovered Olympic weightlifting and quickly excelled in it. In 2010, I bombed out of the American Open and was subsequently kicked out of the Olympic Training Center. Afterward, I had knee surgery and went to Columbus, Ohio, to train with Mark Cannella. In a year and half, I added over 40 kilos to my total to make the Olympic Team.

Q: Describe your average training day.

I train twice a day on Monday, Wednesday, and Friday, and once a day on Tuesday, Thursday, and Saturday. An average training day consists of snatch workouts in the morning (usually snatch presses, snatch pulls, drop snatches, hang snatches, press-in snatches, and snatch pulls), with clean and jerk workouts in the afternoon (hang cleans, clean from boxes, split jerk press from blocks, and back/front squats).

Q: How often do you compete?

I usually compete three to four times a year.

Q: Have you had any media training?

I haven't had formal media training, only what I've learned by watching my brother, who plays for the New York Jets, and having been thrown in the spotlight when I was 16. So, I guess you could say that I learned on the job.

Q: What was the most surprising thing about the 2012 Olympic Games?

What surprised me was how difficult it was for nonathletes or coaches to get access to the Olympic Village. The Village is a special place created for athletes to live and relax, and, security-wise, they take access very seriously.

Q: What endorsements do you have?

Rocktape and City BBQ have given me sponsorship money for wearing their apparel or using their products. Beyond that, it has been difficult to secure endorsements.

Q: What are the most difficult things about obtaining endorsement deals?

First is how hard it is to find them, then how to get the best deal out of them. Most Olympic athletes find it very difficult to find deals. Once an opportunity becomes available, many of us don't have the experience to maximize those opportunities.

Courtesy of Holley Mangold.

Introduction

The 2012 London Summer Olympics illustrate many of the principles discussed in this text. Athletes were going for gold. So were advertisers! The Games have always been a "feel-good" venue for American viewers. Advertisers want to associate themselves with that good feeling. And the potential exposure is mind boggling: 8.8 million tickets were available for sale to the 302 events in 26 sports; 10,500 athletes from 204 countries participated; online and TV viewership numbers worldwide were huge, while live attendance was in the millions.[1] Compared with most sporting events, these are gigantic numbers. This chapter reviews how the topics of this text apply to companies, athletes, and properties using the Olympics to boost their image and sales.

Licensing

The Olympics are a major player in the world of licensing. The United States Olympic Committee (USOC) had a target of $100 million in licensed sales for the 2012 London Olympics. To achieve this, the committee built a plan to work with its 35 licensees and put them in a position to maximize sales. The plan called for licensees to create a tiered product mix that could be sold at high-end retailers such as Bloomingdales, Macy's, and Ralph Lauren Polo and that would work at mass retailers such as Walmart. This tiered merchandise plan allowed the product to reach every level of the retail market and maximized exposure and sales. The new strategy allowed the USOC to double its revenue compared with the 2008 Beijing Games.[2]

This is a great example of how sports marketing goes far beyond simply creating cool products. To be a complete marketer, you must understand pricing, distribution, and the needs of your customer. The tiered pricing strategy and multiple levels of distribution allowed the Olympic licensees to reach a broad demographic of customers.

Athlete Marketing

The 2012 London Olympics sponsorships yielded some winners and losers. All of the endorsers for Citi, Chobani, and Budweiser made their Olympic teams, giving the companies' marketing departments great opportunities to activate the companies' messages. Others such as Procter & Gamble had six endorsers fail to qualify, while Visa and BMW missed on four each. Many Olympic sponsors start to activate their advertising campaigns months and even years before the Games begin.[3] This makes it very difficult to predict not only who will make the team but who will succeed and become a star at the Games.

This is part of the life of an athlete marketer. Although it is impossible to predict injuries, successes, and failures, making educated guesses is part of the job. It is important to be immersed in the sport in which you are working. Read every day and surround yourself with experts who love that sport. By doing so, you have a better chance of making the right marketing decisions and building a successful campaign.

The life of an Olympian can be financially very difficult. I think that it is assumed that most have sponsorship deals and enough money to focus solely on training. The reality is that most don't. Even many gold medal winners struggle to find sponsorship. I've worked with two Olympians in my career. One was a gold medal winner and world champion. The other is now an emerging star. When I first met the track-and-field gold medal winner, he had a small deal with Nike and no other endorsements. Despite being a champion, good looking, and charismatic, he struggled to survive financially.

I recently spent some time at the Olympic Training Center in Chula Vista, California, to discuss athlete marketing. Unfortunately, I heard the same story over and over. The difficulties stem from three areas. First, it appears that the USOC guides sponsors to certain high-profile athletes. The goal is to give advertisers the most bang for their buck. Although it is not a bad policy, it doesn't help in sharing the marketing wealth.

Second, many agents for Olympic athletes end up focused on event scheduling for their clients. Whereas mainstream sports have a defined season and schedule each year, many Olympic sports don't. Picking, choosing, and making the arrangements to attend the potentially most lucrative events around the world take time. This can leave little time to hustle and find marketing deals.

Third, the Olympics happen only once every 4 years. The hype may begin 6 months before the opening ceremony, but it typically ends within weeks of the Games' conclusion. This negatively affects the number of companies willing to use an Olympic athlete in their marketing campaigns. It is already very difficult to secure an athlete endorsement even for a popular mainstream athlete. Shortening that list of potential sponsors makes it nearly impossible for a nonmainstream athlete to land a deal.

With all of those obstacles in the way, it takes creativity from an athlete marketer to develop a portfolio for a client. The most obvious place to start is with the products that the athlete uses while training. It is usually possible to obtain at least free product for the athlete in exchange for marketing rights. Once one deal is finalized, it can be used to promote the athlete to other potential sponsors.

Although landing free product for an athlete is a great start, it can take just as much work as landing a large deal for a major athlete. In the case of free product, however, the athlete marketer doesn't make any money. This is the main reason why most major sports agents have little interest in building an Olympic client base.

Agents

The job of a marketer and agent is clearer in mainstream sports than it is in the Olympics. In mainstream sports, an agent performs very distinct functions that are not called for from an Olympic agent. Drafts, trades, team contracts simply don't happen with Olympic athletes. Team USA won't be trading for a Russian gymnast anytime soon. For these reasons, an Olympic agent focuses more on scheduling events and marketing than does an agent in the Big Four American sports. Whereas there are many high-profile agents in the Big Four mainstream sports, Olympic agents are a small, low-profile group. The main reason is because there simply aren't the financial opportunities in being an Olympic agent. Team contracts, endorsement deals, and appearances either don't exist or are typically much smaller for the Olympic athlete.

Team Marketing

The traditional definition of team marketing doesn't directly apply to the Olympics. That doesn't mean that there isn't team marketing taking place. The USOC definitely markets various sports and those teams more than others. The high-profile swimming and gymnastics teams are visible in the USOC's marketing program. This is not unlike Major League Baseball showing its most popular teams such as the Yankees in its advertising and featuring them on national Sunday night games. The National Football League tries to feature its top draws on Monday Night Football to ensure great ratings.

The USOC marketing its best teams helps drive sponsorship sales. The more that people know about the gymnasts or swim teams, the more likely they are to tune in to those events. High viewership numbers equate to higher advertising revenue. It's in the financial interest of the USOC to promote the best teams and get the public excited to follow them.

Sports Advertising

In the days leading up to the 2012 Olympics, NBC ran advertisements on 20 TV channels and 66 different websites. It also created ads that integrated title sponsors Coca-Cola, Anheuser-Busch, and BMW into the program.[4]

The 2012 London Olympics are a prime example of how sports are leading the way in digital advertising. NBC made $60 million in digital advertising sales. This number more than doubles the $24 million earned for the 2008 Beijing Games and also doubled the percentage of total ad sales from 3% to 6%.[5] This is only the start of the new age of digital advertising. What will the 2016 Rio Olympic Games advertising programs look like? Given the recent advertising possibilities through social media, another revenue doubling seems likely.

A new category of endorsers has been developing in recent years. Athlete moms have become attractive options for companies trying to reach the parent demographic. This is happening because older athletes are now competing more than ever in sports. Many have become mothers, giving companies a credible source to speak to other mothers about the products that they use. The 2012 London Olympics were a perfect example of this emerging market. Athletes such as Kerri Walsh Jennings, Christie Rampone, Dara Torres, Amanda Beard, and Janet Evans are mothers and world-class athletes. They have turned this combination into deals from companies such as Buy Buy Baby, Jersey Mike's, Evofem, and McDonald's.[6]

Public Relations and Media Training

Some athletes live in obscurity for 4 years. Many sports are never shown or even discussed on ESPN. When the Olympics start, even the most obscure sport and little-known athlete can find themselves on the world stage. Holley Mangold is a great example. Not many people closely follow women's weight lifting in the 4 years leading up to the Olympics, and not that many follow it during the Olympics. Despite that, Holley was featured on many interviews and was even mentioned on *Late Night with Conan O'Brien*. Without media training, navigating the world media can be a daunting task for athletes.

New Product Development

Many product trends begin at the Olympics. Sometimes it starts with what the athletes are wearing at the opening ceremonies. In 2002, the Canadian company Roots sure made a splash with its trendy hats. Other times, trends begin with an athlete's performance using new technology. The 2008 Olympic swim competition was defined by the new swim suits that most of the athletes wore. Companies that track trends and put themselves in a position to quickly react can create a new source of revenue for their bottom line. Creativity doesn't happen by accident. Companies should have a defined process in place to help them successfully navigate the development opportunities.

Spotting trends may involve sophisticated analytics or simply observing the world around you. Watching consumer reactions to products and events often gives you a good idea of things that are about to get hot. Keep your eyes open, and you may spot the next great thing.

Companies involved with licensing are always trying to capture a license that will become popular. At Upper Deck, we had a creative team that had the job of trying to find sports and entertainment products and licenses before our competition did. This involved such activities as signing a minor league baseball player to an endorsement agreement before the average fan has even heard of the player. Or licensing an entertainment property such as SpongeBob SquarePants or Yu-Gi-Oh before it becomes popular. Upper Deck sold millions of Yu-Gi-Oh cards because it spotted the trend of popularity in Japanese kids long before Yu-Gi-Oh made it to the United States.

League Properties and Unions

The USOC has similar rules and structure with regard to governance, marketing, and licensing as the Big Four American leagues. Like the Big Four, the USOC controls the use of the Olympic brand by its sponsors and creates programs that guide its athletes and events.

Much like the Big Four, the USOC created rules meant to control athletes' actions and marketing. The controversial Rule 40 gives specific guidelines to control athletes' use of marketing during the Games.

Like all of the major leagues, the USOC is trying to figure out the delicate balance between network television deals and showing content online. For the 2012 Olympics in London, NBC and YouTube struck a technology deal in which YouTube provided the video player so the Games could be watched on NBC.com. This was the first time that all 3,500 events would be streamed live online for individuals to see. NBC saved money on building the infrastructure and hoped to promote the Olympics to YouTube's 4 billion views each day.

In the past, viewers' only option was to watch the evening telecast of the events. The viewers had no choice in what was shown. The more obscure sports received little to no coverage. The 2012 Olympics really were the start of the digital age of Olympic coverage.[7]

Sponsorship and Events

The 2012 London Olympics are a great example of how hospitality at sports events continues to evolve. The days of having a simple place for customers to meet are slowly being replaced by creative ways to engage and interact with customers. Target and GMR Marketing each put a unique spin on hospitality at the Olympics.

Although Target doesn't have any stores in Europe, it had a large presence in London. The company rented Bernie Spain Gardens near Parliament where it hosted a lounge for people to relax and a company-logoed 19-foot by 9-foot cylinder from which 25,000 pieces of branded merchandise were handed out. The strategy allowed Target to interact with its American and Canadian customers who visited the Games.

GRM took a different but equally unique approach to hospitality at the Games. The company had a 5400-square-foot lounge and work area where customers could interact. They called the area The Hub and hosted an invitation-only business forum of leading Olympic executives. The added value of an expert panel discussion turned The Hub into more than just a social gathering space for clients.[8] Is this a developing trend in hospitality or a one-time test of a new idea?

Cause Marketing

The Olympics are a great feel-good marketing opportunity for companies and their brands. A number of interesting campaigns appeared during the 2012 Games. One of the most visible really wasn't a traditional cause campaign in which a company gives money to a nonprofit entity.

Procter & Gamble created the "Thank You, Mom" campaign that let Olympians thank their parents who helped them achieve their dreams of getting to London and participating in the Games. In addition, P&G made a financial commitment to help send more than 2000 parents to London to watch their kids compete in person. Once in London, P&G created the P&G Family Home where 10,000 Olympic families from around the world could relax, eat, surf the Internet, and receive spa treatments featuring P&G products. It will be interesting to see if this becomes a new kind of cause marketing campaign that other companies will use since P&G had such success.

The USOC created an interesting campaign to help raise $400,000 in support of its athletes. The campaign, called "Raise Our Flag," asked supporters to purchase a stitch of the opening ceremony flag. At $12 per stitch, the campaign was a huge success and helped people feel part of the USA team as it entered the stadium.[9]

The company Article 22 created a series of Olympic ring–themed bracelets made out of old bombs. The project, called "PeaceBombs," helps clear bomb fragments left from bombs dropped on Laos in the early 1970s. The money from sales of the bracelets helped local artisans and created awareness for one of the poorest areas in the world.[10]

In 2010, British Petroleum had a PR disaster after the Deepwater Horizon oil spill in the Gulf of Mexico. Looking for a way to help its image, the company chose to develop a cause marketing campaign during the Olympics. BP became one of the official sponsors of the Olympics and Paralympics. The program was called "Target Neutral," which offered Olympic ticket holders the ability to offset the carbon footprint created while traveling to London. The company also provided low-emission specialty fuels for the fleet of 5000 cars used during the Games.

Brawny aired commercials during the Olympics that featured its "Support Our Heroes" campaign. The program was designed to raise awareness and money for the Wounded Warriors Project, which provides support for veterans. Brawny made an initial $250000 donation and, in addition to TV ads, used social media to maximize consumer donations to the campaign.[9]

In campaigns featuring medical themes, the more than 300 beds from the opening ceremonies were donated to hospitals in Tunisia.[10] General Electric's "First Chance" campaign promoted how its donated incubators have saved the lives of babies at a hospital in East London.[11]

All of these companies recognized the power of both cause marketing and the Olympic Games. The combination of a worldwide feel-good event and a brand-promoting social responsibility is a great marketing combination. Although most companies assume that they don't have the revenue to create an Olympic campaign, companies such as Article 22 have shown that even small companies with the right message can make an impact.

Social Media

The International Olympic Committee (IOC) is attempting to become the first sports entity to secure a rights deal with Google or Facebook. The partnership seems like a great idea with the explosion of social media use in sports. In actuality, it opens up a lot of questions for each group. The IOC has been very protective of its broadcast rights. The potential overlap of content with traditional media channels will be an interesting story to watch.[12] As mentioned, NBC streamed all 3500 events live for the first time in 2012. Ironically, the network had the best ratings ever. This shows that there is room for both mediums. Just how the pie gets split up will have to be figured out by the IOC and potential bidders. The days of watching only what is offered in prime time are over. Viewers demand choices, and the networks are responding by covering even the most obscure sports live. Just as the 1984 Los Angeles Olympics changed marketing, the 2012 Olympics will be viewed as the start of modern Olympic coverage.[7]

During the 2012 Olympics, NBC reported that it had surpassed 1 billion page views across all platforms. This more than surpassed the 2008 Beijing Games. In an interesting spin, Yahoo published that it had surpassed 2 billion views.[13] Is this the start of a new form of ambush marketing? Digital ambush marketing will clearly be an issue in the future of online content. For non-Olympic sponsors such as Yahoo to outpace the official site of the Olympics creates an interesting dilemma for the International Olympic Committee. The IOC typically watches over its content rights with great scrutiny. Will it be able to bring companies such as Google and Facebook into the fold when these companies can make a splash around the Olympics without spending millions on rights fees and official status?

The 2012 London Olympics saw a number of athletes increase their Twitter followers by huge numbers. (See **Table 16-1**.) Swimmer Michael Phelps added nearly a million new followers. Diver Tom Daley (825,000), swimmer Ryan Lochte (750,000), gymnast Gabby Douglas (560,000), track and field's Usain Bolt (540,000), and swimmer Missy Franklin (250,000) are a few more who led the way.[14]

Not all Twitter news from the Games was good. Before the events began, Swiss soccer player Michel Morganella and Greek triple jumper Paraskevi Papachristou were both sent home for what were deemed offensive Twitter comments. This proved once again that not all publicity is good publicity. Handling the ease of access to the masses through social media is proving difficult for some athletes to manage.

Table 16-1   2012 Olympic Twitter Followers

Athlete	Number of Followers on Friday, July 27	Number of Followers on Thursday, August 9	Number of Followers Added During Games
Swimming and Diving			
Men			
Michael Phelps	292,207	1,227,843	935,636
Ryan Lochte	143,674	897,783	754,109
Nathan Adrian	13,124	118,173	105,049
Brendan Hansen	10,195	38,290	28,095
Conor Dwyer	8439	42,410	33,971
Cullen Jones	19,419	45,182	25,763
Ricky Berens	12,336	37,622	25,286
Matt Grevers	23,242	39,107	15,865
Tyler Clary	6180	21,860	15,680
Women			
Missy Franklin	82,342	341,067	258,725
Rebecca Soni	18,109	69,167	51,058
Dana Vollmer	9693	59,795	50,102
Allison Schmitt	3577	49,397	45,820
Natalie Coughlin	58,644	88,399	29,755
Elizabeth Beisel	6647	20,392	13,745
Jessica Hardy	15,229	26,281	11,052
Gymnastics			
Men			
Danell Leyva	13,703	66,076	52,373
Women			
Gabby Douglas	35,754	600,967	565,213
Jordyn Wieber	62,457	438,030	375,573
Aly Raisman	39,966	382,413	342,447
McKayla Maroney	35,612	322,674	287,062
Kyla Ross	25,690	183,912	158,222
Track and Field			
Men			
Tyson Gay	37,865	53,735	15,870
Women			
Lolo Jones	182,855	287,350	104,495
Allyson Felix	51,869	85,298	33,429

Table 16-1 2012 Olympic Twitter Followers (*continued*)			
Athlete	Number of Followers on Friday, July 27	Number of Followers on Thursday, August 9	Number of Followers Added During Games
Sanya Richards-Ross	29,830	58,735	28,905
Kellie Wells	7395	28,361	20,966
Carmelita Jeter	8924	21,232	12,308
Beach Volleyball			
Misty May-Treanor	88,188	133,980	45,792
Kerri Walsh Jennings	83,668	110,088	26,420
International Athletes of Note			
Tom Daley (Great Britain/diving)	344,632	1,170,866	826,234
Usain Bolt (Jamaica/track)	634,092	1,174,411	540,319
Jessica Ennis (Great Britain/track)	213,410	602,247	388,837
Bradley Wiggins (Great Britain/cycling)	296,782	510,299	213,517
Oscar Pistorius (South Africa/track)	54,822	125,193	70,371
Yohan Blake (Jamaica/track)	7222	64,143	56,921

Source: Reproduced from: Baucom, Ryan. U.S. Olympians see Twitter followers skyrocket during Games. August 10, 2012. SportsBusiness Daily. http://www.sportsbusinessdaily.com/SB-Blogs/Olympics/London-Olympics/2012/08/twitterfollowers.aspx

College Athletics

The lines between amateur and professional can become blurred when reviewing the careers of Olympic athletes. Although the Olympics were once a competition of the world's best amateurs, the use of endorsements and appearance fees makes it difficult to define what an amateur really is. Swimmer Michael Phelps may not be a part of a professional sports league, but few people would consider him an amateur with his millions of dollars earned from endorsements.

On the other hand, an American athlete who is in or plans to attend college still falls under the rules of the National Collegiate Athletic Association (NCAA). At the 2012 Games, Missy Franklin had a difficult decision to make. The then–high school senior passed up potentially millions of dollars in endorsements so she could keep her amateur status and swim in college. When marketing any athlete, it is important to understand the rules of the game. In the case of Michael Phelps, all marketing options are on the table, whereas with Missy Franklin agents may have to wait 5 years to start building her marketing portfolio.[15]

Case Study

Jim Scharff is the agent for three prominent Olympians. Although he is determined to maximize exposure for his athletes to help them build their brands, he is concerned about their use of social media. He has seen a number of athletes both benefit and create negative publicity during past Games. He also worries about infringing on Rule 40 and creating unnecessary stress on his athletes.

1. What should Jim do to educate his group to avoid controversy?
2. Would you advise Jim to skip social media all together? Do the risks outweigh the benefits?
3. Should Jim have someone in his office do all the posts for the athletes as a way to control the message? If he does this, is he being dishonest to the fans?

Critical Thinking Activity

If you represented an Olympian, are there ways to maximize exposure during the Games for that athlete's endorsers who are not official Olympic sponsors? How would you handle Rule 40? What unique ideas would you create to promote sponsors without infringing on Rule 40?

CHAPTER QUESTIONS

1. Choose an Olympic athlete and describe his or her endorsement portfolio.
2. Why did Missy Franklin forgo sponsorships and endorsements after the 2012 Olympic Games?
3. How are Olympic agents different from mainstream sports agents?
4. Which current Olympic athlete is most active on Twitter?
5. What new category of endorsement has developed in recent years?
6. Which companies were the top USOC sponsors for the most recent Olympic Games?
7. Identify the sponsors of your favorite Olympic athlete.
8. Of the cause marketing campaigns discussed in this chapter, which one do you think was most effective?
9. If you were an advisor to Missy Franklin after the 2012 Games, what would you recommend that she do regarding her endorsement opportunities?
10. What company would benefit most from an Olympic sponsorship? What should that campaign look like?

Notes

1. 2012 Olympics facts and figures, English Club, accessed October 8, 2014, http://www.englishclub.com/vocabulary/sports-olympics-2012-london.htm.
2. Terry Lefton, "U.S. Olympic Committee Targets $100 Million in Retail Sales," *Sports Business Journal*, July 24, 2012, http://www.sportsbusiness-daily.com/SB-Blogs/Olympics/London-Olympics/2012/07/usoclicensing.aspx?print=true.

3. Tripp Mickle, "How Did Brands Fare with Their Rosters of Olympic Hopefuls?" *Sports Business Journal*, July 24, 2012, http://www.sportsbusinessdaily. com/SB-Blogs/Olympics/London-Olympics/2012/07/endorsements.aspx.

4. Tripp Mickle, "NBC's Olympic Promos Will Cover 20 Channels, 66 Websites," *Sports Business Journal*, April 16, 2012, http://www.sportsbusinessdaily. com/Journal/Issues/2012/04/16/Media/NBC-Olympics.aspx.

5. John Ourand, "Digital Sales Now a Key Facet of NBC's Olympic Ad Revenue," *Sports Business Journal*, Published July 2, 2012, http://www.sportsbusiness-daily.com/Journal/Issues/2012/07/02/Olympics/NBC-ad-sales.aspx.

6. Tripp Mickle, "Athletes, Marketers Find New Category: Olympic Moms," *Sports Business Journal*, Published March 19, 2012, http://www.sportsbusi-nessdaily.com/Journal/Issues/2012/03/19/Olympics/Olympic-moms.aspx.

7. Tripp Mickle, "YouTube to Team with NBC on Video for London Games," *Sports Business Journal*, March 5, 2012, http://www.sportsbusinessdaily.com/ Journal/Issues/2012/03/05/Olympics/NBC-YouTube.aspx.

8. Tripp Mickle, "GMR to Utilize Games Hospitality to Test Leadership-Type Events," *Sports Business Journal*, July 25, 2012, http://www.sportsbusiness-daily.com/SB-Blogs/Olympics/London-Olympics/2012/07/gmrhub.aspx.

9. Research & Insights, "Commitments Score Companies Olympic Gold," Cone Communications, August 10, 2012, http://www.coneinc.com/ olympicgold2012.

10. Article 22, "About," accessed October 8, 2014, http://article22.com/world/ about/.

11. "Olympic Hospital Beds from Opening Ceremony to Be Donated to Tunisia," *The Guardian*, July 29 2012, http://www.guardian.co.uk/sport/2012/jul/29/ olympic-hospital-beds-opening-ceremony-tunisia.

12. Tripp Mickle, "IOC Courts Google, Facebook As It Eyes Social/Digital Space," *Sports Business Journal*, August 6, 2012, http://m.sportsbusinessdaily.com/ Journal/Issues/2012/08/06/Olympics/OLY-social.aspx.

13. "NBCOlympics.com Passes 1 Billion Page Views for London Games," *Sports Business Journal*, August 6, 2012, http://www.sportsbusinessdaily.com/Daily/ Closing-Bell/2012/08/06/NBC-Digital.aspx.

14. Ryan Baucom, "U.S. Olympians See Twitter Followers Skyrocket During Games," *Sports Business Journal*, August 10, 2012, http://www.sportsbusiness-daily.com/SB-Blogs/Olympics/London-Olympics/2012/08/twitterfollowers. aspx.

15. Alon Harish, "Missy Franklin Wants to Swim in College, Put Off Endorsement Fortunes," ABC News, August 4, 2012, http://abcnews.go.com/Sports/ olympics/missy-franklin-forgo-millions-swim-college/story?id=16923530.

Glossary

activation The execution of the endorsement contract and marketing plan.

advance Percentage of the minimum guarantee paid to licensor by licensee at the start of contract.

advertising A form of paid communication through mass media.

advertising brief A document that outlines all the key components of the advertising plan and gives direction to all departments involved with executing the plan.

advertising burst Typically some type of an additional callout on packaging to catch the eye of the consumer.

appearances A service provided by an athlete when he or she appears on behalf of a company.

approvals Written documentation that licensee approves of a new product before the product can be sold.

assignment The right of a team to trade a player to another team.

athlete marketability formula (Talent + Success) + (Integrity + Charisma)

athlete marketing Occurs when a brand owner contracts with an athlete in exchange for that athlete's endorsement of the brand.

board A themed folder that contains pins to help others understand the user's vision.

cause marketing Generally, an athlete's involvement with a charity.

client services Meeting the needs of a team's sponsors.

collective bargaining agreement (CBA) The contract between the league and players that spells out their working relationship.

commission Percentage of marketing revenue earned that is paid by the athlete to the athlete's marketing agent; typically between 10% and 20%.

cross-promotional advertising When two companies share an advertising campaign. This usually occurs with two noncompeting companies that seek similar consumer demographics.

direct-to-consumer advertising An ad with a call to action guiding the viewer on how to immediately buy the product.

draft prep The process of preparing the athlete both physically and mentally for the time leading up to the draft.

endorsement An athlete's support of a company or product in exchange for compensation from that company.

engagement The athlete's ability to interact with the fan base through appearances, endorsements, advertising, public relations, and social media.

equity On occasion, companies give an athlete company ownership in exchange for endorsement.

exclusivity When a licensee is the only company licensed in a category.

Facebook A social media site that allows individuals to post thoughts, pictures, videos, and links, which are then shared with the person's network of friends.

fan loyalty Single most important goal for a sports marketer; loyalty to an athlete, company, or brand that reduces the need to sell and increases marketability.

fees Monies paid by a company to an athlete in exchange for the athlete's endorsement of that company or its product.

followers On Twitter, individuals who subscribe to a user in order to read their tweets.

for-profit A company that offers a service or product that it sells to the public.

Foursquare An online service that enables users to check in and share with others where they are and where they have been. Brands are starting to tap into this concept by incentivizing consumers to actively visit certain stores, bars, and restaurants.

frequency The number of times the consumer is exposed to the advertisement.

friends On Facebook, individuals who follow another person in order to read that person's Facebook page.

Friendster Considered to be one of the first social media sites.

group licensing authorization/agreement (GLA) Agreement between the players and the players union that allows union to market and license player's image and likeness as a group.

guest relations Creating the best experience for the ticket buyer.

hashtags A symbol (#) that helps denote trending topics and also express thoughts on Twitter.

image Typically, a photo of an athlete used on a product or in an advertisement.

intellectual property (IP) A copyright, trademark, or indicia.

licensee Party using the licensed marks for a fee.

licensing When the owner of an intellectual property (IP) copyright, trademark, indicia, or "licensed marks" grants use to a third party (licensee) in exchange for a fee.

licensor The owner of the licensed marks.

likeness Some type of artistic rendering of an athlete used for commercial purposes.

lockout A work stoppage created by team owners.

market research The action or activity of gathering information about consumers' needs and preferences.

market segments Definitions of a population based on demographics, geography, psychographics, and product choices.

marketing mix A set of variables used to achieve a company's marketing goals.

media buy The purchasing of space for an advertisement.

media training The process of enhancing someone's communication skills so that person can effectively interact with the media.

medium The delivery options for an advertisement.

mentions When someone uses the @ followed by someone's user name.

minimum guarantee The minimum payment that the licensee will pay to the licensor regardless of earned royalties.

mission statement A formal written declaration that clearly states the purpose of the company.

morals clause A section added to most athlete endorsement contracts that allows the company to cancel the contract if the athlete is involved in questionable activities that might damage or bring negative publicity to the company's brand.

MySpace The first clone of Friendster, this site enabled users to personalize their pages and express their uniqueness.

nonprofit An organization that renders its profits to use toward meeting its goals.

nonsports advertising When the product or company has no apparent connection to the sport but uses sports to reach the desired demographic.

opt out Not participating in Group Licensing.

pay-per-click (PPC) Internet marketing that takes place when a company places an advertisement on a website and agrees to pay a fee each time a consumer clicks on that advertisement.

personal selling The selling of a product on a one-on-one basis. This is often done face to face or over the phone.

Pinterest A virtual pin board where users can share all that they find interesting on the Web.

pin-up A paper cut-out or icon that can be scanned during the checkout process, whether in person or online, that represent a donation to a cause.

place Where a company sells and markets its product.

players unions Groups that represent all players of a sport in regard to marketing, licensing, and labor business.

primary research Research conducted specifically for a project.

proactive product development A strategy companies use to have a formal and constant new product development process in place.

product The item the company is trying to sell. Companies often use product to provide in-kind payment to an athlete instead of cash. Shoe companies almost always use product as part of an athlete's compensation plan.

product development The process of creating and bringing a product to market.

product fit The synergy between the endorser and the brand. A good product fit leads to believability and increases the possibility of a successful campaign.

properties group The entity that collectively represents the team owners in a league.

prospecting When an agency identifies potential business opportunities.

public relations (PR) Use of the media to help build brands and increase an athlete's engagement with the general public.

QR codes QR stands for quick response. QR codes are similar to bar codes and can be used on smartphones to launch a Web page, display a phone number, or show an address.

Q Score A method to measure familiarity and appeal of an athlete's brand image.

reach The number of people an advertiser will meet with its message.

reactive product development A strategy a company uses when it waits to see what innovations are taking place with the competition and then makes changes to its product.

recruiting The process an agent undergoes to convince an athlete to hire the agent as representative.

repins If a user likes an image, that person can then pin the image to one of his or her own boards.

retargeting The process of advertising online to a consumer who came to a site but did not convert to a sale.

retweets A tweet that is sent out by someone other than the original author on Twitter.

royalty A percentage of sales revenue to be paid to a licensor from the licensee.

samples Examples of products that are sent to the league for approval before the products are manufactured.

search engine marketing (SEM) The process of paying for advertisements, inclusion, click-through (pay-per-click), and retargeting online to help promote a website.

search engine optimization (SEO) The process of positioning a website in the optimal way using keywords, links, and site content to make sure that a site is ranked high by search engine results pages.

secondary research Research already conducted that can be accessed and used to help decide the fate of the project.

shortfall When the royalties from sales fail to generate enough revenue to cover the minimum guarantee.

social analytics The use of social media software to analyze the reaction online to marketing initiatives. Teams are starting to use social analytics as a way to gauge customer reactions to ticket pricing, promotions, and many other marketing initiatives.

social media Media which allows for real-time responses as well as two-way communication.

solicitation sell sheets Concise but detailed advertisements for the product that is being developed. Usually used by the sales team to show buyers upcoming concepts.

sponsorship A paid form of marketing between a brand and a property, where the brand is given access to the attributes of the property.

sports advertising When the product, company, or brand is in the sports industry, such as equipment or apparel manufacturers, leagues or teams, or perhaps sports related video game makers, among others.

sports agent A person who represents an athlete in negotiations for team contracts and endorsements in return for a percentage of the athlete's earnings.

sports public relations The crafting and distribution through the media of a message to gain publicity for a team, athlete, or company.

spot An advertisement that creates an image used to influence a consumer.

stock keeping units *SKU* stands for stock keeping unit.

strike A work stoppage created by players of a professional sports league.

SWOT analysis Analysis that enables one to identify the internal strengths and weaknesses of a company while also investigating the external opportunities and threats.

target market A segment of the population to which a company has chosen to promote and sell its product.

team marketing The promotion of a sports team.

tweets Any message sent out on Twitter that is 140 characters or fewer.

Twitter A social media site that allows users to post messages of 140 characters or fewer to express a thought. Pictures can also be uploaded.

venue naming rights Rights granted to a company, for a fee, to have its name associated with a team's stadium.

viral advertising An ad placed only online with the hopes that it will catch on and be spread person-to-person over the Internet.

Web video seeding companies Companies that specialize in making online content available and easily shared.

Index

Note: Page numbers followed by *f* or *t* indicate material in figures or tables respectively.